█║▌█║▌║█║▌║█║▌

D0839478

RIO 2016

RIO 2016

OLYMPIC MYTHS, HARD REALITIES

ANDREW ZIMBALIST

EDITOR

BROOKINGS INSTITUTION PRESS
Washington, D.C.

Copyright © 2017
THE BROOKINGS INSTITUTION
1775 Massachusetts Avenue, N.W., Washington, D.C. 20036
www.brookings.edu

All rights reserved. No part of this publication may be reproduced or transmitted in any form or by any means without permission in writing from the Brookings Institution Press.

The Brookings Institution is a private nonprofit organization devoted to research, education, and publication on important issues of domestic and foreign policy. Its principal purpose is to bring the highest quality independent research and analysis to bear on current and emerging policy problems. Interpretations or conclusions in Brookings publications should be understood to be solely those of the authors.

Library of Congress Cataloging-in-Publication data are available.
ISBN 978-0-8157-3245-7 (pbk. : alk. paper)
ISBN 978-0-8157-3246-4 (ebook)

9 8 7 6 5 4 3 2 1

Typeset in Sabon Roman

Composition by Westchester Publishing Services

Contents

Acknowledgments

The authors would like to thank Nashwa Al-sharki, Allison Stewart, Rodrigo Capelo Nunes, Kaia Sand, Jessi Wahnetah, Gilmar Mascarenhas, Orlando Santos Junior, Christopher Gaffney, Larissa Lacerda, Renata Neder, Andrea Florence, the Fulbright Scholar Program, Pacific University, Smith College, and the remarkable people at Catalytic Communities in Rio de Janeiro. We would like to thank cariocas—the residents of Rio—for their grace and patience with our questions and those affiliated with the Economic Geography group of the University of Zurich for their support, friendship, and a room with a view during a crucial year of research and writing.

ONE

Introduction

"Welcome to Hell"

ANDREW ZIMBALIST

Rio de Janeiro's hosting the 2016 Summer Olympic Games was to be the crowning achievement of three decades of democracy and economic development. Rio and Brazil would enter the first world, Rio's favelas would be modernized, its violent drug gangs rooted out, its sports and transportation infrastructure enhanced, and the city and country would share its good fortunes on the world stage. Reality, however, impinged on what was to have been and played a cruel trick on Rio and Brazil.

Olympics development magic doesn't even work for developed cities.[1] It certainly wasn't going to work for Rio. The depressing economic record of hosting the Olympics has a solid structural basis. The International Olympic Committee (IOC) is an unregulated global monopoly. Every two years it conducts an auction among the world's cities to see which will bid the most extravagantly to earn the honor of hosting the winter or summer Olympics seven years later. Among many other things, the IOC requires the host city to cover any cost overruns. It's a setup conducive to producing a cursed winner. Costs for the summer Games end up in the $15 billion to $25 billion range, while revenues trail in the $3 billion to $5 billion range. After the

1

Games, the host city finds itself with less available land (Beijing dedicated 8,400 acres of real estate to hosting in 2008), more venues of limited use to maintain, environmental degradation, social dislocation, mountains of financial debt, and, generally, a modicum of additional infrastructure, some of which is useful to the city's development but most of which is of low priority.

After each Olympics and the disappointing economic outcome, the IOC puts its well-oiled propaganda machine to work. Try as it does, the IOC public relations effort lately has had little success. City after city is losing interest in hosting the three-week Olympics extravaganza: five European cities dropped out of the competition to host the 2022 Winter Games, and Boston, Budapest, Hamburg, and Rome decided not to go forward with their candidacies to host the 2024 Summer Games. Tokyo won the right to host the 2020 Summer Olympics with a bid of $7.1 billion, but a September 2016 report commissioned by the city of Tokyo projected costs of $30 billion. The IOC could not withstand more bad news, especially after the Rio 2016 experience, and its vice president, John Coates, made this clear, stating that Tokyo's high costs "could scare off cities considering bids for future Olympics."[2] The IOC's concern was its bidding process, not Tokyo's fiscal mess.

It took the International Olympic Committee three months to come up with its definitive characterization of the Rio Summer Games: "the most perfect imperfect Games," declared IOC spokesperson Mark Adams in early December 2016. It's a catchy turn of phrase (albeit grammatically flawed); if we only knew what it meant. Does it mean that the Games were perfectly imperfect—the epitome of imperfection? Or imperfectly perfect—almost perfect? Or is it just obfuscation?

One thing is clear. When the Games ended on August 22, 2016, the IOC breathed a deep sigh of relief and then bid farewell to Rio. To the IOC, Rio now became little more than a historical artifact and an object of spin.

The lead-up to Rio 2016 was harrowing for the IOC. Everything was going wrong and there was legitimate concern that the Games would be disastrous, perhaps Mexico 1968, Munich 1972, and Montreal 1976 all rolled into one. Consider the litany of troubling news emanating from Rio in the months leading up to August 5, 2016.

The Brazilian economy was in deep recession with GDP falling at roughly 4 percent annually for two consecutive years, unemployment over 11 percent, and inflation near 10 percent. Social services were being cut back, and there was a broad sense of government dysfunctionality. At the end of June, state government announced that it owed 310,458 employees an average of $466 each for salaries that were due two weeks earlier. Violence was pervasive and rising, as described by a *Wall Street Journal* article on July 1: "State police have made almost daily raids this week on favelas across greater Rio, waging deadly gun battles in an effort to recapture an alleged drug lord Nicolas Labre Pereira, nicknamed Fat Family. The overweight gangster's posse recently freed him from custody after a shootout at one of the city's biggest emergency hospitals. Since June 20, at least eight people have been killed in shootouts with police."[3] Rio's state government announced that eighty-four people were killed by police in May, a 91 percent increase from a year earlier. Street muggings were up 43 percent during the five months of 2016, with 9,968 cases in May alone. That number rose to a record 10,701 muggings on the streets of Rio in July.

Second, corruption, long a constant in Brazilian politics, began to spin out of control. The oil bonanza and the massive construction projects, many of them connected to hosting the World Cup and the Olympics, were simply too much opportunity for gain for Brazilian politicians and construction companies to forego. Brazil's hosting of the World Cup and Olympics created a wide window for the world to watch the country's biggest corruption scandal (Lava Jato, or Car Wash), along with the graft of World Cup and Olympics contracting, campaign financing, and more. (These scandals are discussed at length in Barbassa's chapter, "Brazil's Olympic Rollercoaster.")

Most notorious perhaps, less than three months before the 2016 Games began, a gang of venal politicians alleged that President Dilma Rousseff was guilty of manipulating the country's budget for political ends. The allegations were never proven, but Rousseff was suspended from office on May 12 and then removed permanently after the Games were over. The impeachment gambit's true purpose was to distract Brazilians from the wider rings of corruption that had infiltrated the government and to prepare for a congressional clemency vote for compromised politicians.[4]

The gambit didn't work out as intended. Eduardo Cunha, the House speaker who led the impeachment effort against President Rousseff, was imprisoned on charges of money laundering and bribery after being discovered with millions hidden away in Swiss bank accounts. Former Rio state governor Sérgio Cabral was arrested in November 2016 for taking $66 million in a graft scheme connected to the renovation of the Maracanã Stadium and other infrastructure. Brazil's new president, Michel Temer, had already lost six of his cabinet ministers to scandal as of mid-December 2016 and was engulfed in his own imbroglio. José Serra, who had been Temer's foreign minister, was accused of receiving a $7 million bribe from Brazil's largest construction company, Odebrecht, and the former CEO of that company is serving a nineteen-year incarceration.[5]

Understandably, the breakdown of services, the revelation of vast corruption, the extensive layoffs and failure to pay workers, the growing violence, and the waste of Olympics spending provoked widespread and militant political protest. Perhaps most visible to the outside world was the protest staged by police and firefighters just five weeks before the opening ceremonies at Rio's International airport, warning visitors that the city was not safe, with one large sign stating "Welcome to Hell." The police, firefighters, and other public workers threatened to go on strike during the Olympic Games.

Amid this social, economic, and political turmoil, the Rio Organizing Committee for the Olympic Games (ROCOG) was scrambling to prepare the city for the event. And not everything was going so well. It was unclear if the new Line 4 metro to Barra da Tijuca would be functional or if many of the competition and related venues would be ready. ROCOG had run out of money. In July 2016 the Rio city government allocated an extra $46 million to help with last-minute preparations, and following a declaration of a state of calamity by the state governor, a further $890 million was committed by the federal government in emergency aid to help complete the Line 4 metro and provide Games-related security, including the payment of wages to police to patrol the streets. The sports venues were supposed to have test events. Many didn't. Some that did failed. Power supply to all venues was in question. ROCOG announced that many venues with temporary seating would have significant reductions in capacity. Meanwhile, the temporary seating in some arenas was not stress tested before the competition. Only 15 percent of the planned promotional, decorative, and directional signage was installed. Construction was rushed and, in many places, shoddy. As athletes arrived at their village days before the competition began, they found lodging with dysfunctional plumbing and electricity. Some teams were forced to relocate temporarily and the Australian team refused to move in. There were ten reported construction-related deaths.

A 3.9-kilometer bike path that passed by a sheer cliff at ocean's edge—heralded as one of the city's infrastructural improvements from the Games—collapsed, sending two bikers plunging to their deaths. The path was constructed by the construction group Concremat and funded by a loan with public funds from the state development bank, BNDES. After the collapse it was revealed that "the number of contracts signed between the city of Rio and Concremat went up by 2,132 percent since 2009, when mayor Eduardo Paes took office for the first of his two terms. Of those contracts, 46 percent were offered without public bidding, under the allegation they pertained to emergency works. The group belongs to family members of Rio's tourism secretary, who was also treasurer of both of Paes' campaigns for mayor."[6]

But matters turned still uglier for Rio 2016. Rio was hit by a virulent outbreak of the mosquito-borne Zika virus. Hundreds of *cariocas* (as residents of Rio are known) fell ill, and dozens of babies born to Zika-infected mothers suffered from microcephaly. This alarming news led many star athletes to bypass Olympics competitions, beginning with the world's number-one ranked golfer, Jason Day. Rio 2016 was supposed to herald golf's triumphant return to the Olympics after a 112-year hiatus, but Jason Day led an embarrassing exodus. Because of Zika, an international group of eminent doctors, bioethicists, and scientists signed a petition calling for the Games to be moved or postponed.

The ugliness continued to spread. Guanabara Bay, site of three of the five sailing courses, was supposed to be cleaned up for the Games. The bay is the dumping ground of waste from the surrounding communities and factories. The plan from the 2009 hosting document was to increase the treatment of water going into the bay to above 80 percent, but by August 2016 less than half of the water was treated. The Associated Press commissioned a sixteen-month-long study of the bay; the Rodrigo de Freitas Lagoon, host of rowing events; and Copacabana Beach, site of the open swimming competition, and here's what they found:

> The first results of the AP study published . . . showed viral levels at up to 1.7 million times what would be considered worrisome in the United States or Europe. At those concentrations, swimmers and athletes who ingest just three teaspoons of water are almost certain to be infected with viruses that can cause stomach and respiratory illnesses and more rarely heart and brain inflammation—although whether they actually fall ill depends on a series of factors including the strength of the individual's immune system.[7]

The next blow to Rio 2016 was that the World Anti-Doping Agency (WADA) noticed irregularities in Rio's new testing laboratory and shut it down. (It was later restored.) Given all the above and ticket prices out of reach to middle-class Brazilians, it should come as no surprise that ROCOG had to contend with severely lagging ticket sales.

Conditions did not improve once the Games began. Ben Fischer, who covered the Games for the *Sports Business Journal*, wrote: "The problems started out of the gate for Olympic partners, when sponsor guests waited two hours to enter the opening ceremony. Volunteers guided regular fans to a gate designated for sponsors, just the first of many complaints about poorly trained or unaware local staff."[8] Rio 2016 initially had 70,000 volunteers, the majority of whom received just a few hours of training at most. Many stopped reporting to duty after a day or two, happy to have been fed and given uniforms. Fischer's assessment continued: "Signs of budgetary collapse were common, from the poorly managed volunteer program, to the lack of wayfinding signage, to the precarious sewer system that couldn't handle toilet paper being flushed."[9]

Joshua Paltrow and Dom Phillips, writing for the *Washington Post* after the first week of the Games, characterized the steady mishaps as follows:

Before the bus windows got blasted out and the water in the aquatics center turned emerald, before the Australian coaches got robbed at knifepoint and the Belgian sailor fell sick after tumbling in the sewage-strewn bay, before gang members in a favela killed a Brazilian police officer and a stray bullet landed in the media tent, one could make the case that Rio's Olympics were going well. But the scares, mishaps and inconveniences have started to pile up. Olympics organizers have been bombarded by questions about the safety and efficiency of arenas and transportation routes, about the spotty attendance and officials' tough response to political protests, and about the level of contamination in swimming pools, which turned an algal green this week, forcing organizers to cancel a dive training session Friday morning. . . . Last Saturday, a stray bullet pierced the roof of the media tent at the equestrian venue. Three days later, two windows on an Olympics bus were struck by projectiles—organizers claimed they were rocks, passengers suspected gunfire. The next day, a pickup carrying police officers working security for the Olympics took a wrong turn into a favela and were met by a hail of bullets. One officer since died. Throughout the Games, Olympics fans and participants have been mugged, sometimes in harrowing circumstances. Two Australian rowing coaches were robbed at knifepoint near Ipanema Beach, and Portugal's education minister was assaulted near a downtown lagoon.[10]

Paltrow and Phillips neglected to mention that an overhead camera at Olympic park fell sixty-five feet on August 15, injuring at least seven people.

Writing for the *New York Times* about the horrors of transportation in Rio during the Games, Rebecca Ruiz and Ken Belson observed that it sometimes took two hours or longer to travel from one Olympics cluster to another—and that would be once you were able to find a taxi, assuming that the driver knew the route to the venue.[11] The largest impact of the transportation bottleneck fell on cariocas going to and from work. One commuter told Ruiz and Belson, "What makes me really outraged is that even with eight years of preparation, the organizers planned it to be this way, knowing how much it would impact a large part of the local work force." She said her normal commute time of thirty minutes ballooned to more than two hours during the Games.

Probably Rio 2016's biggest scandal had little to do with Rio. The president of the Irish Olympics council and a longstanding board member of the IOC, Pat Hickey, was arrested in Rio and charged with heading a massive, lucrative ticket-reselling scheme. People knew about corruption in FIFA and Brazilian politics, but the executives of the IOC were generally deemed to be free of corrupt behavior, at least since the Salt Lake City bidding scandal prior to the 2002 Olympics. With Hickey's arrest, it appeared that profiteering and graft had penetrated all the way to the top of the IOC. (Chade's chapter on press coverage of the Games reveals some implicating news about the Hickey affair.)

So, the fact that the Games were pulled off was, as IOC president Thomas Bach proclaimed at the closing ceremony, "a miracle." Other than very visible empty seats on television at most venues, the competitions all took place and did so with few serious incidents—at least incidents that were visible to the international audience.

Long-time Canadian IOC member and former director of WADA, Richard Pound, put it poignantly: "Ninety-nine percent of the folks who experience the Olympics do so by television or whatever platform . . . the world has no idea about the back-of-the-house shambles that are here. . . . Let's . . . get out of town, and the world will forget how close it was to disaster on many occasions."[12] Rio had limped to the finish line—and then collapsed.

Since the Games ended in late August, Rio's problems have only grown worse. Violence has escalated dramatically. The economy has continued to sink steeply. Mountains of debt augur fiscal austerity, if not paralysis. Corruption scandals have become more extant and every week touch more politicians. Thousands of workers, including hundreds involved with the Games, have continued to be unpaid. Numerous Olympics white elephants mock the passersby.[13]

Meanwhile, the IOC, turning now to spin the Tokyo Games and the Russian doping quagmire, has evinced little concern over the actual impact that the Games had on Rio and Brazilian society. That's the oversight that this volume aims to rectify. In the next chapter, "The Olympics in the Twenty-First Century: Where Does Rio 2016 Fit In?," Jules Boykoff describes how the task of hosting the Olympics has changed over the years, how the experience of host cities has varied, and how Rio's record compares to that of others. In chapter 3, "Brazil's Olympic Rollercoaster," Juliana Barbassa situates Rio 2016 in its historical context, tracing the arc of the 2016 Games from the euphoria of being selected as host by the IOC in 2009 to the depressing decomposition of the city's political and economic life.

In chapter 4, "Not Everyone Has a Price: How the Small Favela of Vila Autódromo's Fight Opened a Path to Olympic Resistance," Theresa Williamson discusses the centrality of the favela in carioca life and tells the story of one favela adjacent to the Olympic park. The city made promises it didn't keep and trampled on the rights of the *favelados* in Vila Autódromo. Williamson extracts lessons from the resistance tactics used in this favela.

In the next chapter by Renata Latuf de Oliveira Sanchez and Stephen Essex, "Architecture and Urban Design: The Shaping of Rio 2016 Olympic Legacies," the architectural and urban planning that went into Rio 2016 is discussed as well as many of its infelicitous outcomes. Chapter 6, "Strictly Confidential: Access to Information and the Media in Rio," relates the frustrations of Jamil Chade, an award-winning journalist and European correspondent for the newspaper *O Estado de São Paulo* who has covered numerous Olympic Games and the 2014 World Cup, and the manipulated accounts of Olympics-related events that were presented to the public.

In "Safety for Whom?: Securing Rio for the Olympics," Juliana Barbassa elaborates the prejudicial plan to keep executives, athletes, and fans safe at the expense of Rio's residents before, during, and after the Games. The environmental challenges and costs of hosting the Games are related by Jules Boykoff in chapter 8, "Green Games: The Olympics, Sustainability, and Rio 2016." The final chapter, "The Economic Legacy of Rio 2016," by Andrew Zimbalist, analyzes the economic impact on Rio from hosting the Olympics.

Together these chapters seek to provide a fuller picture of how hosting the Olympics affected life in Rio de Janeiro—an issue to which the IOC gave only lip service. A consistent theme resonates throughout these pages that buttresses the ascendant cautionary narrative surrounding hosting the Olympic Games. The chapters herein detail the economic, social, environmental, and political pitfalls that impacted Rio and that should be red flags for all prospective hosts.

NOTES

1. There is an occasional exception to this generalization. See Andrew Zimbalist, *Circus Maximus: The Economic Gamble Behind Hosting the Olympics and the World Cup* (Brookings Institution Press, 2016).

2. "IOC: Tokyo Olympics' Huge Cost Could Give Wrong Message," *NBC Sports*, December 1, 2016 (http://olympics.nbcsports.com/2016/12/01/tokyo -2020-olympics-cost/). Since Coates issued this admonition, it is interesting to note that Tokyo in December 2016 was estimating costs between $15 billion and $18 billion. That is, magically, the costs were reduced practically in half from those estimated in the September study, without any significant change in the plan for the Games. One has to wonder whether the technique for cost reduction is the same as is being used in Beijing 2022 and has been used elsewhere; namely, Olympic-related costs are simply moved off budget. Beijing did this with its high-speed rails going to the Nordic and Alpine ski areas, 60 and 120 miles north of Beijing, that will cost $5 billion or more. They simply declared that the rail lines would be built anyway (a highly dubious proposition) and so would not be counted as part of the Olympics' expense.

3. Will Connors and Paul Kiernan, "Woes Confound Rio in Run-Up to Olympic Games," *Wall Street Journal*, July 1, 2016.

4. Of course, the success of the impeachment process was a function of Rousseff's abysmally low popularity rating. Although Rousseff was not directly implicated in the Lava Jato scandal, she was chair of the board of Petrobras during the years of its misdeeds. Further, many interpret her removal as part of a larger plan by Brazil's Social Democratic Party and the PSDB-led coalition to carry out the austerity program demanded by international financial institutions.

5. Odebrecht pleaded guilty to providing bribes for construction contracts worldwide to the tune of billions of dollars, at least $349 million of which went to Brazilian politicians. See, for one, Samuel Rubenfeld and others, "Brazil Giant Settles Bribery Case," *Wall Street Journal*, December 22, 2016, p. B2.

6. Juliana Barbassa, "Rio de Janeiro's Olympic Gamble," *ICSSPE Bulletin* (Journal of Sport Science and Physical Education), no. 70 (May 2016), pp. 33–34.

7. See, for one, Jenny Barchfield, "Expert to Rio Athletes: Don't Put Your Head Under Water," *Associated Press: The Big Story*, August 1, 2016.

8. Ben Fischer, "After All the Problems, Rio '16 Is the Olympics that Succeeded in Spite of Itself," *Sports Business Journal* (August 22–28, 2016), p. 42.

9. Ibid.

10. Joshua Paltrow and Dom Phillips, "The Olympics Are a Test that Brazil Has Yet to Pass," *Washington Post*, August 12, 2016.

11. Rebecca Ruiz and Ken Belson, "No Way Around Rio's Gridlock, Even for Olympic Officials," *New York Times*, August 17, 2016.

12. Quoted in Fischer, "After All the Problems," p. 42.

13. One excellent discussion of the utter state of disrepair of multiple Rio Olympic venues is Anna Jean Kaiser, "Legacy of Rio So Far Is Series of Unkept Promises," *New York Times*, February 16, 2017.

TWO

The Olympics in the Twenty-First Century

Where Does Rio 2016 Fit In?

JULES BOYKOFF

The morning after the 2016 Summer Olympics closed in Rio de Janeiro, Games honchos convened for an exclusive breakfast where International Olympic Committee (IOC) President Thomas Bach bestowed special Olympic Order awards to Rio 2016 Organizing Committee President Carlos Nuzman, Rio Mayor Eduardo Paes, and Rio 2016 CEO Sidney Levy. While conferring Olympic Orders to the Rio 2016 luminaries—gold medallions for Nuzman and Paes, silver for Levy—Bach heaped on the plaudits. "These were marvelous Olympic Games in the *cidade maravilhosa*," he enthused. "The Olympic Games Rio 2016 have shown the best of the Cariocas and Brazilians to the world." Speaking from a similar script, Nawal El Moutawakel, the IOC vice president who headed the Rio 2016 Coordination Commission, asserted, "Brazil and Rio de Janeiro delivered marvelous Olympic Games to the world. The Olympic Games Rio 2016 will forever be remembered for sporting excellence, the passion and warmth of the Cariocas and for their tremendous legacy to the people of Rio de Janeiro, Brazil and South America."[1]

A few days later, outside the cozy Olympic echo chamber, journalists grilled Bach about the questionable economics undergirding the first-ever Olympics staged in South America. Bach deflected: "You can say very clearly that the financial model of the Olympic Games has really stood a stress test which I hope we will not have to stand again in the future."[2] Three months later, Olympic powerbrokers continued to push the party line that the Games were an unequivocal success. While attending the general assembly of the Association of National Olympic Committees in Doha, Qatar, Nuzman stated, "The mood in Brazil is very good, everybody loved the Olympics, they are happy thanks to all they have in Rio. The transformation in the city, the new way of life. They are very proud and honored with the success of the Games."[3]

Such bland blandishments have become an Olympic tradition of sorts, with Games organizers routinely claiming their Olympics to be the best Olympics to date. But in the twenty-first century, the Olympic Games have left a discernible, material pattern of ramifications in their wake, a set of legacies, many of them shadow legacies not touted in shiny Olympic bid materials. This chapter compares the Rio 2016 Games to previous Summer Olympics in the twenty-first century in regard to social displacement, the militarization of the public sphere, and transportation network development. The 2016 Games in Rio transpired in a ferociously unequal city and hosting the Olympics did not help matters. Tens of thousands of people were displaced to make way for Olympic stadiums and transport structures. Although athletic venues were blanketed with security officials, making them some of the safest spaces in Latin America, Rio's exurbs and favelas experienced an uptick in violence. While the Olympics and Paralympics received a public bailout, local hospitals were shuttered and social services reduced. And while members of the International Olympic Committee's Executive Board enjoyed $900 per diems, people cleaning the athletes' village earned just $1.83 an hour.[4] The Rio 2016 Olympics also failed to deliver significant legacy promises such as cleaning up Rio's notoriously polluted waterways. Though it would be easy to simply wag a finger at the *Cidade Maravilhosa*—to blame it on Rio—the reality is much more complicated. What may seem like Rio problems are actually Olympic problems. This chapter examines Rio 2016 within the wider context of recent Olympic history: Sochi 2014, London 2012, Vancouver 2010, Beijing 2008, Athens 2004, and Salt Lake City 2002.

DISPLACEMENT

Hosting the Olympics requires vast swathes of space, a significant geographical reorganization. This can have major ramifications for the host city's social topography. Restructuring the political space of a city harkens Trevor Paglen's observation that geography "sculpts the future. The spaces we create place possibilities and constraints on that which is yet to come, because the world of the future must, quite literally, be built upon the spaces we create in the present. To change the future, then, means changing the material space of the present."[5] The Summer Games, with their array of relatively obscure sports that demand particular spatial configurations, can swallow up huge parcels of urban turf. Accommodating Winter Olympics events like skiing and luge can mean slicing paths through the pristine mountain terrain. Beyond this, the construction of an Olympic Village for athletes has become de rigueur. For the Summer Games this means finding housing for more than 11,000 people, which often translates into fresh construction and a demand for land.

The requirements bricked into hosting the Olympic Games can lead to social dislocation in two forms: the velvet glove of gentrification and the iron fist of displacement. In the twenty-first century, we see different combinations of these two methods depending on the social and political-economic conditions in the host city and wider host country. The general trend is that Olympic host cities in developed countries emphasize gentrification while host cities in developing countries tend to deploy more brass-knuckle displacement and eviction.

The latter dynamic—forced eviction through state power—was in sharp relief ahead of the 2008 Summer Games in Beijing. Organizers adopted the slogan "One World, One Dream," but the dreams of the more than one million people who were displaced to make way for Olympic venues and infrastructure were hardly realized. To wrest control of the space necessary to host the five-ring festival, the Chinese government deployed administrative measures to acquire land. These processes routinely circumvented democratic consultation. Fiscal compensation for those who were displaced was uneven at best; land confiscation was essentially the order of the Olympic day. The Centre on Housing Rights and Evictions (COHRE) adduced that 1.5 million people were displaced from their homes because of Olympics-induced development and urbanization. In their report *One World, Whose Dream?: Housing Rights Violations and the Beijing Olympic Games*, the group asserts that Olympic organizers in Beijing

> have been responsible for destroying affordable rental housing stock, and authorities have used tactics of harassment, repression, imprisonment, and even violence against residents and activists. The Municipality has also subjected people, including alleged unlicensed taxis operators, street vendors, vagrants and beggars, to 'Re-education through Labour'—a form of imprisonment without charge. Moreover, demolitions and evictions have often been undertaken without due process, without the provision of adequate compensation sufficient to attain alternative accommodation, and without access to legal recourse. In some cases, tenants were given little or no notice of their eviction and did not receive the promised compensation. Compensation rates have rarely enabled affected people to relocate while retaining the same standard of living. Instead, residents have been forced to move further from sources of employment, community networks, and decent schools and health care facilities.[6]

To be sure, not every single one of the 1.5 million evictions resulted directly from the Beijing Olympics, but COHRE found ample evidence that Chinese authorities took full advantage of the state of exception that the Games created. Government officials coerced residents into 'voluntarily' relocating in order to assist with the wider goal of showing the world China's best face. On the practical side, rebuking the state could mean earning a lower compensation sum or no sum at all. To get residents on board, Chinese authorities covered neighborhoods with pro-Games propaganda. Slogans like "Welcome the Olympics," "Treasure the Opportunity," "Switch to a New Look," "Improve Our Surroundings," and "Initiate a New Life" were plastered around the city to inspire compliance.[7] Amid the whirling swirl of propaganda, residents were often shortchanged. For instance, Beijing resident Guo Tiehui was booted from his home and only received compensation for one-third the square footage he occupied. Capturing the complexity of the situation, or at least reflecting the intimidation in the air, he told the *Washington Post*, "Chinese people do support the Olympics, but we also need reasonable compensation." He added, "We don't believe that our houses were torn down for the Olympics. The real purpose is moneymaking."[8]

At the London 2012 Games, gentrification was the dominant dynamic, although around 1,200 people in East London were displaced to make way for the Games, including 450 from Clays Lane Estate, a thriving housing cooperative eviscerated by the Olympics. Londoner Julian Cheyne, who was displaced from his home in Clays Lane Estate, told me, "You are swept aside—it's just like a juggernaut." He described the experience as "a very stressful situation" and added, "The only reason Clays Lane was demolished was because of the Olympics."[9] Gentrification ravaged sections of Newham, one of the host boroughs. Estelle du Boulay, director of the Newham Monitoring Project, an East London–based, antiracist organization, told me, "There is a reality to these sports events when they land on your town, they basically overturn the community life that is already there and the progress that was happening organically. This is a huge project of gentrification. There's a lot of money in this project and we don't see it coming back to local communities." Because of the economic pressure of rising rents, the Newham Monitoring Project had to relocate from Stratford. According to du Boulay, the Olympics-induced gentrification was sure to "widen the gap between the rich and poor in the borough."[10]

Rio witnessed both significant gentrification and widespread eviction. Rampant real estate speculation and the financialization of urban land was the order of the day. The geographer Christopher Gaffney points out that "different processes of gentrification" were "happening in different parts of the city."[11] This gentrification took many forms, from huge rent spikes in Flamengo to state-driven commercial ventures in Porto Maravilha to new-build construction in Barra da Tijuca.[12] Barra da Tijuca, the sprawling western zone of Rio de Janeiro, was a central hub for the Olympics where numerous venues and stadiums were built specifically to service the Games.

In the process, Rio 2016 shifted public resources into private hands, ginning up sizable profits for well-connected impresarios with links to people in high places. A prime example of this was the construction of the Olympic Village. At the center of the Olympic Village scheme sat Carlos Carvalho, the Brazilian real estate baron whose firm Carvalho Hosken took responsibility for building the housing project, alongside Odebrecht, the scandal-wracked contractor embroiled in the Petrobras bribery imbroglio known as Lava Jato (Car Wash). Rio's Olympic bid innocuously stated, "Carvalho Hosken, acting as land owner and developer, will assume responsibility for the construction of the Olympic and Paralympic Village. Carvalho Hosken has already entered into a cooperative and collaborative development relationship with Rio 2016." The plan was to have Rio 2016 rent the Olympic Village—more than thirty high-rise buildings—from Carvalho at a capped cost of around $19 million.[13]

However, the bid fails to note that billionaire Carlos Carvalho stood to make astronomical profits from the Games by converting the Olympic Village into more than 3,600 unapologetically high-priced condos in a gated community called Ilha Pura (Pure Island). Units were slated to sell from $230,000 to $925,000. All this was done on the back of a R$2.3 billion loan from Caixa, a Brazilian public bank, at a heavily subsidized interest rate and with a healthy contribution of public land. Meanwhile, critics pointed out that Carvalho and another developer in Barra da Tijuca donated more than R$1 million to Eduardo Paes's election campaign. Geophysically speaking, Ilha Pura isn't even an actual island; it's a social island where class matters. Carvalho told Jonathan Watts of *The Guardian* that he wanted to create, "a city of the elite, of good taste. . . . For this reason, it needed to be noble housing, not housing for the poor."[14] Yet, in a way, "the poor" had a role to play. A year before the Games, Brazilian media revealed that construction workers at the Olympic village were laboring under slave-like conditions, inhabiting living quarters teeming with rats and cockroaches. Carvalho's role in building the Olympic village and Olympic stadium helped make him the thirteenth richest person in Brazil, with a net worth of $4.2 billion. But the real-estate karma gods may have intervened: thanks to Brazil's economic downturn, condo sales lagged. Two weeks before the Games' opening ceremony, only 240 of the 3,600 units had sold.[15]

In the wider picture, between the time the International Olympic Committee awarded Rio the Games back in 2009 and the Games' kick-off in 2016, around 77,000 *cariocas*, or residents of Rio, had been displaced to make way for Olympics infrastructure and venues.[16] Theresa Williamson, founder of Catalytic Communities, a Rio-based NGO that monitors human rights issues in favelas, told me, "The number is likely much higher, since these are official statistics that traditionally undercount favela residents in all aspects of data collection, much less eviction." She added, "Without the pretext of the Olympic deadline, very few of the evictions undertaken by the Paes administration would have been possible."[17] A study from the Rio-based think tank Instituto Igarapé estimated that the Rio Olympics could displace 100,000 people.[18]

One favela that gained significant international media traction was Vila Autódromo, a small, working-class neighborhood along the Jacarepaguá lagoon on the edge of Barra da Tijuca. The favela found itself in front of the Olympics steamroller, but residents battled the city-driven displacement every step of the way. As legendary Brazilian journalist Juca Kfouri put it ahead of the Games, "Vila Autódromo . . . still resists the merciless displacement driven by the Olympics."[19] Originally more than 600 families lived in Vila Autódromo, but by the time the Games arrived, only about twenty remained, and this after a protracted political battle with the city. Partway through the Rio Olympics, the community held a celebration of its tenacity as well as its ability to fight an asymmetrical power battle and win. Amid the festivities, around one hundred activists peeled away to walk over to the Olympic stadium area wielding large protest banners that read *Jogos da Exclusão* (Exclusion Games), "*#CalamidadeOlímpica*" ("#OlympicCalamity"), and "*Terrorista É o Estado*" ("The State Is Terrorist").[20] It should be emphasized that the dynamics of social dislocation that these activists courageously resisted crop up in every twenty-first century Olympic city, whether it be market-driven gentrification or iron-fisted displacement.

MILITARIZATION OF THE PUBLIC SPHERE

When residents of Vila Autódromo and their allies marched over to the nucleus of Olympic stadiums to protest during the Olympic Games, they waded into a sea of militarized security officials. In this instance, police looked the other way and allowed the demonstration to transpire.

Nevertheless, the security presence at Rio 2016 was formidable. Around a year before the Games began, Olympics security head Andrei Augusto Rodrigues announced that Rio 2016 would deploy 85,000 personnel to police the Games, more than doubling the number at London 2012. He said, "There has never been anything like this in the country."[21] Although Rio's Olympic bid stated, "Brazil has no history of any significant international or domestic terrorist activity and Brazilian authorities have not identified any terrorism threats to the 2016 Games in Brazil," the security force included 1,500 people whose sole focus was antiterrorism.[22] In other words, the Olympics had potentially transmuted Rio into a terrorism target.

Such militarized policing in the name of terrorism prevention has become par for the Olympic course in the twenty-first century. There was an intensification of policing practices after the 1972 Munich Olympics, where members of a Palestinian group calling itself Black September snuck into the Olympic village and kidnapped Israeli athletes. This eventually led to a gun battle where all the sequestered Israeli athletes and five Palestinians were killed on the airport tarmac as they prepared to board a plane. But the militarization of Olympic security saw an even bigger boost after the terrorist attacks in the United States on September 11, 2001. The Salt Lake City Winter Olympics were the first Games staged after those attacks. A 12,000-strong security force policed the Games, replete with biometric surveillance technologies, chemical weapons, riot gear, and paint-pellet weapons for dispersing crowds. Even before the attacks of September 11, the Salt Lake City Organizing Committee was planning on cordoning off "designated forums" where protesters could demonstrate only if they secured permits in advance. Just before the Games began, the city council passed an ordinance that forbade demonstrators from donning masks in public during the Olympics.[23]

The 2004 Athens Games upped the security ante. Organizers spent approximately $1.5 billion on security measures, which amounted to nearly $143,000 per athlete and an increase of more than 700 percent over the prior Summer Games in Sydney.[24] Greek officials created what security scholar Minas Samatas calls an "Olympic superpanopticon" comprising surveillance cameras, vehicle tracking devices, satellites, and much more. The U.S.-based security firm SAIC provided a centralized "C4I" (Command, Control, Communication, Computer and Integration) security system to filter the surveillance-derived data. The system was originally developed for military use, but in Athens it was used to not only monitor terrorist threats but also activists who were expressing dissent.[25] According to Samatas,

> The military security umbrella was activated on July 27, 2004, just before the Olympic Games were to start. Hundreds of CCTV cameras swept the main avenues and squares of Athens, whereas three police helicopters and a zeppelin, equipped with more surveillance cameras, hovered overhead. The helicopters and the zeppelin were flying almost around the clock throughout the games. Dozens of new PAC 3 (Patriot Advanced Capability) missiles were armed and in position at three locations around the capital, including the Tatoi Military Base near the athletes' Olympic Village, to provide a defense umbrella over Athens. Security forces also received 11 state-of-the-art surveillance vans that received and monitored images from around the city. . . . By the August 13 opening ceremony, authorities had installed thousands of CCTV cameras and deployed all over Greece more than 70,000 military and security staff on patrol.[26]

According to Olympics organizers in Athens, the security force also included around forty explosives detection devices, more than 4,000 automatic vehicle locators, and chemical and radiological detection systems.[27] At the time, the Athens Games were the most expensive peacetime operation ever.[28]

Subsequent Olympics followed a similar path. The 2010 Winter Games in Vancouver saw the creation of the Vancouver Integrated Security Unit (VISU), a force headed by the Royal Canadian Mounted Police (RCMP) and consisting of more than twenty policing agencies. Ostensibly designed to thwart terrorism, VISU doubled as an activist intimidator. Security officials purchased military-grade weaponry such as a Medium Range Acoustic Device (MRAD). (However, due to pushback from civil libertarians, activists, and the media, the MRAD was not used during the Games.) The security price tag totaled more than $1 billion, far surpassing the initial estimate of $175 million.

Officials deployed 17,000 security personnel, including agents from the Canadian Border Services Agency, the Canadian Security Intelligence Service, city police forces, and the RCMP. The Office of the Privacy Commissioner of Canada reported that approximately 1,000 surveillance cameras were installed across metropolitan Vancouver. The state both infiltrated activists groups and harangued individual dissidents on the streets.[29]

The London 2012 Olympics conformed to the trend. Games organizers threw a spotlight on the dynamic whereby security forces that are ostensibly marshaled to squelch terrorism can also be used to quash, or at the very least intimidate, political activists. This dynamic was in clear evidence when in late 2011 the national coordinator of Olympics security briefed the London Assembly on policing costs for the Olympic and Paralympic Games. He singled out "four key risks to the Games"— terrorism, protest, organized crime, and natural disasters.[30]

To address these "four key risks," Olympics security officials militarized public space in London. The Ministry of Defense located surface-to-air missiles in the city (including atop residential apartment buildings). Typhoon fighter jets and Puma helicopters zinged through the city's airspace. The Metropolitan Police purchased more than 10,000 plastic bullets and constructed mobile stations for quicker bookings. The *BBC* reported that Olympics security had even acquired a Long Range Acoustic Device, as if to outdo Vancouver's MRAD. The Games featured a literally militaristic element, with more than 18,000 military personnel policing Games venues. Another 17,000 police officials joined them. Scotland Yard organized "dispersal zones" where police freely banned people they deemed to be engaging in antisocial behavior. Estelle du Boulay of the Newham Monitoring Project told me that in the state of exception created by the Olympics, local police were "rolling out more draconian measures and more attempts to increase the power of the police." She observed that in the year ahead of the Games, London experienced "a different kind of policing, a harder form of policing against our communities, and just a far greater police presence on the ground."[31] This intimidating police presence was a shadow legacy of the Games.

The Sochi 2014 Winter Olympics featured similar dynamics, in part because of the fact that the Games were staged in a political tinderbox. Russia was enmeshed in a longstanding disagreement with Georgia over the Abkhazia region, and Sochi is also located near Chechnya, Dagestan, and Ingushetia, where anti-Russian sentiment was rampant. One prominent Chechen rebel beseeched his supporters to "do their utmost to derail" the Games, which he described as "satanic dances on the bones of our ancestors."[32]

Meantime, Russian officials were already moving to crack down on domestic dissent. Ahead of the Games, Human Rights Watch pronounced:

> The Russian government has unleashed a crackdown on civil society unprecedented in the country's post-Soviet history. The authorities have introduced a series of restrictive laws, harassed, intimidated, and in several cases imprisoned political activists, interfered in the work of nongovernmental organizations (NGOs), and sought to cast government critics as clandestine enemies, thereby threatening the viability of Russia's civil society.[33]

One of these "restricted laws" required NGOs engaging in "political activity" and receiving funds from outside Russia to register as "foreign agents," a term thrumming with subtext from the Soviet era. The Russian Duma also crafted legislation with a broad, imprecise definition of "high treason." Civil libertarians voiced concern that this capacious definition could be applied to any Russian—especially political activists—who worked with foreign groups. Astride all this, Russian security forces ramped up their intimidation in March 2013, doing impromptu inspections at hundreds of NGO headquarters. Then, only six months ahead of the Sochi Olympics, Russian President Vladimir Putin decreed that all non-Olympics "gatherings, rallies, demonstrations, marches and pickets" in Sochi between January 7 and March 21 would be illegal. After pushback from the international human rights community, Russian officials backpedaled, instead establishing "protest zones." One was located in Khosta, a village more than seven miles from the nearest Olympics site. Not surprisingly, no protests were staged in Khosta, where the protest zone was tucked under a highway overpass.[34]

All this set the security stage for Rio de Janeiro. When Rio bid for the 2004 and 2012 Olympics, it was criticized by the IOC for lacking proper security. With that in mind, when Brazilian President Luiz Inácio Lula da Silva traveled to Copenhagen in 2009 to pitch Rio's Olympic bid, he was joined by Captain Pricilla Azevedo, commander in the Pacification Police Units (or UPPs, *Unidades de Polícia Pacificadora*), a program set up to stymie violence in favelas.[35] When it came time to vote, IOC members appeared satisfied that Brazil had addressed its alleged deficiency—they voted to send the Games to Rio rather than Chicago, Madrid, or Tokyo.

Security officials plunged ahead, stockpiling military-grade hardware. Ahead of the 2014 soccer World Cup, the Brazilian Defense Ministry purchased Black Hawk and Sabre helicopters as well as A-29 Super Tucano aircraft outfitted for aerial surveillance and counterinsurgency. This high-tech weaponry was also available for the Olympics.[36] One group of Brazil-based researchers asserted that the *perception* of safety—"*the sale of the sense of security*"—was vital to the Olympic spectacle.[37] Along these lines, Rio 2016 organizers hired Giuliani Security and Safety, the security firm headed by former New York mayor Rudy Giuliani, as a consultant who could impart guidance regarding policing, technology, and weapons.[38] In reality, a powerful security presence was always part of the Rio 2016 master plan. According to the original candidature file, the Brazilian Defense Forces would be integral, offering "a significant contribution to Games security planning and operations." The bid went on to assert, "The Army will have a key venue security role in the Deodoro Zone, and the Air Force and Navy will provide airspace control and protection and maritime security for Games venues." In addition, bidders stated that the Army would "be an important part of the counterterrorism plan for the Games."[39]

For many human rights observers, this was hardly comforting. Amnesty International reported a year before the Rio Olympics that Brazil's military police had carried out 1,500 killings in the previous five years. The group viewed many of the deaths as "extrajudicial executions" via excessive force or occurring after the victim had surrendered or was previously injured. Additionally, between 2010 and 2013, 79 percent of the victims were cariocas of color (51 percent brown and 28 percent black) and 75 percent were young (between fifteen and twenty-nine years old).[40] Plus, Rio's police have a history of mass violence during sports megaevents. Ahead of the Pan American Games of 2007, security officials killed dozens of civilians in Rio's Complexo do Alemão.[41] During the 2013 Confederations Cup, police killed at least nine people from the Maré favela complex, firing a hail of bullets from helicopters floating above.[42]

Anyone considering protesting during the Olympics had additional grounds for pause: the Rio bid explicitly conflated activism and terrorism. In a section of the bid curiously titled "Activist/Terrorist Risks" the bidders contended, "The risk to the Games from protest action and domestic terrorism is low." However, the bid then specifically identified "issue motivated groups" that are "concerned with indigenous rights, environmental or anti-globalization issues." Although the protest repertoires of these groups are typically legal and nonviolent, Brazilian security officials were concocting "comprehensive civil order plans" and "establishing designated protest areas."[43]

Before and during the Olympics, protests occurred across the city. The *Comitê Popular da Copa do Mundo e das Olimpíadas* (The Popular Committee of the World Cup and the Olympics) organized a four-day teach-in just before the Olympics kicked off on August 5.[44] On the opening day of the Olympics, there were two sizable street mobilizations that connected the Games to the broader political crisis and threw a spotlight on the opportunity costs involved in accommodating Games goers while health and education budgets were being slashed. Around 15,000 people attended a rally along Copacabana Beach in a "Fora Temer" ("Temer Out") protest challenging the legitimacy of then interim president Michel Temer. Choreographed by groups like Brasil Popular, Esquerda Socialista, and Povo Sem Medo, the rambunctious event diverted the route of the Olympic torch relay. Later that day, activists from the *Comitê Popular* coordinated a rally under the banner *Jogos da Exclusão* (Exclusion Games) at Praça Sáenz Peña, a public plaza close to the Maracanã Stadium, which hours later would be the site of the opening ceremony for Rio 2016. These mobilizations received markedly different police responses. The former was allowed to proceed with a light security touch while the afternoon protest was met with blunt repression by police outfitted in riot gear. These militarized police units occasionally shifted formation, marching in a tight pattern with hands on the shoulder of the officer in front of them. Later, they were bolstered by busloads of additional riot police. At one point a police helicopter circled overhead. Tear gas was sprayed at protesters below. It was a policing style designed to maximize intimidation.[45]

As mentioned above, Olympic athletic venues were filled with an overwhelming security presence. Meanwhile, however, Rio's exurbs and favelas experienced an uptick in violence where policing was thinned to accommodate the Games. The first week of the Olympics saw an average of more than eight firearms shootings per day, almost double that of the previous week. Understaffed police forces resorted to violent operations across the city: Acari, Cidade de Deus, Borel, Manguinhos, Alemão, Maré, Del Castilho, and Cantagalo all saw police violence resulting in at least five deaths and numerous wounded individuals. Renata Neder of Amnesty International in Brazil wrote, "Security operations in the context of Rio 2016 are violating the rights of a large part of the population of Rio de Janeiro."[46]

After the five-ring juggernaut departed Rio de Janeiro along with its massive security detail, the bloodshed intensified. In the wake of the Rio Olympics, violence soared across the city. By September 2016, the city's murder rate saw an uptick of nearly 18 percent compared to the same period in 2015.[47] From January through October 2016, street robberies leaped by 48 percent compared to the same months in 2015.[48] These figures reflect a dynamic inherent to hosting the Olympics in the twenty-first century: domestic security forces use the Games like their own private cash machine, leveraging all the special laws and weapons that would be more difficult to secure during normal political times.

TRANSPORTATION NETWORK DEVELOPMENT

Over the course of the Olympics, aspiring host cities have ramped up their legacy promises in regards to providing improved transport structures—roads, subways, train lines, airport terminals, and more—that will remain in the wake of the Games. Hosting the sports megaevent can provide local developers, politicians, and urban planners with a socially acceptable means to justify an infusion of public investment in transport infrastructure.[49] The development of transport networks tends to be one of the few legacy promises that actually gets met, in part because these transportation systems are integral for the Games to function. In addition, transport network construction benefits from the IOC's Transfer of Knowledge program, created in 1998 and renamed the Olympic Games Knowledge Management Program in 2005. "Olympic Transport System" requirements have been successfully implemented in numerous Olympic cities. Urban and transport planning researcher Eva Kassens-Noor contends, "The Olympic Games can be a powerful stimulus for transport improvements in host cities," in particular when they "follow a very specific Olympics-driven or Olympics-catalyzed agenda."[50]

Exhibit A is the 2004 Athens Games. The city used the Olympics to spur significant upgrades to its bus, rail, and road networks. Step one was securing the requisite land. Athens took full advantage of the state of exception that the Olympics bring. Organizers noted in their official report:

> With the expert support provided by ATHOC and with the new legal framework, the process of land expropriation was significantly accelerated. Land for all the major Olympic Works that were initially assigned to ATHOC (e.g. the Olympic Village, the Equestrian Centre and Racecourse, the Rowing Centre) as well as for the other Olympic Works, sports venues or non competition, and also for the infrastructure projects, such as roads and rail track transport, was secured in record time.[51]

Step two was contracting out the work for the ambitious transport plans that Athens organizers charted out in their Olympic bid. Although the organizing committee's Transport Division got a late start, which contributed to the last-minute nature of systems delivery, it eventually got its traction and managed to coordinate strategic and operational plans that were executed during the Olympics.[52] The Athens transport plan aimed to alleviate two intractable transport problems in the city: massive road congestion and limited airport access.[53] Ahead of the Games, Athens was the beneficiary of 120 kilometers of fresh roads and another 90 kilometers of revamped roadways as well as forty new junctions. In addition, the city received three major metro lines, with Metro Line 1 serving as a central travel artery during the Games. The region also received a tram and suburban rail lines. In addition, the city got "Olympic express bus lines" as well as an increase in the frequency of extant bus lines servicing Games venues.[54]

The Rio 2016 candidature file forecast a similar revitalization of transport infrastructure. The Games took place in four separate zones spread across the city. In an effort to facilitate smooth passage between venues and across the city, bidders promised "a High Performance Transport Ring" that involved a "completely renovated suburban railway system, an upgraded metro system and three new Bus Rapid Transit (BRT) systems." Numerous transfer stations were planned to help connect spectators to the sports events they wished to watch. The long-term idea was to forge for cariocas "a legacy with a significant social impact."[54] Undoubtedly there was a real need in Rio, and Brazil more widely, for high-capacity, top-quality public transportation infrastructure. As Andrew Zimbalist noted ahead of the Olympics, "The Brazilian economy is in dire need of light rail, metros, intercity train transport, roads, bridges, ports, and airport improvements, yet it spends only 1.5 percent of its GDP on infrastructure, compared to the global average of 3.3 percent."[55] This lack of reliable infrastructure hurts Brazilian businesses.

Arguably the most important transport development was the extension of the Rio Metro from the tourist-friendly Zona Sul area that includes upscale Ipanema and Copacabana to Barra da Tijuca, the major Olympic hub. Known as Linha 4, it served as a vital pipeline for Games goers. Although the decision to prioritize Metro extension deserves criticism for leapfrogging more pressing transport needs— such as connecting workers north of the city to their jobs in the Zona Sul—it was a significant advance for the people of Rocinha, Rio's largest favela, as a Metro stop sits at the base of Rocinha. However, during the actual Olympics, residents of Rocinha were not allowed on the Metro unless they possessed both a ticket to an Olympic event and a special daily Metro pass, which cost a pricey R$25 (approximately $8). In short, during the Games the subway served as a non-stop pipeline for Olympic tourists traveling from the south zone to the Olympic zone. Everyday cariocas were boxed out.

CONCLUSION: LEGACY PROMISES, MET AND UNMET

In advance of each Olympic Games, the media descend on the host city, sniffing out controversies and problems. In the twenty-first century, with the Games under the influence of what seems like ever-ballooning gigantism, there are plenty of disagreements to be found. When the media put Rio 2016 under the analytical microscope it found, in varying degrees, problems with social dislocation, militarized policing, and transport development. What this chapter aims to make clear is that simply chalking these up to ineptitude in Rio is misleading. The ugliest variant of this line of thinking is that South Americans simply were not equipped to host the Games. To be sure, organizers in Rio offered hefty doses of arrogance and maladroitness along the way, and endemic government corruption raised both the cost and inefficiency of the Games. But the reality is that the significant problems that we saw in Rio are actually Olympic problems. A similar pattern of issues occurs in Olympic cities regardless of whether they are in the developed or developing world.

Residents of aspiring host cities are waking up to this reality. In fall 2014, elected officials in Oslo, Norway, rejected the city's bid to host the 2022 Winter Olympics. Norway's Prime Minister Erna Solberg stated, "A big project like this, which is so expensive, requires broad popular support, and there isn't enough support for it."[57] This followed other cities in the bidding war for the 2022 Games coming to similar conclusions. Everyday people and elected officials squelched bid efforts in Kraków, Poland; Munich, Germany; Stockholm, Sweden; and Lviv, Ukraine, as well as in Davos and St. Moritz, Switzerland. In the end, this left only two cities in the running: Almaty, Kazakhstan, and Beijing, China, neither of them places where political freedom flourishes. IOC members chose Beijing, making it the first city to host both the Summer and Winter Games. Then, in September 2016, the mayor of Rome, Virginia Raggi, quashed the city's bid for the 2024

Summer Olympics. She was actually elected on an anti-Olympics, anti-corruption platform; in fact, she connected the two hot-button issues, campaigning on the idea that sports megaevents like the Olympic Games were hotbeds for bribery, malfeasance, and false hope.[58] Further, there is very little accountability among IOC members who hop straight to the helipad after the Games conclude, zipping off to the next five-ring destination.

Still, diehard boosters in Rio pressed ahead with the rote script. In mid-November 2016, Rio 2016 President Carlos Nuzman took what *Around the Rings* described as a "victory lap" at a gathering of the Association of National Olympic Committees. He said the Rio Games were "the most connected, the most scrutinized, and maybe the most influential" Games in the entire history of the Olympics movement.[59] More and more, such blind enthusiasm is being curbed by fact patterns, fiscal caution, and fiery dissent.

NOTES

1. "President Thomas Bach Awards the Olympic Order to Rio 2016 Organisers," August 22, 2016 (www.olympic.org/news/president-thomas -bach-awards-the-olympic-order-to-rio-2016-organisers).

2. David Wharton, "IOC President Thomas Bach Faces Questions about Olympic Troubles," *Los Angeles Times*, August 27, 2016.

3. Ed Hula, "Carlos Nuzman: 'I Never Give Up,'" *Around the Rings*, November 12, 2016 (http://aroundtherings.com/site/A__58149/title__Carlos -Nuzman-'I-Never-Give-Up'/292/Articles).

4. Jonathan Watts, "Cleaners at Rio's Athletes' Village Paid Just £1.40 an Hour," *The Guardian*, August 18, 2016.

5. Trevor Paglen, *Blank Spots on the Map: The Dark Geography of the Pentagon's Secret World* (New York: New American Library, 2010), p. 280.

6. *One World, Whose Dream?: Housing Rights Violations and the Beijing Olympic Games* (Geneva, Switzerland: Centre on Housing Rights and Evictions [COHRE], July 2008), pp. 6–7.

7. *One World, Whose Dream?*, p. 11.

8. Maureen Fan, "China Defends Relocation Policy," *Washington Post*, February 20, 2008, p. A14.

9. Jules Boykoff, *Activism and the Olympics: Dissent at the Games in Vancouver and London* (New Brunswick, NJ: Rutgers University Press, 2014), pp. 110–11.

10. Ibid., pp. 111–12.

11. Christopher Gaffney, "Gentrifications in Pre-Olympic Rio de Janeiro," *Urban Geography* (2015), p. 3.

12. Ibid., pp. 1–22.

13. Rio 2016, "Candidate City Bid," vol. 2, pp. 203, 205. For a more robust discussion of Olympic Village construction, see Jules Boykoff, *Power Games: A Political History of the Olympics* (New York and London: Verso, 2016).

14. Jonathan Watts, "The Rio Property Developer Hoping for a $1bn Olympic Legacy of His Own," *The Guardian*, August 4, 2015 (https://www .theguardian.com/sport/2015/aug/04/rio-olympic-games-2016-property -developer-carlos-carvalho-barra).

15. "MP Resgata 11 Trabalhadores Escravos em Obras para as Olimpía-das," *O Dia*, August 14, 2015; Blake Schmidt, "Rio Olympics Developer Car-valho Becomes 13th-Richest in Brazil," *Bloomberg*, August 21, 2015 (https:// www.bloomberg.com/news/articles/2015-08-21/rio-olympics-developer -carvalho-becomes-13th-richest-in-brazil); Stephen Eisenhammer, "Rio Risks Empty Legacy as Real Estate Stalls," *Reuters*, July 19, 2016 (http://www .reuters.com/article/us-olympics-rio-realestate-insight-idUSKCN0ZZ179).

16. Cerianne Robertson, "Popular Committee Launches Final Human Rights Violations Dossier Ahead of Rio 2016 'Exclusion Games,'" *RioOn-Watch*, December 10, 2015 (http://www.rioonwatch.org/?p=25747).

17. Jules Boykoff, "Six Months Out from Olympics, Rich, Not Poor, Are the Big Winners," *Folha de São Paulo*, February 5, 2016.

18. Raphael Martins, "Obras das Olimpíadas Podem Tirar Até 100 Mil de Suas Casas," *Exame*, August 30, 2015.

19. Juca Kfouri, "A Vila Autódromo Resiste," *Folha de São Paulo*, February 4, 2016.

20. Dave Zirin and Jules Boykoff, "One Community's Resistance Will Be the Rio Olympics' Longest-Lasting Legacy," *The Nation*, August 17, 2016 (www.thenation.com/article/one-communitys-resistance-will-be-the -rio-olympics-longest-lasting-legacy/).

21. "Rio 2016 Olympics to Hire 85,000 Security Staff," *BBC*, July 31, 2015 (http://www.bbc.com/sport/olympics/33729359).

22. Rio 2016, "Candidate City Bid," vol. 3, p. 27; "More than 1,500 Anti-terrorism Troops to Guard Rio Olympics," *AFP*, September 10, 2015.

23. Boykoff, *Power Games*, pp. 111–15, 153.

24. Minas Samatas, "Security and Surveillance in the Athens 2004 Olympics: Some Lessons from a Troubled Story," *International Criminal Justice Review* 17 (2007), pp. 220–38, at 225; John Sugden, "Watched by the Games: Surveillance and Security at the Olympics," in *Watching the*

Olympics: Politics, Power and Representation, edited by John Sugden and Alan Tomlinson (London: Routledge, 2012), pp. 228–41, at 231–32; Philip Boyle, "Securing the Olympic Games: Exemplifications of Global Governance," in *The Palgrave Handbook of Olympic Studies*, edited by Helen Jefferson Lenskyj and Stephen Wagg (Basingstoke, U.K.: Palgrave Macmillan, 2012), pp. 394–409, at 394.

25. Minas Samatas, "Security and Surveillance in the Athens 2004 Olympics: Some Lessons From a Troubled Story," *International Criminal Justice Review* 17 (2007), pp. 224, 221.

26. Ibid., p. 224.

27. *Official Report of the XXVIII Olympiad*, vol. 1 (Athens 2004 Organising Committee for the Olympic Games, November 2005), p. 190 (www.la84foundation.org/6oic/OfficialReports/2004/or2004ap1.pdf).

28. John Horne and Garry Whannel, *Understanding the Olympics* (London: Routledge, 2012), p. 136.

29. Jules Boykoff, "The Anti-Olympics: Fun at the Games," *New Left Review* 67 (Jan–Feb 2011), pp. 41–59.

30. Boykoff, *Activism and the Olympics*, p. 117.

31. Ibid., pp. 118–19.

32. Jules Boykoff, "Celebration Capitalism and the Sochi 2014 Winter Olympics," *Olympika: The International Journal of Olympic Studies* 22 (2013), pp. 39–70, at 57–58.

33. "Laws of Attrition: Crackdown on Russia's Civil Society after Putin's Return to the Presidency," *Human Rights Watch*, April 24, 2013, p. 1 (www.hrw.org/reports/2013/04/24/laws-attrition-0).

34. Boykoff, *Power Games*, pp. 200–2.

35. Juliana Barbassa, *Dancing with the Devil in the City of God: Rio de Janeiro on the Brink* (New York: Touchstone, 2015), p. 40.

36. "Aeronáutica Esclarece Medidas de Restrição de Voos Nas Cidades-sede," *Ministério da Defensa, Força Aérea Brasileira*, March 21, 2014 (www.fab.mil.br/noticias/mostra/18005/).

37. Demian Garcia Castro, Christopher Gaffney, Patrícia Ramos Novaes, Juciano Rodrigues, Carolina Pereira dos Santos, and Orlando Alves dos Santos Junior, "O Projeto Olímpico da Cidade do Rio de Janeiro: Reflexões sobre os Impactos dos Megaeventos Esportivos na Perspectiva do Direito à Cidade," in *Brasil: Os Impactos Da Copa Do Mundo 2014 e Das Olimpíadas 2016*, edited by Orlando Alves dos Santos Junior, Christopher Gaffney, and Luiz Cesar de Queiroz Ribeiro (Rio de Janeiro: Observatório Das Metrópoles, 2015), p. 411, emphasis added.

38. Samantha R. McRoskey, "Security and the Olympic Games: Making Rio an Example," *Yale Journal of International Affairs* (Spring–Summer

2010), p. 102; Rio 2016 Organizing Committee, "Rudolph Giuliani Visits Rio 2016 Committee and Praises the Games Project," *Rio 2016*, September 11, 2013 (www.rio2016.com/en/news/news/rudolph-giuliani-visits-rio -2016-committee-and-praises-the-games-project-i-m-very-impresse).

39. Rio 2016, "Candidate City Bid," vol. 3, p. 43.

40. Amnesty International, "You Killed My Son: Homicides by Military Police in the City of Rio de Janeiro," August 3, 2015 (https://www .amnesty.org/en/documents/amr19/2068/2015/en/), pp. 33–35.

41. "Fight in the Favelas," *The Economist*, August 2, 2007 (www .economist.com/node/9597408).

42. Marianna Aravjo and Vitor Castro, "Maré de Terror," *Agência Pública*, July 1, 2013.

43. Rio 2016, "Candidate City Bid," vol. 3, p. 33.

44. For a full treatment of the *Comitê Popular*, see Christopher Gaffney, "An Anatomy of Resistance: The Popular Committees of the FIFA World Cup in Brazil," in *Sport, Protest, and Globalisation: Stopping Play*, edited by Jon Dart and Stephen Wagg (New York: Palgrave, 2016), pp. 335–363.

45. Jules Boykoff, "The Olympic Calamity," *Jacobin*, August 8, 2016 (www.jacobinmag.com/2016/08/olympics-protests-rio-temer-coup-brazil/).

46. Renata Neder, "10 Dias de Rio2016: Um Balanço da Insegurança Pública na Cidade Olímpica," Anistia Internacional, August 16, 2016 (https://anistia.org.br/10-dias-de-olimpiada-um-balanco-da-inseguranca -publica-na-cidade-olimpica/).

47. Paulo Prada, "Police Helicopter Crashes, Kills 4, After Rio Shoot-out," *Reuters*, November 19, 2016 (www.reuters.com/article/us-brazil -violence-helicopter-idUSKBN13F017?il=0).

48. Will Carless, "Three Months After the Olympics, Rio De Janeiro Is Broke," *Public Radio International*, December 1, 2016 (www.opb.org /news/article/olympics-brazil-rio-money/).

49. Stephen Essex and Brian Chalkey, "Olympic Games: Catalyst of Urban Change," *Leisure Studies* 17 (1998), pp. 187–206.

50. Eva Kassens-Noor, "Transport Legacy of the Olympic Games, 1992–2012," *Journal of Urban Affairs* 35, no. 4 (2012), p. 406.

51. *Official Report of the XXVIII Olympiad*, p. 148.

52. John M. Frantzeskakis and Michael J. Frantzeskakis, "Athens 2004 Olympic Games: Transportation Planning, Simulation and Traffic Management," *Institute of Transport Engineers Journal* (October 2006), pp. 26–32.

53. Eva Kassens-Noor, "Sustaining the Momentum: Olympics as a Catalyst for Enhancing Urban Transport," *Transportation Research Record*, no. 2187 (2010), pp. 106–13.

54. *Official Report of the XXVIII Olympiad*, pp. 171–75.

55. Rio 2016, "Candidature File," vol. 3, p. 97.

56. Andrew Zimbalist, *Circus Maximus: The Economic Gamble Behind Hosting the Olympics and the World Cup* (Brookings Institution Press, 2015), p. 70.

57. Lynn Zinser, "Oslo Withdraws Bid to Host 2022 Winter Games, Citing Cost," *New York Times*, October 2, 2014, p. B13.

58. David Wharton, "L.A. Likely Has Lost One of its Rivals for 2024 Olympics," *Los Angeles Times*, September 21, 2016.

59. Aaron Bauer and Kevin Nutley, "Rio Victory Lap at ANOC," *Around the Rings*, November 16, 2016 (http://aroundtherings.com/site/A__58080 /title__Rio-Victory-Lap-at-ANOC/292/Articles).

THREE

Brazil's Olympic Rollercoaster

JULIANA BARBASSA

When Jacques Rogge stood before a gathering of the International Olympic Committee in Copenhagen on October 2, 2009, and pulled Rio de Janeiro's name from an envelope, declaring it the host of the 2016 Summer Games, the Brazilian delegation exploded into celebration. President Luiz Inácio Lula da Silva, the country's first working-class president, cracked under the emotional strain and cried, declaring, "the world has recognized that the time has come for Brazil."[1]

On Copacabana Beach, a crowd decked in yellow and green leapt in celebration. Their enthusiasm was fueled by much more than the chance to host the Olympics. Brazil was experiencing a unique moment in its history: Its economy was strong, fed on Chinese demand for its export commodities—soybeans, iron ore, sugar, beef, and coffee. Foreign direct investment in Brazil had reached record levels. Under the aegis of the Workers Party, or PT in its Portuguese acronym, millions of Brazilians emerged from poverty and began buying everything from stoves to cars to dinners out, stoking domestic consumption and fueling further growth. Discovery of oil just beyond Rio de Janeiro's coast prompted Lula to joke, "God is Brazilian."[2] The petroleum bounty and the political alignment of Rio's mayor, Eduardo Paes; Rio state's governor, Sérgio Cabral; and the president augured well for Rio de

Janeiro, a once-grand national capital fallen on hard times. Finally, there was enough money and political will to tackle the persistent inequality and underdevelopment that defined Brazil.

The Rio Olympics would be the window through which the world would see this bright, new Brazil in which they staked their own futures. For Paes, Cabral, and Lula, the Games would provide a showcase for their handiwork: a Rio de Janeiro refashioned by the preparations for the 2016 Games and an economy forged under PT rule that was on its way to becoming the sixth largest in the world.

Seven years later, when the world turned to Rio de Janeiro for the opening of the 2016 Olympic Games, the state of Rio de Janeiro was broke,[3] and Brazil was gutted by scandals and misrule. Police had hauled Lula in for questioning in connection to a wide-ranging corruption scandal; his handpicked successor Dilma Rousseff was facing impeachment; the interim president was booed in the opening ceremony, as Rouseff herself had been at the opening match of the 2014 World Cup. The national economy shrank for the second year in a row.

To many citizens, the Games that were supposed to signal Brazil's arrival on the world stage had become a symbol of their government's misplaced priorities, wasted opportunities, and graft: two weeks before the start of the opening ceremony one in two Brazilians were against hosting the Olympics, and two out of three believed that hosting would do more harm than good.[4] This chapter will examine this reversal of fortune and how preparations for the 2014 World Cup and the Olympics, once a key part of a narrative of urban renewal in Rio and of Brazil's rise to political and economic prominence, became enmeshed in, a catalyst for, and ultimately a symbol of the corruption plaguing Brazil.

THE COUNTRY OF THE FUTURE, AGAIN

For decades, Brazilians weathered their country's political and economic crises by offering up an old punch line: "Brazil is the country of the future—and it always will be." This inability to live up to its potential had held true during the country's 1964–85 military dictatorship. During those years, rapid growth (dubbed "the Brazilian economic miracle") and investment in high-profile projects, such as hydropower dams, nuclear energy plants, and highways, had come at the price of political repression and fiscal imbalance, ultimately leaving the country mired in the hyperinflation, unemployment, and recession of the 1980s and 1990s.

When Lula ran for president in 2002—his fourth attempt—the country was still in recovery. The possibility of his victory and the fear that Brazilian economic policy would make a hard left under a PT administration rattled the markets and scared investors. Moody's cut its outlook on Brazilian government debt to negative and Fitch downgraded its ratings. The Brazilian real plummeted from two to nearly four to the dollar. Foreign investment shriveled along with lines of credit. Nevertheless, Lula won, a remarkable achievement built on a long fight for democracy and for the political relevance of Brazil's working class that had led the *New York Times* to call him "the Brazilian equivalent of Lech Walesa" in 1981.[5]

Soon after his win, Lula set about reassuring the Brazilian business class and international investors, imposing a stringent fiscal orthodoxy that earned him the praise of IMF and World Bank officials even as it shocked many of his supporters.[6] The trepidation soon turned to euphoria, on the right and on the left, within Brazil and beyond. Fueled by high commodity prices, the country sailed through years of political stability and growth. At home, Lula won the loyalty of millions who benefited from the economic good news and from specific income distribution policies that helped shrink inequality, broaden the middle class, and strengthen the citizenship rights of the poor.[7] Abroad, he promoted Brazil as a profitable place to invest, a growing geopolitical power, and a flourishing democracy where a steel worker could rise from the factory floor to become president.

Two years into Lula's first term investigators revealed a campaign slush fund and a cash-for-congressional-votes scheme involving the Workers Party.[8] This rocked his credibility, but Brazilians, inured to the venality of their legislators, let their desire for more growth and stability sweep aside their concerns.[9] In 2006 Lula was reelected for a second term by a landslide.[10] His broad appeal, which went over as well in world summits as in Rio's favelas, and his ability to weather accusations that could have brought down a lesser political operator were made clear in the headlines that greeted his victory: "Brazil's Working Class Leader Wins Landslide Second Term Victory," in *The Guardian*; "Brazil's President Roars Back to Win Vote," in the *New York Times*; and "Wall Street Loves Lula, Too," in the *Financial Times*.

During this second term (2006–10), Lula presided over a country that seemed to be finally fulfilling its geopolitical and economic potential. Despite the advances of his first administration, much remained to be done. Education and health services were chronically underfunded; an aging infrastructure and a convoluted tax code increased the cost of doing business in the country. But Lula's reelection seemed to indicate that there would be time, political will, and funds to work on those problems, too. Even as the United States' economy tanked, brought down by the subprime mortgage and financial derivative debacle, Brazil's had hiccupped in 2009 but continued to grow, winning three coveted investment-grade ratings. On the strength of this growth and the certainty of its continuation, Lula pushed for greater political clout for Brazil by strengthening alliances with other BRIC countries—Russia, India, and China—raising the profile of the G20, and seeking a permanent seat at the United Nation's Security Council.[11] *The Economist* captured the optimism of the time in a November 2009 cover that showed Rio's *Christ the Redeemer* statue rocketing into space under the headline "Brazil Takes Off."

By the time Lula went to Copenhagen in October 2009 to pitch Rio de Janeiro's Olympic bid against Chicago, Madrid, and Tokyo, he was one of the world's most popular leaders. He was also nearing the end of his second mandate, driven by the desire to cement his domestic legacy and ensure the country's rise to a higher geopolitical echelon. Brazil had already secured the 2014 World Cup. Rio's Olympic candidacy was an extension of this bid for greater visibility and international legitimacy. The International Olympic Committee had played this role before: the 1988 Games helped brand Korea and its industrial power; the 2008 Games served to recognize China's growing international clout. Lula sought the IOC's vote as an indication that his forever-emerging nation had finally arrived.[12]

In his impassioned speech to the IOC, Lula implied that denying Brazil the 2016 Games would perpetuate a historical injustice and deny a new world order. As a self-styled representative of the Global

South, he framed Rio's candidacy as Brazil's and South America's, assuming the mandate to correct geopolitical power imbalances and give greater prominence to the developing world as a whole:

> It's our time. Among the 10 largest economies in the world Brazil is the only country that has not hosted the Olympic and Paralympic Games. Among the countries that now seek the indication we are the only one not to have had the honor. For the others, it would be just another Olympics. For us, it would be an opportunity without equal, increasing Brazilians' self-esteem, consolidating recent achievements, and inspiring new progress. The bid is not only our candidature, it is also that of South America, a continent with almost 400 million men and women and about 180 million young people which has never hosted the Olympic Games. It's time to fix this imbalance.
>
> My friends, Brazil is living through an excellent time. We have worked hard in the last decades. We have a thriving economy, which smoothly confronts the crisis that plagues many nations. . . . Rio's candidature to the Olympic family takes into account this new scenario in which our country has found its place.[13]

BRAZIL'S CONSTRUCTION-INDUSTRIAL COMPLEX

When Lula spoke of the opportunities and the progress that would be inspired by the Olympics, he was likely thinking not only of Brazil's soft power. One of the tangible results of hosting the Olympics would be the construction of new infrastructure. Rio's bid for the 2016 Games was the most costly of the four candidates in 2009, with an initial budget of $11.1 billion for capital investments.[14] It was also the most geographically diffuse, requiring the greatest number of new venues and urban interventions, including extensive and expensive transportation arteries. The Rio 2016 bid committee spent a reported R$100 million on the candidature alone.

The IOC was well aware of the costs and problems of Rio 2016 but found reassurance in Brazil's robust economic health. In the month preceding the IOC vote, the organization released its "Report of the 2016 IOC Evaluation Commission," with assessments of each candidate's plans for hosting the Games. In Rio's Sport and Venues section, the report states that of the thirty-three venues proposed, only ten were in place. Under Transport, it said, "infrastructure development scheduled for completion by 2016 is extensive." However, the IOC reported no cause for concern, pointing to the political and economic context: "All planned projects and related investments are fully guaranteed, with funding provided by the three levels of government." In the Finance section's conclusion, the Commission said it was "confident that the growing Brazilian economy would be able to support the necessary infrastructure development needed for the delivery of the 2016 Games."[15]

Indeed, with China's seemingly insatiable demand for Brazil's raw materials and high commodity prices bringing in a steady increase in revenue (exports went from $118 billion in 2005 to $256 billion in 2011, when they accounted for 14 percent of GDP),[16] Lula's administration had already embarked on a construction spree reminiscent of the extravagant building that took place during the military regime's "economic miracle."[17] His administration was pursuing monumental projects much like those engineered under the dictatorship. These included a controversial string of megadams in the Amazon region,[18] even a number of ventures that had been first proposed during the military years, such as transposing the bed of a northeastern river, the São Francisco; erecting a new thermonuclear plant; and paving the Transamazônica, a highway that traverses Brazil from east to west, cutting right through the Amazon forest.[19] Many of these works fell under the rubric of the PAC, the Programa de Aceleração de Crescimento, or Growth Acceleration Program, launched in 2007 to "increase private investment and public investment in infrastructure," thereby "clearing the logjams that impede investment," in the words of then Finance Minister Guido Mantega.[20] The initial phase of the PAC projected R$503.9 billion in investment.[21] It mushroomed over the following nine years to encompass a budget of R$1.9 trillion by 2015.[22]

Petrobras, the state-controlled oil company, was leading its own ambitious infrastructure development plan to explore the deep offshore oil fields discovered in 2007. This made the company a prime source of hefty government contracts. In 2010, it raised $69.97 billion in the largest share offering to date, making it even more flush with cash. The event had heavy political overtones. It took place one week ahead of the 2010 presidential elections in which Dilma Rousseff, Lula's chief of staff and the chair of Petrobras's board from 2003–10, would be elected president. Lula himself presided over a ceremony that marked the offering in an unmistakable reminder of the federal government's increasing control over the oil giant.[23]

The plan was that, among Petrobras's investments, the PAC projects, the World Cup, and the Olympics, Brazil would create jobs for its workers and the infrastructure it needed to catch up with the developed world.[24] The companies that landed these handsome contracts, paired with low-interest government loans extended through Brazil's development bank, the BNDES, and tax privileges would also fare very well. Lula once remarked that Gen. Ernesto Beckmann Geisel, who led the dictatorship from 1974 to 1979, was "the president who commanded the last great period of development in the country."[25] Even as it followed a similar developmentalist approach as the military regime, his administration also worked with the same companies that had developed a symbiotic relationship with the state during those years, under similarly profitable conditions.

For Brazil's military regime had not only invested heavily in public works but had centralized much of its investment in the hands of increasingly large, powerful construction giants, chief among them Odebrecht, Andrade Gutierrez, and Camargo Corrêa. Together with Mendes Júnior and Cetenco, these firms went from earning one-third (31.2 percent) of the total netted by Brazil's one hundred biggest construction firms in 1978 to earning more than half (56.9 percent) of that total in 1984.[26] Despite shifts within the governing bloc, the construction companies

> were part in various ways and to various degrees of the ruling groups (and) were able to fully develop their modes of organizations throughout the regime, such that, together with the limitation imposed on popular participation, the influence of these businessmen on the machinery of the state and on state policies grew. . . . These construction magnates obtained highly

favorable policies throughout the regime, allowing them to reach the end of the dictatorship even more powerful than before 1964.[27]

When Brazil transitioned to democracy these construction giants were primed to take advantage of the privatization of public companies and services that took place. In the 1990s they entered essential areas like road maintenance and tolls, water and basic sanitation, telecommunications, administration of landfills, and other urban services.[28] Brazil might have gone through a regime change, but much as during the dictatorship, the "public policies of the period allowed not only the continuity and survival of these companies, but also a new cycle of high revenue rates which capitalized and reinforced these groups, taking them to a higher level, no longer as economic conglomerates at a national level or as international construction companies, but as conglomerates with global projection."[29]

These were the powerful entities Lula found in place when he was elected—with minor reshuffling, such as the rise of OAS, a company founded in Bahia by the son-in-law of the powerful northeastern kingmaker Antonio Carlos Magalhães. Political patronage helped OAS rise rapidly in the ranks of national companies, first on the strength of contracts in Bahia, then by winning contracts in regions governed by Magalhães's political allies.[30] By 1984, it was the tenth largest in Brazil. By the time Lula's PAC program was launched in 2007, OAS, Odebrecht, Andrade Gutierrez, Camargo Corrêa, and Queiroz Galvão were the powerful core of Brazil's construction-industrial complex, though by then they had international interests in areas ranging from telecommunications to fashion, arms manufacture to agribusiness.

During Lula's two terms in office and into the first term of Dilma Rousseff (dubbed the "mother of the PAC" by Lula),[31] these companies dominated the national construction scene and reaped massive profits from public works. OAS, Odebrecht, Andrade Gutierrez, and Camargo Corrêa alone concentrated 38 percent of the revenue of Brazil's fifty largest construction firms in 2009. Another way of understanding this relationship is to look at these companies' dependence on public contracts during that same year. In 2009, municipal, state, federal, and state-controlled companies like Petrobras formed 62 percent of Odebrecht's revenues, 35 percent of Camargo Corrêa's, 72 percent of Andrade Gutierrez's, and 100 percent of Queiroz Galvão's.[32]

These same conglomerates also benefited during this period from billions of reais in cheap loans from Brazil's development bank, the BNDES, for projects within Brazil and abroad.[33] The bank's assets grew fourfold between 2007 and 2014, when its disbursement was estimated at R$190 billion, on par with the output of neighboring Uruguay. It is a lender to tycoons—60 percent of its loans go to large conglomerates—but its rates are subsidized by the taxpayer.[34]

Securing the 2014 World Cup (which included twelve host cities, requiring twelve new or refurbished stadia and attending infrastructure) and the 2016 Olympics allowed the Brazilian government to embark on a new wave of bidding and building public works. Contracts flowed into the same waiting hands. This was particularly evident in Rio de Janeiro, where the biggest four firms—Odebrecht, Andrade Gutierrez, Camargo Corrêa, and OAS, known as the "four sisters," controlled directly or through subsidiaries all of the twenty largest undertakings. This included the new bus rapid transit routes promised as part of the Olympic or World Cup legacy (Transolímpica, Transcarioca), the new light rail system (VLT) by the port, the refurbishment of the port itself, as well as the construction of specific megaevent infrastructure like the Olympic Park and the renovation of Engenhão and Maracanã stadiums[35]—the latter at a cost of over R$1 billion, less than six years after its last, costly improvement for the 2007 Pan American Games.

The relationship between the government and Brazil's powerful construction sector, consolidated during the military years, had been nurtured throughout the subsequent administrations and into the PT era with, on the one hand, political donations from the companies and, on the other, a steady flow of contracts arising from state-controlled companies like Petrobras, the PAC programs, and the megaevent construction, as well as with BNDES loans. This governmental largesse fed back into the political parties whose elected officials handed out the contracts. In 2014 alone, the campaign contributions from Andrade Gutierrez to various parties amounted to R$83 million; OAS, R$69

million; and Queiroz Galvão, R$56 million. Looking at this relation-
ship from the PT's perspective, that year the party received R$132
million from companies that would eventually be charged in the Lava
Jato (Car Wash) corruption probe.[36] These contributions resulted in
specific returns: a study found that public works firms could expect a
boost in contracts that was at least fourteen times the value of their
donation when they gave to a legislative candidate from the PT and
that candidate won.[37]

THE BEGINNING OF THE END

By the time Rousseff took office on January 1, 2011, the years of
growth that had propelled Brazil's global ambitions had slowed. The
7.5 percent GDP expansion in 2010, which crowned Lula's last year
in office and helped secure his nearly 90 percent approval rating at the
time,[38] rested on the commodity boom and on domestic consumption
but also on loose spending and tax breaks; it left a fiscal mess and a
spike in inflation for Rousseff to face. She responded much as Lula
had at the beginning of his first term, with a fiscal tightening that
earned her the approval of the financial press.[39] The economy con-
tracted, however, first to more sustainable levels of growth (2.7 percent
in 2011) then into a worrisome slump (1 percent in 2012). Her administration reacted by changing course again, lowering interest rates,
reducing the cost of energy, and cutting taxes. But the economy did not
respond. Commodity prices, known to be volatile, sank, and China's
demand for Brazil's offerings had stabilized and would begin to contract; Brazil's economy, grown dependent on this influx, would follow
along the path into a gripping recession.[40]

Expectations among Brazilians, especially among those who made
up the new middle class, were higher than ever: they paid the highest
taxes among any country outside the developed world (36 percent of
GDP) and wanted public services to match.[41] Not only that, they wanted
government that was transparent, accountable, and responsive to
their needs and priorities; Brazil's middle class was making conven-
tional middle-class demands. In June 2013, their growing dissatisfaction exploded into massive demonstrations that drew hundreds of

thousands to the streets across Brazil and took everyone by surprise—even, or perhaps particularly, the Workers Party, which had once achieved prominence through such popular demonstrations. The swell of anger had experts scrambling for explanations, but a look at the placards the protesters carried showed a broad set of concerns over public services like health care, transportation, education, and governance.

These protests revealed a widening of fault lines that ran through the administration. Writing in *Critical Sociology*, A. Saad-Filho offered this interpretation: "First, [they are] symptoms of a social malaise associated with the contradictions of left-wing policy-making under neoliberalism. Second, they illuminate the limitations arising from the achievements of these administrations, including higher expectations of economic performance and public service provisions. Third, they reveal the atrophy of traditional forms of social representations . . . which have been unable to channel discontent and resolve disputes between social groups."[42]

The immense sums being poured into controversial construction projects such as megaevent-related infrastructure of dubious utility underscored the dissonance between government spending and the population's priorities.[43] As the Confederations' Cup—a dress rehearsal for the World Cup—started in June 2013, the triumphalist stadiums cast as sites of Brazil's consecration into a global elite via the hosting of prestigious international sporting events became lightning rods and symbols of this dissatisfaction. The world watched as fans pushed through clouds of tear gas to enter venues and police clashed violently with protesters.[44] A typical protest banner called for "FIFA-quality health care and education."[45]

With the population focused on the largest protests in a generation and puzzled by Rousseff's delayed reaction (she did not address Brazilians directly until June 21, after weeks of turbulence; her popularity plummeted to 31 percent by July of 2013[46]), few paid much attention to a federal investigation into a money-laundering scheme that had operated through a fueling station in Brasília. A wiretap generated enough information for Sérgio Moro, the judge behind the sting operation, to call for the arrest of a black-market currency dealer with a long record, Alberto Youssef.[47] Youssef, facing indefinite preventive imprisonment and encouraged by laws that rewarded plea bargaining, started to talk.

The tale Youssef spun would reveal a vast corruption scheme in which he, as a money launderer and cash smuggler, played a key role. It centered on Petrobras, whose capitalization and growing array of activities had transformed it into the fourth most valuable company in the world, with operations that amounted to 10 percent of Brazil's GDP and made it a source of contracts worth billions.[48] Youssef described a system by which, between 2006 and 2014, key company executives installed in their posts by political parties worked with a cartel involving sixteen of the country's largest construction companies—among them Odebrecht, Camargo Corrêa, OAS, Queiroz Galvão, and Andrade Gutierrez—to rig bids for public contracts, fixing the results and overinvoicing. The rules were written up in a two-and-a-half-page encoded guide that described contract bidding as a sports championship, with leagues and teams.[49] The goal was to funnel cash back into the pockets of all participants: politicians, Petrobras executives, construction magnates, and operators such as Youssef himself.[50] Over the next two years, this investigation would reveal a graft scheme that went far beyond the oil company and permeated Brazil's construction-industrial complex.

The case broke publicly in 2014, when Rousseff was campaigning for her second term and Brazil was preparing for the World Cup. The country was tense, erupting into protests and strikes in the months leading up to the championship.[51] Lava Jato, or Car Wash, as the case became known, played out like a soap opera on the nightly news, with new plea bargaining deals dredging up more names and more arrests, leading to more plea bargaining deals, in a cycle that brought down Brazil's powerful like dominoes. The principal political parties involved were the Partido do Movimento Democrático Brasileiro (PMDB), long the éminence grise of Brazilian politics and the party of then Vice President Michel Temer, Rio's Mayor Paes, and Rio's Governor Cabral; the Partido Progressista (PP), a conservative party whose roots, like the PMDB's, stretched back to the military years; and the PT. Brazilians expected little of the first two, ideologically amorphous and clientelistic creatures of the country's venal political culture. The Workers Party faced the brunt of popular reaction because it was the governing party but principally because it was supposed to be different. It had a coherent ideology, popular support, and moral underpinnings that other political organizations largely lacked.

Rousseff campaigned through it all, promising to maintain the social gains made under the previous three PT administrations and to prioritize the needs of working Brazilians. Protests dimmed as the World Cup started in earnest, turning the focus of soccer fans—which includes most Brazilians—to matches and street parties and leaving Brazil with a good reputation as host. Despite Lava Jato's aspersions on the PT and PMDB, Brazilians gave Rousseff a new term in office (albeit by a very narrow margin: 51.4 percent of the vote to her challenger's 48.5 percent).[52] With inflation ticking up and a wobbly economy, the population, especially the poorest, was increasingly concerned about maintaining the gains achieved. Rousseff represented continuity.

More of the same was no longer possible, however; by the end of Rousseff's first term in 2014, the long wave of high commodity prices that had buoyed the country through the previous three administrations had broken. Raw materials made up more than half the value of all of Brazil's exports, but the prices were spiraling downward: iron ore went from $180 to $55 a ton, soy beans from $18 to $8 a bushel, and crude oil from $140 to $50 a barrel.[53] Even before transitioning into her second term, Rousseff reversed her stance, cutting social spending, curtailing credit, and raising taxes.[54] Within three months, hundreds of thousands of Brazilians took to the streets demanding her ouster in a wave of protests that would escalate throughout the year.[55]

By the opening of the 2016 Olympic Games, Rousseff had been forced from the presidency pending an impeachment trial on charges that her administration improperly used money from state banks to obscure the size of the country's budget gap. She did not attend the opening ceremony. Neither did Lula, whose emotional appeal had been key to securing the IOC's vote for Rio. The acting president, Temer, was roundly booed. By then, the Lava Jato investigation and the series of political dramas it unleashed had thoroughly discredited Brazil's political and business class and had led to the arrest of more than 150 of the country's top executives and elected officials.[56] The list included the heads of Odebrecht,[57] Andrade Gutierrez,[58] OAS,[59] Queiroz Galvão,[60] and Camargo Corrêa.[61]

Among the more than fifty politicians investigated were the PT's senate leader, Delcídio do Amaral; the former head of Congress, Eduardo Cunha of the PMDB; and the president of the senate, Renan Calheiros, also of the PMDB. This turmoil diverted the attention of legislators and further hamstrung the economy. During 2015–16, Brazil had its credit ratings cut to junk and faced escalating debt levels as it sank into the deepest downturn in a century.[62] Petrobras wrote off $17 billion in losses from graft and overvalued assets in 2015, with alleged bribe payments alone amounting to $2.1 billion.[63] Brazilians suffered as unemployment shot up to 11 percent and average earnings declined.[64] The state of Rio was broke, missing debt payments, and forced to shutter hospitals and delay salaries of teachers, nurses, firefighters, police officers, and public servants in general.[65]

What was supposed to be Brazil's crowning moment became a representation of what ailed it: the Olympic ceremonies were scaled back due to the economic crisis and no political leader in government or the opposition had enough credibility to step out in public without jeers from the population. In the months following the Games, Rousseff was impeached; Lula was charged in several corruption cases connected to Lava Jato or the companies involved, such as OAS and Odebrecht;[66] a state court froze the personal assets of Rio mayor Paes as it investigated improprieties during the building of the Olympic golf course; and former Rio governor Cabral (and his wife) were arrested on suspicion of taking bribes from construction companies in exchange for publicly-funded infrastructure contracts, including the renovation of the Maracanã Stadium.[67]

The venues and infrastructure associated with the World Cup and the Olympics, which were supposed to showcase the country's capacity, modernity, and ambitions, became the embodiment of the most clichéd of Brazilian vices: corruption. Construction companies, including Odebrecht, Queiroz Galvão, OAS, Camargo Corrêa, and Andrade Gutierrez, colluded to defraud the bidding process and overcharge taxpayers in as many as eight of the twelve World Cup stadia that were built or refurbished, according to Brazil's antitrust agency Conselho Administrativo de Defesa Econômica (CADE).[68] The agency has used *acordos de leniência*, a type of plea bargaining available to companies, to uncover evidence pointing to similar cartels behind the bidding for PAC projects like the Belo Monte Dam, the thermonuclear plant Angra 3, and the north-south and east-west railroad projects.

At the time of this writing, in December 2016, CADE had thirty ongoing investigations into cartel practices involving the companies at the center of Lava Jato,[69] and federal prosecutors were looking into evidence of corruption in all Olympic venues and services that used federal funds. This includes projects conducted by Odebrecht—which got half of Olympic contracts (by value)—OAS, and Queiroz Galvão.[70] Even the PAC project intended to improve infrastructure in Rio's favelas was fair game for this gang of businessmen grown fat at the trough of public funding.[71]

The declared revenue of Brazil's top construction companies tripled from R$15 billion in 2004 to R$44.4 billion in 2013, according to the Câmara Brasileira de Construção Civil, the Brazilian Chamber of Civil Construction.[72]

CONCLUSION

The economic growth that propelled Brazil into greater international prominence rested on a China-driven commodity boom, domestic consumption, and the promise of oil discovered off the coast of Rio. This bonanza and the promise of its continuation were used to achieve laudable social progress under the Workers Party. Brazil, a country marred by a deep race and class divide and an inequality gap that is among the world's widest, made steps toward remedying these disparities. The Bolsa Família program in particular helped lift twenty-five million people out of poverty. This windfall was also harnessed to fund immense investments in infrastructure, from roads to ports to dams. The promise was that these developments would catapult Brazil into a place among developed nations. Brazil's hosting of mega sporting events, culminating with the Olympic Games of 2016, was widely portrayed as a recognition of these achievements. Lula, who managed at once to be the country's first working-class president and a friend of business, was the charismatic embodiment of this progress and of an even brighter future.

When the price and demand for Brazil's raw materials plunged, the nation's increased dependence on commodities exporting left its economy teetering.[73] Domestic consumption shriveled as inflation reared its head, unemployment rocketed, and credit tightened. Oil production, central to Brazil's strategy, did not come through: worldwide prices plummeted, making the expensive deep offshore oil reserves less appealing, even as Petrobras crumpled under the weight of the Lava Jato investigation.

The years of growth had fostered multiple opportunities for tendering generous bids for public works: through Petrobras, through the PAC projects, and through the construction of megaevent venues and infrastructure. Many of these contracts went to powerful construction companies that had developed strong, long-lasting, and profitable relationships with the state over decades.[74]

As investigations revealed (and are still uncovering at the time of this writing), most of the construction contracts were not legitimate. The bidding system was often rigged through bribery and cartelization by a select group of companies in collaboration with elected officials. In several instances, the projects themselves were ill conceived, irresponsible allocation of resources that came at tremendous cost for the country. Many of them were never finished and stand abandoned.[75] The cost of this graft and waste and of the political and economic instability generated by the revelation of these schemes is hard to calculate. Now that Brazil's games are over, the venues that were intended to symbolize the country's inexorable rise stand as empty reminders of the profligacy and corruption that foiled its dreams and continue to hamper its growth.

NOTES

1. Stuart Grudgings, "Olympics Affirms Brazil's Rise, Lula Legacy," *Reuters*, October 2, 2009.

2. Chico de Gois, "Lula Diz Que Megacampo de Petróleo Mostra Que Deus É Brasileiro," *O Globo*, November 20, 2007 (http://oglobo.globo.com /economia/lula-diz-que-megacampo-de-petroleo-mostra-que-deus -brasileiro-4139780).

3. Francisco Dornelles, "Decreto No 45,692 de 17 de Junho de 2016. Decreta Estado de Calamidade Pública No Âmbito Da Administração Financeira Do Estado Do Rio de Janeiro, E Dá Outras Providências," *Diário Oficial Do Estado Do Rio de Janeiro*, June 17, 2016.

4. "Olimpíada," *Datafolha Instituto de Pesquisas*, July 2016 (http://media.folha.uol.com.br/datafolha/2016/07/18/olimpiada.pdf).

5. "Gdansk, Brazilian Style," *New York Times*, February 23, 1981.

6. Kenneth Marxwell, "Lula's Surprise," *New York Review of Books*, July 3, 2003 (www.cfr.org/brazil/lulas-surprise/p6062).

7. Anthony W. Pereira, "*Bolsa Família* and Democracy in Brazil," *Third World Quarterly* 36, no. 9 (September 2, 2015), pp. 1682–99, doi:10.1080/01436597.2015.1059730.

8. "What Is Brazil's '*mensalão*'?" *The Economist*, November 13, 2013 (www.economist.com/blogs/economist-explains/2013/11/economist-explains-14).

9. Perry Anderson, "Lula's Brazil," *London Review of Books*, March 31, 2011.

10. Larry Rohter, "Brazil's President Roars Back to Win Vote," *New York Times*, October 30, 2006.

11. John Paul Rathbone, "UK Backs Brazil Bid for UN Security Council Seat," *Financial Times*, November 10, 2010 (www.ft.com/content/6718897e-ec1e-11df-9e11-00144feab49a).

12. Andreia Soares e Castro, "2014 FIFA World Cup and 2016 Olympic Games: Brazil's Strategy 'to Win Hearts and Minds' through Sports and Football," *PD Magazine* (Winter 2012), pp. 28–35.

13. Luiz Inácio Lula da Silva, "Rio 2016: Lula's Speech (English subtitled) and Olympic Bid Video" (speech to the International Olympic Committee), Copenhagen, 2009 (www.youtube.com/watch?v=R3rO8xhHxMs).

14. Associated Press, "Rio Bandwagon: IOC Keeps on Loving City's Bid." *ESPN*, September 2, 2009 (www.espn.com/espn/wire/_/section/oly/id/4441833).

15. The IOC Evaluation Commission, *Report of the 2016 IOC Evaluation Commission: Games of the XXXI Olympiad* (International Olympic Committee, September 2009) (https://stillmed.olympic.org/media/Document%20Library/OlympicOrg/Documents/Host-City-Elections/XXXI-Olympiad-2016/Report-of-the-IOC-Evaluation-Commission-for-the-Games-of-the-XXXI-Olympiad-in-2016.pdf).

16. Peter Kingstone, "Brazil's Reliance on Commodity Exports Threatens Its Medium- and Long-Term Growth Prospects," *Americas Quarterly* (Summer 2012) (www.americasquarterly.org/kingstone).

17. Pedro Henrique Pedreira Campos, *"Estranhas Catedrais": As Empreiteiras Brasileiras E a Ditadura Civil-Militar, 1964–1988* (Niterói, RJ: Editora da UFF, 2014).

18. Charles Lyons, "The Dam Boom in the Amazon," *New York Times*, June 30, 2012.

19. Campos, *"Estranhas Catedrais."*

20. "Discurso de Guido Mantega No Lançamento Do PAC," *Congresso Em Foco*, January 22, 2007 (http://m.congressoemfoco.uol.com.br /noticias/leia-o-discurso-de-mantega-no-lancamento-do-pac/).

21. Murilo Rodrigues Alves, André Borges, and Alfredo Mergulhão, "Das Dez Maiores Obras Do Primeiro PAC, Apenas Duas Foram Concluídas," *Estado de São Paulo*, January 23, 2016 (http://economia.estadao.com .br/noticias/geralnova-noticia,1824792).

22. Ministério do Planejamento, "Em Nove Anos, Investimentos Executados Pelo PAC Somam R$1,9 Trilhão," *PAC*, May 11, 2016 (www.pac .gov.br/noticia/68777baf).

23. Christ V. Nicholson, "Petrobras Raises $70 Billion in Share Issue," *New York Times DealBook*, September 24, 2010 (http://dealbook.nytimes .com/2010/09/24/petrobras-raises-70-billion-in-share-issue/).

24. Alex Cuadros, *Brazillionaires: Wealth, Power, Decadence, and Hope in an American Country,* 1st ed. (New York: Spiegel & Grau, 2016).

25. Demétrio Magnoli, "Lula Celebra Geisel Em Belo Monte," *Estado de São Paulo*, April 29, 2010 (http://opiniao.estadao.com.br/noticias/geral,lula -celebra-geisel-em-belo-monte,544519). Author's translation from the original Portuguese.

26. Campos, *"Estranhas Catedrais,"* p. 121.

27. Ibid.

28. Ibid., p. 132.

29. Ibid.

30. Ibid., p. 104.

31. Kelly Lima, "Dilma É a 'Mãe' Do PAC, Diz Lula Em Morro Do Rio," *Estado de São Paulo*, March 7, 2008 (http://politica.estadao.com .br/noticias/geral,dilma-e-a-mae-do-pac-diz-lula-em-morro-do-rio, 136437).

32. "Quatro Empreiteiras Concentram R$138 Bilhões Em Obras No País," *O Globo*, May 7, 2011 (http://oglobo.globo.com/economia/quatro -empreiteiras-concentram-138-bilhoes-em-obras-no-pais-2773130).

33. Adriano Belisário, "As Quatro Irmãs," *Pública*, June 30, 2014 (http:// apublica.org/2014/06/as-quatro-irmas/).

34. Joe Leahy, "BNDES: Lender of First Resort for Brazil's Tycoons," *Financial Times*, January 11, 2015 (www.ft.com/content/c510368e-968e -11e4-922f-00144feabdc0).

35. Adriano Belisário, João Roberto Lopes Pinto, and Rafael Rezende, "The Owners of Rio," *Henrich Böll Stiftung*, June 6, 2014 (www.boell.de /en/2014/05/23/owners-rio).

36. "Operação Lava Jato—Lista Das Empresas Relacionadas," *Meu Congresso Nacional* (http://meucongressonacional.com/lavajato/empresas).

37. Taylor C. Boas, F. Daniel Hidalgo, and Neal P. Richardson, "The Spoils of Victory: Campaign Donations and Government Contracts in Brazil," *The Journal of Politics* 76, no. 2 (April 2014), pp. 415–29, doi:10.1017/S002238161300145X.

38. "Brazil's Lula to Leave with Record-High Popularity," *Reuters*, December 16, 2010 (www.reuters.com/article/us-brazil-lula-poll-idUSTRE6BF4O620101216).

39. "How Tough Will Dilma Be?" *The Economist*, February 17, 2011 (www.economist.com/node/18178315).

40. John Lyons and Paul Kiernan, "How Brazil's China-Driven Commodities Boom Went Bust," *Wall Street Journal*, August 28, 2015.

41. "The Streets Erupt," *The Economist*, June 18, 2013 (www.economist.com/blogs/americasview/2013/06/protests-brazil).

42. A. Saad-Filho, "Mass Protests under 'Left Neoliberalism': Brazil, June–July 2013," *Critical Sociology* 39, no. 5 (September 1, 2013), pp. 657–69, doi:10.1177/0896920513501906.

43. Clara Velasco, "Na Véspera Da Copa, Apenas 50% Das Obras de Mobilidade Foram Entregues," *G1*, June 11, 2014 (http://g1.globo.com/economia/noticia/2014/06/na-vespera-da-copa-apenas-50-das-obras-de-mobilidade-foram-entregues.html).

44. "Brazil Maracanã Stadium Protest Ends in Clashes," *BBC News*, June 16, 2013 (www.bbc.com/news/world-latin-america-22930402).

45. "The Signs of the Brazilian Protests," *The New York Times*, June 21, 2013.

46. Mariana Oliveira, "Aprovação Do Governo Dilma Cai de 55% Para 31%, Aponta Ibope," *G1*, July 25, 2013 (http://g1.globo.com/politica/noticia/2013/07/aprovacao-do-governo-dilma-cai-de-55-para-31-aponta-ibope.html).

47. Francisco Marcelino and Sabrina Valle, "The Talented Mr. Youssef, Brazil's Black-Market Central Banker," *Bloomberg*, January 13, 2015 (www.bloomberg.com/news/articles/2015-01-14/the-talented-mr-youssef-brazil-s-black-market-central-banker).

48. Perry Anderson, "Crisis in Brazil," *London Review of Books*, April 21, 2016.

49. "*Regras Do Clube*" (Catta Preta Advogados, 2011, unpublished).

50. "Por Onde Começou—Caso Lava Jato," *Ministerio Publico Federal* (http://lavajato.mpf.mp.br/atuacao-na-1a-instancia/investigacao/historico/por-onde-comecou).

51. Simon Romero, "Brazil on Edge as World Cup Exposes Rifts," *New York Times*, June 9, 2014.

52. Simon Romero, "Brazil Stays With Rousseff as President After Turbulent Campaign," *New York Times*, October 26, 2014.

53. Anderson, "Crisis in Brazil."

54. Ibid.

55. Shasta Darlington, "Protestors in Brazil Push to Impeach President Dilma Rousseff," *CNN*, April 12, 2015 (www.cnn.com/2015/04/12 /americas/brazil-protests/index.html).

56. Andrew Jacobs and Paula Moura, "At the Birthplace of a Graft Scandal, Brazil's Crisis Is on Full Display," *New York Times*, June 10, 2016.

57. Blake Schmidt and Sabrina Valle, "Brazil's Marcelo Odebrecht Gets 19 Years in Jail in Carwash," *Bloomberg*, March 8, 2016 (www.bloomberg .com/news/articles/2016-03-08/brazil-s-marcelo-odebrecht-gets-19-years -in-jail-in-carwash-case).

58. Rogerio Jelmayer, "Brazil's Andrade Gutierrez Reaches Plea Deal in Corruption Case," *Wall Street Journal*, May 9, 2016.

59. Luciana Magalhaes, "Brazilian Builder OAS's President Arrested in Bribery Probe," *Wall Street Journal*, December 11, 2015.

60. Rogerio Jelmayer, "Brazil Police Re-Arrest Former Executives of Builder Queiroz Galvao," *Wall Street Journal*, August 2, 2016.

61. Rogerio Jelmayer and Luciana Magalhaes, "Three Former Construction Executives Sentenced in Petrobras Graft Case," *Wall Street Journal*, July 20, 2015.

62. Luciana Magalhaes, "Fitch Downgrades Brazil," *Wall Street Journal*, May 5, 2016.

63. Paul Kiernan, "Brazil's Petrobras Reports Nearly $17 Billion in Asset and Corruption Charges," *Wall Street Journal*, April 23, 2015.

64. Paul Kiernan and Rogerio Jelmayer, "Brazil's Recession Deepens," *Wall Street Journal*, June 1, 2016.

65. Paul Kiernan and Luciana Magalhaes, "Brazil's Rio de Janeiro State Misses Debt Payment," *Wall Street Journal*, May 25, 2016.

66. Simon Romero, "'Lula,' Brazil's Ex-President, Is Charged With Corruption," *New York Times*, September 14, 2016; Brad Brooks, "Lula Charged over Odebrecht Angola Work in Brazil Graft Probe," *Reuters*, October 10, 2016 (www.reuters.com/article/us-brazil-corruption-idUSKCN 12A2C8).

67. Vinod Sreeharsha, "Sérgio Cabral, Ex-Governor of Rio de Janeiro, Arrested on Corruption Charges," *New York Times*, November 17, 2016.

68. Paul Kiernan, "Brazil's World Cup Stadium Construction Contracts Were Inflated, Officials Say," *Wall Street Journal*, December 5, 2016.

69. "Lava Jato Provoca Corrida de Empresas Em Busca de Acordos de Leniência," *BOL Notícias*, November 18, 2016 (http://noticias.bol.uol.com .br/ultimas-noticias/brasil/2016/11/18/cade-investiga-30-carteis-formados -por-empresas-envolvidas-na-lava-jato.htm.

70. Brad Brooks, "Exclusive: Brazil Investigating Possible Corruption at Olympic Venues," *Reuters*, May 26, 2016 (www.reuters.com/article/us -olympics-rio-corruption-exclusive-idUSKCN0YG2WT).

71. Vladimir Netto and Marcelo Parreira, "Em Acordo de Leniência, Empreiteira Revela Cartel Para Fraudar Obras No Rio," *G1*, November 30, 2016 (http://g1.globo.com/economia/noticia/2016/11/em-acordo-de-leniencia -empreiteira-revela-cartel-para-fraudar-obras-no-rio.html).

72. "Faturamento de Empreiteiras Da Lava Jato Triplica Na Era Petista," *UOL*, March 10, 2016 (http://noticias.uol.com.br/politica/ultimas-noticias /2016/03/10/faturamento-de-empreiteiras-da-lava-jato-triplica-na-era -petista.htm).

73. Lyons and Kiernan, "How Brazil's China-Driven Commodities Boom Went Bust"; Kingstone, "Brazil's Reliance on Commodity Exports."

74. "Faturamento de Empreiteiras."

75. Simon Romero, "Grand Visions Fizzle in Brazil," *New York Times*, April 12, 2014.

FOUR

Not Everyone Has a Price

How the Small Favela of Vila Autódromo's Fight
Opened a Path to Olympic Resistance

THERESA WILLIAMSON

It was exactly one hundred and twenty years ago. As history, now thoroughly intertwined with legend, has it, downtrodden soldiers, poverty-stricken and scarred after the long, bloody battle of Canudos, Brazil's deadliest ever civil war, headed from Bahia to the nation's capital at the time: Rio de Janeiro. The soldiers, formerly slaves who'd just been freed and then immediately drafted for the fight, had been promised land there for serving in battle.[1]

Rio de Janeiro was one of the world's largest cities in 1897 and certainly the largest in Brazil, with over half a million inhabitants. Brazil urbanized relatively early for a developing nation, and Rio was the first major city to do so. Due to its importance as both the nation's fastest-growing city and federal capital, land there represented a major opportunity.

(RE)INTRODUCING FAVELAS

But as they arrived, soldiers found no such land set aside for them, so they squatted outside the Ministry of War in downtown Rio, awaiting

57

what would turn out to be an empty promise. Weeks later, a colonel with some land on a nearby hill in Rio's downtown port area gave them permission to squat on his hillside. And so they climbed up the hill and settled, naming their settlement Morro da Favela, or Favela Hill, after the robust, spiny, oily, and flowering Favela bush that had characterized the Canudos hills where they had served in battle, hills also named after the Favela plant and where some of them had met their wives.[2] They thereby coined *favela* as the go-to word to describe Brazil's informal settlements, which became the mainstay of affordable housing in Brazilian cities during the century to come.[3]

Over the subsequent decades, more and more rural migrants and former urban and rural slaves and their descendants joined the Canudos soldiers in occupying Rio's hills,[4] and all of Rio's informal settlements became known as *favelas*, so Morro da Favela changed its name to Morro da Providência, or Providence Hill. Despite attempts at eviction throughout its history, the residents of Providência have resisted, and the community celebrates its 120th birthday this year.[5]

Sprouting initially on central hillsides and later in peripheral low-lying areas as the city expanded—nearly always on public land— favelas came to be such an integral part of the city that, by 2012 when Rio's landscape was declared a UNESCO World Heritage Site, UN Special Rapporteur on Adequate Housing Raquel Rolnik declared "Rio's favelas between the mountain and the sea" an integral part of that world heritage status.[6] Georgetown University's Brazil historian Bryan McCann explains: "about the only things that today's Vidigal (a favela in Rio's South Zone) has in common with the same neighborhood in 1978 is the absence of property title and the continuing discrimination against its residents, yet everyone still recognizes it as a favela."[7]

The century in between was marked by a number of policies toward Rio's favelas, the primary policy being one of neglect that led to these communities' marginalization.[8] Descendants of slaves who comprised the bulk of the favela population were not deemed full citizens and favelas were, as a result, described as "backward, unsanitary and oversexualized."[9] They were deemed "illegal" occupations and thus it was argued they were not entitled to urban improvements. Yet they were also not terminated for the most part and were even encouraged at times because they "offered cheap labor nearby," as a municipal official informed a Rio audience in April 2014; as he also explained, this was "convenient, until now."[10] Thus, one can summarize policy toward favelas historically as one of finding ways to maintain the structure of a slaveholding society, even post abolition.

Three other broad and interrelated policies were applied toward Rio's favelas in the twentieth century. The first is a policy of forced eviction, which was mainly applied under Governor Carlos Lacerda during the military regime between 1962 and 1974, when 140,000 people were removed from their homes, though the fear of eviction has characterized favela residents' experiences from day one until now.[11] Second were sporadic, incomprehensive, and insufficient upgrading policies, intended to provide minimal infrastructure in some favelas, with the most robust program, Favela-Bairro, taking place in the 1990s.[12] Third has been a policy of criminalizing and repressing the urban poor, with Rio's Military Police as its principal enforcer, dating back to the institution's founding in the first decade of the 1800s and compounded during the institution's history.[13] Today, favela residents regularly criticize the occupation of favelas under the current Military Police's Pacifying Police Units program as the only arm of the state residents experience, when they "always demanded long-term policies" and what they "want [is] the end of open sewers and of electricity and water outages."[14]

Over a century, however, favela residents did not all remain passive recipients of such policies. Instead, they have increasingly organized and reacted. Vidigal, in Rio's South Zone, is notable in its early resistance to eviction during the military regime, which essentially halted the regime's forced eviction campaign in 1978.[15] And housing groups that grew out of the decades of insufficient affordable housing and poor policies led a movement that secured adverse possession as a clause in Brazil's new "People's Constitution" of 1988, and other forms of housing rights in state and municipal laws to follow.[16] In addition, by the 1990s a trend began which is now widely held, among the Brazilian architecture, engineering, and urban planning establishments, to view comprehensive and participatory favela upgrading as the correct policy approach to improving the lives of residents.[17]

As a result of this history, today Rio de Janeiro is the Brazilian city with the largest number of people living in favelas.[18] Approximately 1,000 individual favelas, ranging in size from hundreds of residents in small communities like Recreio II, which was removed for the TransOeste bus corridor and highway in the West Zone, to 200,000 in Rocinha in the city's South Zone, comprise the 1.5 million *favelados*, or 24 percent of the city's population, living in favelas.

And in fact, despite significant challenges to comprehensive upgrading that would guarantee quality public infrastructure and services in these communities, there are numerous qualities—urbanistic, economic, and sociocultural—that have developed out of informality in Rio's favelas.[19] Favelas naturally tend to be characterized by a number of qualities that urban planners around the world are currently working to integrate into sustainable communities but often have a hard time building into already-consolidated urban centers: affordable housing in central areas, housing near work, low-rise/high-density construction, mixed-use developments, pedestrian-first roads, high use of bicycles and transit, organic (flexible) architecture, high degree of collective action and mutual support, cultural incubators, and a high rate of entrepreneurship, among other factors.[20] In fact, during Brazil's recent ten-year boom, favelas fared better in developing than society as a whole on average.[21]

Unlike other developing regions, namely in Africa and Asia, which have been urbanizing in recent decades, Brazil's population has been more than 80 percent urban since the 1990s.[22] Given their presence in Brazil's fastest developing early city, favelas in Rio are thus some of the most long-lived informal settlements (still seen as such) in the world today. Their struggles, successes, and challenges thus offer incredibly rich sources of wisdom and knowledge, inspiration and warnings, about what can happen when communities are left to develop themselves over a long period of time. Urban planners and international development practitioners are starting to pay attention to what can be learned from these communities, what sort of innovative new treatments are necessary to ensure their effective integration without compromising community attributes, and how their stories can inspire a new approach to city-making in the decades to come.[23]

Despite this reality, a deeply biased and inaccurate narrative dominates the view of Rio's favelas locally and around the world.[24] In the early 1900s, shortly after their settlement, favelas were labeled "backward and unsanitary." Such views quickly found their way into the monopolistic Brazilian media's narrative, where they were consolidated over many decades through to the present day. Maintaining a public perception of favelas as inherently illegal, criminal, precarious, and unmanageable allowed for the perpetuation of an image of these communities as temporary and in need of dramatic punitive intervention, whether that be through evictions or policing, and has allowed the authorities to maintain a policy of neglect and poor upgrading, which further exacerbates community challenges, keeping favelas in a never-ending spiral of legitimized neglect. Meanwhile, as an important world city and tourist destination for two centuries, Rio has always been of interest to international news outlets, though not important enough to dedicate significant resources to it. As a result, historically the global media picks up on the dominant local media narrative and amplifies it via telephone or parachute journalism, quoting authorities or citing press releases issued by authorities or local newspapers, which are deeply committed to maintaining the status quo. Sensational and big stories are the only ones deemed important enough to cover, so the global narrative on these communities has produced intense prejudice, which further justifies societal stigma among elites who care about global perceptions of their city and depend on them for investment, in another vicious cycle.

INTRODUCING VILA AUTÓDROMO

It is in this complex context that the inspiring and rich story of the small, punch-above-their-weight favela of Vila Autódromo unfolds. As with virtually all favelas, the community ties its founding to a subsistence or employment opportunity, in this case one that generated on the shores of the Jacarepaguá Lagoon. Settled by fishermen in 1967, fifty years ago, the small favela around eight kilometers southwest of City of God began just one year after the founding of its (in)famous regional compatriot (City of God is perhaps the prime example of a favela made famous over sensationalized violence with the 2002 film by the same name). But whereas City of God was settled initially as public housing—hours from the employment hubs of the time, filled with military regime evictees globbed together against their will despite originating in different communities—Vila Autódromo was settled by a small group of fishermen choosing the location for their subsistence and to settle,[25] unconcerned with the lack of development in the region at the time. In fact, the entire region was characterized by what were seen by many as impenetrable wetlands.

In 1971, workers came to the area to build the Nelson Piquet International Autodrome, Rio de Janeiro's Formula One racetrack, which would occupy the bulk of the peninsula on which Vila Autódromo was located.[26] This is when the small community took its name, Vila Autódromo, or "Racetrack Village," as those workers joined the original fishermen in expanding the community's footprint. Again, the favela expanded around employment, as is typically the case.

Over the subsequent decades Vila Autódromo consolidated itself into a favela of some 700 families, filling all the potential lots available between the lagoon on one side, the racetrack on a second side, and a canal on the third. Original settlers eventually sold what were considerably large favela lots, allowing for some homes, decades later, to occupy 400 square meters of land on the edge of the lagoon or within what became the core area of the favela, nearer the Ambassador Abelardo Bueno Avenue. In some cases, large lots allowed families to grow, from one small home to two or three on the same compound, with several generations of a single family benefitting from their individual homes located on a family compound with trees and space allowing for an active outdoor private family life within the compound. Others grew their houses into quite large individual homes. Some used the outdoor space to plant fruit trees, open mechanic repair shops for Formula One cars, or establish Candomblé *terreiros* for Afro-Brazilian spiritual rituals requiring intense relationships with the land. Still others opened businesses in front of or below their homes, and churches were established, both Catholic and evangelical. Eventually, many also subdivided their plots, so the community also hosted a number of small, more precarious dwellings of those who moved in more recently and were beginning the process of iterative development that characterizes favela consolidation and informal development. Meanwhile, a small subset of fishermen continued living on and off the water throughout the decades.

Some twenty-five years after it was founded, in the early 1990s, Vila Autódromo faced its first battle against eviction.[27] This was when the up-and-coming neighboring area of Barra da Tijuca began expanding into the wetlands nearby. Barra da Tijuca was a response of real estate developers to high levels of crime in the wealthy South Zone of the city and redemocratization after the fall of the military regime: the whole region developed since the 1980s as thousands of gated community condominiums that were packaged for exclusivity and exclusion.[28] The pretext for eviction at the time was environmental. Rio would host the UN Earth Summit, the UNCED (United Nations Conference on Environment and Development), in 1992 and the city administration used this as justification for removing the favela, which it said posed a visual and environmental threat to the area.

Residents organized, however, via their highly active Vila Autódromo Residents, Fishermen, and Friends' Association (Associação de Moradores, Pescadores e Amigos da Vila Autódromo, or AMPAVA). The recent adverse possession clause in the federal constitution,[29] combined with Rio state's own 1989 constitution's similar determination that land must fulfill a social function, were key to the community's victory. They worked with public defenders and, in the early 1990s, were able to secure two leases from Rio governors. Termed *Concessão de Direito Real de Uso*, these "real use concessions" were provided by the state government because the peninsula on which Vila Autódromo sat was state-owned land. The more robust concession, delivered in 1998, provided occupancy rights for ninety-nine years, with the right to renewal for another ninety-nine.

Vila Autódromo then continued its self-styled development for another two decades, further consolidating itself with each passing year, residents being well employed given the labor opportunities associated with the Barra da Tijuca region's boom over this period. During this period, the community also fought for public investment in sewerage infrastructure, road paving, and other upgrades. But at no point did the city government invest there, even despite the community's now-official status. The only investment made by a public official was when a political candidate running for office provided resources for a small playground in an attempt to attract votes. The poor-quality equipment was thereafter maintained by residents.

One date stands out in Vila Autódromo's story like no other. On October 2, 2009, the International Olympic Committee (IOC) voted on which city would win the bid to host the 2016 Summer Olympic Games. Rio, unlike Chicago, had suffered no public protest in response to the bid, and along with other elements of planning and projection that had been "fixed" in relation to its three earlier bids, appeared a solid choice.[30] In Rio's traditional wealthy South Zone, a state-sponsored celebration had been organized on Copacabana beach with 100,000 in attendance. When Rio was declared 'winner,' the crowd erupted in elated joy in a way that only a party city marked by three decades of stagnation and finally getting a glimpse of life postlimbo could experience. The excitement and hope was palpable across the city.

Meanwhile, Vila Autódromo artisan and director of the residents' association, Jane Nascimento, was dozing off later that night in front of her television.[31] In a drowsy haze she heard a press conference taking place. Rio de Janeiro Mayor Eduardo Paes, elected just a year prior, was responding to questions about Rio's successful bid. In one of his responses, he announced that Vila Autódromo would be "the only community removed" for the Olympic Games.[32]

Nascimento had fought eviction threats before. In addition to the threats of the early 1990s, Vila Autódromo had also resisted eviction in the lead-up to the 2007 Pan American Games nearby.[33] The mayor's announcement shook her to her core, and once again, Nascimento, together with Altair Guimarães—the popularly elected president of AMPAVA—other directors, and dedicated community members from across the favela, began organizing, starting by reaching out to the state's public defenders' office, for legal protection.

VILA AUTÓDROMO'S STORY AND RISE AS A SYMBOL OF OLYMPIC RESISTANCE

I first visited Vila Autódromo two weeks later. Catalytic Communities—the NGO I founded in 2000 that supports favela organizing and development of homegrown solutions as well as advocating for favela-led urban planning policies—was partly inspired by the community of Asa Branca, the closest favela to Vila Autódromo, due to their extensive community planning programs. When I read about Vila Autódromo being slated for eviction in the newspaper, I reached out to the president of the Asa Branca Residents Association, and he introduced me to Guimarães.

On my first visit to Vila Autódromo in early November 2010, Guimarães provided a rundown of the community's history, his own incredible personal struggle with eviction—Guimarães had been removed by the government from his homes in two other favelas[34]—and walked me around the calm and livable, family-centered community. Guimarães explained how he'd chosen Vila Autódromo due in part to its peace and quiet when he was evicted from City of God in the 1990s.

As we walked, Guimarães pointed out that the residents' association headquarters had a stack of recently purchased, long, thin steel reinforcement beams carefully piled up. He explained that these were acquired thanks to weekly fundraisers the community had been holding, and they would allow the association to cover the soccer pitch on its property, guaranteeing an enclosed space for community events. Their other dream for the plot of land, he told me, was a neighborhood day care center. Eventually, he said, the plot would host the association, an enclosed soccer pitch and event hall, and a day care center.

This dream was completely shoved aside in the months and years that followed, and those reinforcement beams eventually grew rusty, as the residents' association and a wide gamut of community members stopped living their everyday lives, instead dedicating themselves exclusively to resisting the City of Rio's campaign to evict them. Hearing of their ensuing fate through media channels—rather than from the mouths of municipal officials—residents were confused. Planning maps submitted by the city government to the IOC in the bidding process and later—those approved by the architecture firm AECOM for the final works—maintained Vila Autódromo in place.[35] After all, the favela was not located on the land assigned for the Rio 2016 Games—that land was where the Nelson Piquet Racetrack was—but simply adjacent to it. Yet Rio's main media channel, *O Globo*, reported occasionally about the community's pending removal "for the Games," and, as they began to visit the community and increasingly did so, municipal workers claimed the same.

Without a moment to waste, Vila Autódromo residents began organizing. In early 2010, association members met weekly with lawyers representing the community from Rio state's public defenders' Land and Housing Nucleus (Núcleo de Terras e Habitação or NUTH). The NUTH was on firm ground in claiming the community's rights, given Vila Autódromo was one of few favelas where residents held written documentation conceding the right to use the land. In 2005 Vila Autódromo had also been declared an Area of Special Social Interest (Área de Especial Interesse Social or AEIS) via Municipal Law 74, thus recognizing the community's role as a site of affordable housing, protecting the community from speculative development, and declaring it a priority area for investment in infrastructure and public services.[36] With these legal supports in hand, the community's case was as solid as is possible for any favela in Rio de Janeiro.

In addition to opening a case against the City of Rio, the NUTH prepared an eighty-page memorandum to the IOC, describing the human rights and broader legal violations being witnessed in Vila Autódromo. The letter attempted to bring to the IOC immediate, direct knowledge of the nature of the unsettling behavior being exhibited by Mayor Paes's administration toward Vila Autódromo, its legal ramifications, and context about what was at stake. The history and nature of the community was at risk. At the end of 2010, the IOC responded with a direct inquiry to Rio de Janeiro State Governor Sérgio Cabral, who proceeded to "resolve" the problem by disbanding the NUTH, reassigning all the public defenders from the office elsewhere in the state, and temporarily closing the office.[37]

Over the course of 2011, municipal workers increasingly visited the community and attempted to knock on residents' doors individually, but they were barred entry by organized residents who insisted that any negotiations had to be done collectively. The city's "divide and conquer" eviction tactic had by this point been well documented in communities that experienced sudden evictions in 2010 and were caught unprepared to react, such as Recreio II and Favela do Metrô.[38] Municipal workers were therefore ineffective in reaching individual households during this period.

While some residents held watch, barring entry by municipal agents, others took extroverted organizing roles. Early on Nascimento, Guimarães, and Inalva Mendes Brito were a sort of all-star team of organizers, each entirely dedicated to the community's permanence yet characterized by a unique skill set and audience. Nascimento, a soft-spoken militant and mother of two teenage girls, was exceptional at building emotional bonds and often left the community for meetings with human rights and church groups and broader networks of communities suffering eviction. Guimarães held his ground in the residents' association, generally always there when not at his construction job, often flanked by his young daughter Naomy, welcoming visitors and sharing his story of repeated eviction and thus his absolute determination to not allow the same to happen in Vila Autódromo. Brito, a school teacher who had been able to build her home up over decades, into one of the community's largest with an organic tropical fruit garden near the lagoon, was a popular speaker on university and school campuses as well as academic conferences. All worked together to host community-wide meetings, engage with NUTH attorneys, and generally make strategic decisions.

During 2011 the government's determination to remove Vila Autódromo became explicit. Not only in the governor's dismantling of NUTH but in the constant reinterpreting of the "need" to remove Vila Autódromo. Justifications for eviction vacillated constantly and continued to do so over the subsequent years.[39] Initially, in 2009 it was said the community actually occupied the future media center needed for the Games. When the future media center's location was moved, the new justification became a "security perimeter" around the Olympic park. The community, via legal counsel, quickly defended against this justification, citing the towering condominiums being built across the street from the future park as a much greater risk. And indeed, statistically they were right: not only were the hundreds of new high-rise condos on that land more difficult to police, offering high platforms from which to execute threats, but Vila Autódromo, in its nearly five decades, had coexisted next to Formula One races and massive events like Rock in Rio (on the neighboring plot) without a criminal incident.

At this same time, left in the lurch while awaiting the reestablishment and preparation of a new group of lawyers at NUTH, leaders of Vila Autódromo's resistance began working with urban planning partners at Rio's two top universities, the Federal University of Rio de Janeiro (Universidade Federal do Rio de Janeiro or UFRJ) and Fluminense Federal University (Universidade Federal Fluminense or UFF). They summoned their help to respond to a 2010 comment by Mayor Paes in which he challenged the community to "come up with an alternate plan (to removal)."

In what constituted the city's next chess play, however, Rio de Janeiro's housing secretary, Jorge Bittar, called a meeting in Vila Autódromo for Sunday, October 16, 2011, not to negotiate, but to make an announcement.[40] No high-ranking city official had yet set foot in the community since declaring its removal two years earlier. And neither did Bittar, as his staff set up the "circus" (the meeting literally took place in a circus tent) just outside the community's entrance that morning.

Citing simply a vague "we need this area for the Olympics," Bittar shared a thorough PowerPoint presentation with a packed audience of well over one hundred residents and an equal number of supporters and journalists, displaying flashy sketches and blueprints of the Parque Carioca housing development that would be built especially to house the residents of Vila Autódromo.[41] A bright blue swimming pool with a toboggan waterslide was promised and afforded much attention on the shiny brochures. A map showed the housing project would be just one kilometer away on the well-transited Estrada dos Bandeirantes. Apartment sketches included state-of-the-art appliances, including an espresso machine.[42] The presentation was clearly intended to seduce while also sending the message that this was a done deal. He then opened the floor to questions and reactions.

Residents got up, one after the other, posing a number of questions. Some simply wanted more information about the diagrams and maps. Others gave deep testimonials about why they would not consider the city's proposal and would resist to the end, citing the community's legal defenses. Still, a few got up and angrily fired back at their resisting neighbors, saying they were eager to learn more and would accept the city's plans. I recognized these residents—they tended to live in the newer, more precarious area of the community near the lagoon and canal's intersection. These residents, at their peak equaling some

10 percent of the community, indeed had reason to consider the city's proposal better than their current conditions, and they felt unrepresented by their resident association.

In previous months, however, with technical support from UFRJ's Experimental Nucleus of Conflictual Planning (NEPLAC by its Portuguese acronym) and Institute of Urban and Regional Research and Planning (IPPUR) and UFF's Nucleus of Housing and Urban Studies and Projects (NEPHU), AMPAVA and these technical experts had been leading a series of broadly attended public meetings in the community, debating, developing, and fine-tuning an alternate plan that would allow for the community's full upgrading and integration with the Olympics site next door. Named the Vila Autódromo Popular Plan, the first thirty-two-page report was completed in December 2011 and launched in mid-2012, demonstrating how, for R$13,526,000 ($6,627,700 at the time), the entire community could be upgraded, including providing affordable housing on site for those in precarious dwellings while making final improvements on established homes and integrating sewerage, lighting, paving, and even the community's sought-after day care center and enclosed soccer pitch, all outside the boundaries of the Olympic park.[43]

Bittar's office, the Municipal Housing Secretariat (Secretaria Municipal de Habitação or SMH)—which became known internationally for marking homes for eviction without warning in a Naziesque fashion, with the famous "SMH" and a number—had uncovered an opportunity through the public display of vulnerability at the October event. Now the SMH argued that the community could not block access from the office visiting individual homes because some residents were clearly interested in the public housing option. So in the weeks and months that followed, while urban planners from the federal universities were holding public meetings debating the Popular Plan, which included community-based affordable housing for those more vulnerable families, SMH workers began going door-to-door, collecting information from residents allegedly interested in the public housing option.

The SMH notably sent large, intimidating groups of workers door-to-door, in many cases pressuring residents into allowing entry by saying if their information was not captured they would have no claim to eventual compensation should relocation take place or claiming they were registering residents for the Bolsa Família federal welfare program or simply asking questions about the home's size to register something on their spreadsheets.[44] This process went on for many months, throughout 2012 and into 2013, while a large group of residents increasingly organized their resistance.

Meanwhile, in 2012 Vila Autódromo began making its way into the global media spotlight. The first major visibility came from the *New York Times* in March under the headline "Slum Dwellers Are Defying Brazil's Grand Design for the Olympics."[45] Thus, the stage was set for what would grow into one of the key narratives in coverage of the Rio 2016 Olympic Games: how this small peaceful favela resisted the largest of corporate interests, interests represented not only by the IOC but especially by Brazil's mega–real estate developers who were the ones investing in the Olympic park next door with massive government subsidies and who would thus reap the post-Games benefits of inheriting what was once prime public land. After 2016, the Olympic park would be converted to luxury housing and moguls such as Marcelo Odebrecht and Carlos Carvalho were set to gain.[46]

By the end of 2012 all of the ingredients were thus in place for what would unfold over the next critical year. Vila Autódromo's resistance was on a very strong footing and continued expanding in early 2013. The compelling Popular Plan was being distributed, a strong network of community leaders assembled and organized, a diverse range of partners engaged, the global media beginning to pay attention, and the community's legal battle firmly unresolved. Legally speaking, the mayor would not be able to remove the community without their consent or a justification for the application of eminent domain. And given the community's visibility and organizing, a violent forced lightening eviction was increasingly out of the question politically.

In April 2013 urban planning professor Lawrence Vale at MIT published the first extensive summary of the Vila Autódromo struggle, comparing it with the Atlanta Olympics, in *Places, The Design Observer*. Entitled "The Displacement Decathlon: Olympian Struggles for Affordable Housing from Atlanta to Rio de Janeiro," the article's publication made clear the international reach and reputation of Vila Autódromo's resistance.[47] That same month, Vila Autódromo made its compelling case on Australia's *Special Broadcasting Service* (SBS) via the short documentary "Reshaping Rio."[48]

At this point the mayor of a city in an advanced democracy might have stopped and negotiated collectively or recognized the political damage that insisting on the eviction of a small, well-supported community like this would cause and might have changed course. But in Rio, Mayor Eduardo Paes instead buckled down in his approach, obviously committed to the behind-the-scenes demands of the real estate moguls who would ultimately benefit from the eviction and who were responsible for building the Olympic park.

What had started in late 2011 only intensified in the early months of 2013, when the municipal housing secretariat expanded its door-to-door pressure over the community.[49] Municipal workers used a variety of means to fill out forms on which they listed everything from resident names and addresses to how interested they were in relocation and how large their homes were. Some residents testified that they refused to speak to these workers, while others said that relatives provided information without realizing what was at stake or that they responded in fear that they would be left out of an eventual forced resettlement.[50]

The purpose of this extensive and highly questionable surveying process was made clear on July 1, 2013, at OsteRio, an exclusive debate series hosted by the Institute for the Study of Labor and Society (Instituto de Estudos de Trabalho e Sociedade or IETS), a well-respected labor and urban economics think tank in Rio. At the event, to an audience of some sixty executives, journalists, researchers, and NGOs, the mayor announced that 70 percent of Vila Autódromo's residents wanted to leave. Having had their names added to the survey forms, regardless of their reason for doing so, effectively served as an admission of willingness, or even desire, to relocate, according to the mayor's claim.

Vila Autódromo residents followed up by organizing a large protest on July 20, 2013.[51] The competing narratives were coming to a head when, in early August, Mayor Eduardo Paes called a meeting with Vila Autódromo's leaders, municipal secretaries of environment and housing, submayors for Barra da Tijuca and Jacarepaguá, a representative of the Municipal Olympic Corporation, and the city's attorney general.

At the meeting on August 9, 2013, Vila Autódromo was represented by a number of community leaders and residents, public defenders, the Catholic Church's favela outreach group, and technical partners from UFRJ and UFF who had helped draw up the Popular Plan. Leaders left the meeting hopeful, declaring themselves victorious, after the mayor had publicly acknowledged mistakes in how the community had been treated and agreed to open a round of collective negotiations to upgrade and "guarantee the community's permanence," stating that eventual cases of resettlement would be made only "in the same area, if a resident so desires."[52]

Over the next month, into September, a working group composed of residents and their university technical aids worked with the city's environment secretary, housing secretary, and municipal architects over a series of weekly meetings to agree on the upgrading plan. Vila Autódromo's working group was clear in its commitment to permit no evictions and used the jointly developed Popular Plan as the basis for negotiation. City officials, however, came to these meetings with an entirely different set of plans, requiring significant removals, which they would not relinquish. They refused to speak of other details without agreeing to some removals. As a result, community organizers did not negotiate further. They knew of the city's common tactic, using scattered removals to initiate larger evictions in other communities.[53] In these cases, the demolition of a handful of homes resulted in a domino effect, with frightened neighbors giving up one by one and entire communities eventually dismantled. From such divergent positions, the meetings were inconsequential, and by mid-September it was clear to community members that the mayor had made his public statements in bad faith, "for the English to see."[54]

Within two weeks of these negotiations, approximately one hundred Vila Autódromo residents received an invitation from the mayor for a closed-door meeting to be held down the road in Rio's convention center, RioCentro, on October 6, 2013. These one hundred residents were decidedly not those elected by residents to represent the community in the public negotiations. Nor were they among the hundreds of resisters. It was clear that the SMH workers' data on those willing to negotiate formed the basis of whom would be invited to the big event. The city had selected only those willing to negotiate, and the mayor would see just them.

The small rift in the community exposed at Bittar's event in late 2011 thus ultimately proved catastrophic to the community as a whole two years later. Sunday morning, hundreds of Vila Autódromo residents who had not been invited to the meeting were joined by an equal number of journalists and supporters when they stormed Rio-Centro, barging through a fence across a security outpost, traversing a pool, and finally accessing the building, where they were barred entry from the large hall where Paes addressed invited residents for over half an hour.[55] Not only were uninvited community residents and their elected leadership barred entry but the *BBC* was too, as were all the alternative and freelance journalists in attendance.

Meanwhile, inside the mayor had nearly a full hour's private audience with those one hundred residents. The only media outlet allowed in during this time was *O Globo*, and executives of Olympic park construction companies were also in the room. After several Vila Autódromo residents were injured by private security guards in their attempts to enter, unable to accept the idea that such a closed-door meeting would decide their future, the mayor finally approved entry of community residents, one of the university planners assisting them, and a handful of professional journalists. All other supporters and media were forced to remain just outside the double doors.

Inside, those who had received invitations to attend were given priority in taking the microphone, and very few others had an opportunity to speak. During his long presentation highlighting plans for rehousing the community in Parque Carioca, the public housing project advertised with a toboggan waterslide "especially for Vila Autódromo," Mayor Paes made announcements that broke with his previous statements and with standard protocol regarding public housing rules.[56] He stated, for example, that owners of multiple properties in Vila Autódromo would be compensated with several properties, when public housing is supposed to be issued on the basis of need and not speculation. He also stated that residents would be permitted to sell their new public housing units immediately, when normally there would be a ten-year permanency requirement, and that renters in

Vila Autódromo would be given apartments in Parque Carioca, when renters normally would not receive any compensation during eviction. Finally, he declared that more valuable homes could opt for "market rate" compensation. Those residents that asked for upgrading according to the Popular Plan were told by the mayor that they could make their way to the city's regional office to sign up for relocation or compensation.

By this point it had become clear that the mayor found himself caught between a rock and a hard place. His personal interests and political promises to developers were his sole commitment, yet the legal system was not concluding the case in the city's favor, and time would eventually run out to meet those commitments. Otherwise, there would be no need to negotiate separately—he could have kept his August promise to relocate only those who wanted it while upgrading the remainder of the community. If his goal was to remove the entire community, something that could be argued to be "consensual relocation" would be his only viable option, so identifying and convincing those families that had not participated in the broader community resistance and which were living in precarious situations to leave first was his most viable strategy.

So beginning with this meeting, and despite Vila Autódromo's Popular Plan being chosen from among 170 Rio de Janeiro–based projects as winner of the December 3, 2013, prestigious Deutsche Bank Urban Age Award,[57] the city entered a phase of mixing endless and diverse forms of intimidation with negotiations family by family, detecting what would convince each to move instead of upgrading their neighborhood. The administration even went so far as to forge a protest *in favor* of relocation, hiring two buses to carry twenty residents to city hall where they "protested" to be assigned to public housing.[58] That same night, community organizers were hosting a community meeting with nearly 200 residents signing a commitment to staying.

And so it happened, one by one, families living in more precarious situations, attracted by the glossy ads, were the first to go, taking apartments in Parque Carioca. Once their homes were demolished, fear began settling in among their neighbors, with one wave after another of residents taking various levels of compensation over the course of

2014, with the largest wave following the Evangelical Church's settlement offer. The community's Evangelical Church had received a very large offer to relocate, leading its parishioners to follow suit. Offers began at just one apartment, but shortly after families began receiving two or even multiple apartments. Once no one was willing to take an apartment, the city began offering financial compensations, which increased from tens of thousands of reais to their peak at R\$3 million (\$1 million), delivered to a colonel who owned a property there.[59] These offers, in the context of a community crumbling under bulldozers, dust, cut services, and other forms of duress, led even some who had declared themselves utterly committed to staying to ultimately leave.

In May 2014 at a second OsteRio event, just as the university planners and community residents issued a map showing that hundreds of residents remained committed to staying,[60] Mayor Paes told the audience that it was "difficult to prepare an upgrading plan when there [were] so many people coming to [them] looking to leave" but that they would "see what remains of the community [after compensations were all provided to those leaving], and that of what remain[ed] . . . so long as they [were] not in access areas [for the Olympic Park], [they would] upgrade as promised."[61]

One year later, even with Rio de Janeiro's first-ever market-rate compensations to favela residents, even under so much physical and emotional stress, by May 2015 the mayor had reached that limit and was unable to convince 170 of the remaining families to leave.[62] Rather than upgrading what was left of the community to permit the smaller portion of remaining residents to remain, however, Paes had shifted to an entirely new approach.

On March 20, 2015, fifty-eight homes had been marked for removal via an eminent domain decree, with future decrees offering the possibility of more homes suffering a similar fate.[63] It was by way of this decree that all of the community's earlier leaders were eventually evicted, and as a result of the eminent domain decree stipulating that the courts determine the value of the land in question, their compensations were a fraction of those provided to residents who had taken prior compensations. Thus, those most committed to the community, who fought so hard on its behalf and wanted so deeply to remain, were ultimately those who received the worst compensations, a form of searing revenge by the mayor. Guimarães, Nascimento, and Brito were all removed in August, in one excruciating eviction after another, as were numerous other organizers who had come to represent the cause.

Perhaps the single most critical turning point in the community's struggle came during this period. Building a home, particularly in a favela, can take decades. Tearing it down takes a matter of seconds. Municipal workers targeted homes covered by the eminent domain decree in those weeks, assigning houses for attention by hungry bulldozers following compensations being deposited in the bank accounts of their owners. And so there was a gaping threat that homes that had not yet been compensated for would be torn down. To protect themselves from ending up homeless, residents formed groups to watch over demolitions.

On June 3, 2015, such a scenario unfolded.[64] Two homes that had not yet been compensated for were targeted for demolition. Residents formed a ring around the houses as they attempted to explain that the demolition could not go forward. Public defenders and supporters were regularly in the community during those weeks and months and joined them. Yet on this fateful day the municipal guard reacted violently, using rubber bullets, pepper spray, and batons on the protesters and injuring several residents. Some required surgery. The images of the municipal guard's barbarity circulated on Brazil's TV networks, in newspapers, and around the world.[65]

This day was a game changer for the resistance movement remaining in the community. One of those most injured was Maria da Penha Macena, a small, agile woman in her fifties and one of the friendliest people one will ever meet, beaming with positivity and optimism steeped in her Catholic faith. Penha had by now assumed a leadership position in the community's struggle and was widely known by media outlets covering the resistance.

Penha was nearly the only hopeful person left in Vila Autódromo by the time of this incident. Morale had been at an all-time low. But the violent clash propelled remaining residents to recommit to the struggle. Over the ensuing months, and through to today, the community and its supporters have led campaigns, including cultural occupations, festivals, and the launch of the Evictions Museum, expanding on Vila Autódromo's sense of community to include the now tens of thousands who were following and supporting them in their struggle.[66]

By the time the most symbolic community structure was demolished—the residents' association—on February 24, 2016, Vila Autódromo was no longer felt by its remaining residents or their supporters to be simply the original blueprint of their community. The concept of Vila Autódromo had expanded to represent a broad, even global, social struggle reflected in one of the community's many slogans,[67] which was stamped on its walls: "Not Everyone Has a Price." Penha coined the slogan, summarizing the movement for visitors and the press. And it was exactly that notion that captivated so many who grew to embrace the community as their own.

The eminent domain decree ultimately led to the eviction of almost all of the community's remaining inhabitants. The two final houses demolished within the decree belonged to Maria da Penha and Heloisa Helena Costa Berto. Berto was a Candomblé priestess whose home had served as a spiritual center and who was chronically mistreated by city workers, even receiving death threats.[68] Berto and Penha along with two other women, Sandra Maria de Souza and Nathalia Silva (Penha's daughter), became Vila Autódromo's best-known leaders in the final stages of the community's resistance and have since received widespread recognition and awards from city and state governments, as well as international human rights organizations.[69]

The final eminent domain evictions took place during the last week of February and the first week of March 2016, witnessed and documented by remaining residents along with support from dozens camped out overnight in the community on those final weeks. Vila Autódromo was now down to twenty families that were both outside the decree and had remained steadfast in their unwillingness to negotiate with the city throughout the entire process.

The final stage of Vila Autódromo's pre-Olympics struggle now began. It was clear that the city would not leave the area looking like a war zone come August 5 and the Olympic Games' opening ceremony. And, of course, at least a couple of months would be needed to prepare the site. So whatever was to happen to Vila Autódromo's twenty remaining families would have to be decided by early June. This was just two months away.

Once again taking control of the broader narrative and keeping spirits high during those few remaining demolitions, on February 27, 2015, Vila Autódromo residents and supporters launched the #UrbanizaJá (#UpgradesNow) social media campaign, calling on supporters to post videos on social media using the hashtag and declaring why they wanted Vila Autódromo to be fully upgraded now. On the same day, they launched an updated version of the Popular Plan, considering the reduced nature of the community.

Mayor Paes had declared publicly over the years, on numerous occasions, that he would not remove anyone who didn't agree to relocation.[70] His administration had sent in municipal workers to do the dirty work of "convincing" residents through a variety of means and then made use of a questionable eminent domain decree. But now no such option was left. The final twenty families had never even entertained the idea of negotiating, and nothing short of a violent eviction would remove them.

The #UrbanizaJá campaign quickly produced dozens if not hundreds of videos on social media, including high-visibility posts from Brazilian celebrities Camila Pitanga, Gregório Duvivier, and Bruno Gagliasso, as well as internationally known figures like David Harvey.

On March 8, 2016, the same emotional day that the home of Maria da Penha was demolished *and* she went on to receive a major award from the Rio State Legislative Assembly,[71] Mayor Paes held a press conference that community members were restricted from to announce his plan for the community. The mayor's plan ignored recommendations made in the updated Popular Plan and instead proposed not the upgrading of the community but the construction of a set of new homes on a single street, maintaining only the Catholic church from the original community's blueprint.[72] Residents insisted on a meeting with the mayor to discuss the proposal directly, and it took place on March 15. On that day, the community and mayor reached a tentative agreement, based mainly on the city's proposal.[73] The final agreement would come to be the first collectively signed relocation agreement in favela history.[74]

As a result of their extraordinary resistance efforts, and with supporters and the media watching, over the subsequent months the remaining residents held firm, watching and waiting, then actively participating, in relocating to their new homes. Several lived in temporary trailers on the site for a number of weeks, while others remained in their original homes as the new houses were prepared. Maria da Penha had the opportunity to speak of the community's struggle to the United Nations in Geneva.[75] Media outlets from around the world made daily visits, reporting on the community's struggle and relative success. Technical partners from the federal universities watched over construction quality. The entire original community was paved over, parts became parking; others became access roads (the final justification used by the city for demolitions).[76] But the bulk of the community's land was paved over with no apparent purpose. The hundreds of trees Vila Autódromo residents had planted over decades were toppled at some point during the demolition process, leaving the area barren and synthetic, like its modern neighbor, the Olympic park.[77]

Vila Autódromo launched the Evictions Museum on May 18, 2016, and kept up weekly cultural events and meetings in the months building up to the Games, during the Games, and afterward.[78] The original 700-family, relatively bucolic and green favela with large-lot homes by the lagoon exists only in the memories of those who lived there or visited prior to the onset of 2014 demolitions. In its wake are twenty small, identical, white homes lining a wide street, named Vila Autódromo Street, surrounded by asphalt and pounded by the hot sun. One resident, Delmo Oliveira, caught in a legal battle with the city that excluded him from the twenty units built prior to the Games, has managed to maintain his original home.[79]

In the end, the drawn out and painful eviction of Vila Autódromo's residents cost the city of Rio over R$327 million, as compared to the Popular Plan's budget, which would have upgraded the original community for under R$14 million.[80] More than R$105 million was spent on the Parque Carioca public housing complex alone.[81] At least another R$220 million was paid out in financial compensations.[82] And the city's final rebuilding of Vila Autódromo cost at least R$2.9 million.[83] Today, the city also faces a lawsuit: 110 of the families that received compensations are suing the city over the unjust natures of those compensations in relation to those of their neighbors.[84]

While not the victory residents fought for, and certainly not the victory those evicted under eminent domain (and even many who took compensations) longed for, the fact that those who held out succeeded in staying on their original land in the face of such tremendous pressure and power is an unequivocal success. And these community members have gone on to represent Rio's favelas in international forums like Habitat III and the United Nations,[85] and their archives delivered to Brazil's National Historical Museum during a ceremony on International Museum day, May 18, 2017, one year following the founding of the Evictions Museum. The story of the community's steadfast early Residents' Association President, Altair Guimarães, evicted during the eminent domain period, was in April 2017 recognized in a documentary titled "One Man, One City, Three Evictions: The Human Cost of Rio's Growth."[86]

Vila Autódromo's illustrative story serves as a glowing example and inspiration to communities in Rio and around the world. The small favela forged a path that communities facing eviction in the name of the Olympic Games or any other megaevent or megainvestment project can look to for inspiration or strategic lessons and on which they can base their movements. And the residents who succeeded in remaining on the new Vila Autódromo Street have set the community up to host and support such organizers.[87]

VILA AUTÓDROMO IN THE CONTEXT OF RIO'S OLYMPICS EVICTIONS

Unfortunately, Vila Autódromo represents just one of dozens of communities that suffered forced evictions in the lead-up to the 2016 Olympic Games. In all, nearly 80,000 people were removed.[88] Two to three thousand of these were from Vila Autódromo. By some estimates more people were evicted in the pre-Olympics years in Rio than in both previous Rio administrations associated with evictions combined: those of Francisco Pereira Passos in the first decade of the 1900s and Carlos Lacerda in the 1960s.[89]

The Olympic Games offered the perfect pretext for eviction. Over the previous century favela residents had acquired basic land rights, and their communities were being slowly upgraded under the growing conclusion that this was the only way to justly integrate them. Opportunities for mass eviction would no longer be justifiable—that is, until the Olympics deadline provided a state of exception.[90] The city's population yearned for investment. There was a broad assumption that municipal decisions were being well made in the public interest. And there were few checks to make sure they were.

So as city workers pulled up at favelas from Recreio II to Metrô, Manguinhos to Harmonia, Tanque to Restinga, few residents resisted. Most did not know they had any rights to claim, often struggling to make ends meet from multiple jobs or hampered by little education. Twenty-six percent of evictees during this period were in and near the rapidly expanding upper-class Barra da Tijuca region, despite this region only housing 12 percent of the city's favela residents.[91] Evictees were generally bused to distant housing projects in the extreme West Zone of Rio de Janeiro, in neighborhoods like Cosmos and Santa Cruz, two hours from employment opportunities and now at the mercy of vigilante cop mafias, known in Rio as *milicias*. In other cases, the government offered rent subsidies of R$400 per household (about $120) per month, insufficient to rent a favela home in most of Rio de Janeiro.

This broader context helps put Vila Autódromo's remarkable resistance into perspective. The community carved out a strategy to resist greed of Olympic proportions that relied on seven keys to successful resistance: the community's relative unity in its commitment to stay, access to information,[92] legal defense, diverse and resolute leadership, broad networks of support ranging from peer communities to technical partners, creative responses such as the Popular Plan and Evictions Museum, and early and ongoing documentation and visibility.

Residents will attribute the success at each moment of their struggle to one or the other of these keys to resistance. For example, in the first year the community's legal defense was the most critical, in particular allowing the community time to organize on other fronts. And as the struggle went on, creative responses allowed them to solidify their commitment, become more united, and get over psychological hurdles while attracting partners and media attention. And finally, mass attention from the global media and broad networks of support emboldened residents during their most trying period,[93] when so many of their neighbors had been removed, services were cut, and demolition debris left morale low. And all along, it was the community's diverse and resolute leadership, able to evolve and adapt among a large number of compelling community members as the struggle continued, that resulted in the relative success of the final outcome.

Though ultimately dismantled in virtually its entirety, Vila Autódromo's victories in the broad context of the history of Rio de Janeiro's favelas and housing rights in Brazil as a whole (and perhaps ultimately around the world) are many and its lessons far-reaching.

Vila Autódromo was up against the most powerful real estate interests in Brazil, one of the world's most unequal societies. Yet its battle was uniquely successful on numerous levels. Oversold as some sort of paradise,[94] Parque Carioca was nonetheless one of the better examples of public housing built under the Paes administration, and those who moved there were able to remain in the same region as their jobs and schools. In many cases, families moving to Parque Carioca received multiple apartments—one per adult child plus the parents and grandparents, for example. And there were those who received market-rate compensation, the first-ever favela compensations recognizing land value in Rio's history.

Finally, and perhaps most importantly, those twenty families who remained to the end were able to prove to those who gave up—perhaps ultimately more importantly to communities at threat elsewhere—that firm, creative resistance pays off. And they signed their agreement collectively, rather than individually with the city.

The Rio Olympics proved that, at least somewhere, not everyone has a price. The Games have also inadvertently spread that gospel.[95]

APPENDIX: VILA AUTÓDROMO TIMELINE

From "Timeline: Vila Autódromo, Story of Resistance," *RioOnWatch* (www.rioonwatch.org/?page_id=28610). Links to relevant dates available on the site.

Before 2009

1967	Construction of homes begins
1992	Struggle against eviction begins
1993	Court battles over removals begin
1994	Residents are granted ninety-nine-year titles to land
2005	Community is declared Zone of Special Social Interest

2009

October 2 Rio is awarded the 2016 Olympics and residents learn of the mayor's plan to evict them

2010

February 10 Protest against city-wide evictions

March 3 Residents meet mayor and propose plan for remaining

March 11 Rock in Rio site construction begins in "Protected Area" that includes Vila Autódromo

2011

February 27 Court authorizes demolitions of some homes

May 3 Competition to design Olympic Park begins

August 22 Winning AECOM Olympic park design maintains Vila Autódromo

2012

January Judge suspends private bids for Olympic Park

March 4 *New York Times* first covers Vila Autódromo

June 6 Four thousand–strong protest in Vila Autódromo

July 26 Popular Plan created

August 16 Residents present Popular Plan to mayor

November 8 Public meeting about BRT highways planned for Vila Autódromo area

2013

March 4 City employees go door-to-door to convince residents to leave

March 5 Evictions discussion with threatened communities across Rio

April MIT report "Displacement Decathlon" published

May 15 2013 Popular Committee Human Rights dossier is launched

June 5 Vila Autódromo team participates in Evictions Cup

June 24 Five homes marked for removal

June 28 Confrontation between residents and city officials

June 30 Protest against evictions in Rio

July 17	Vila Autódromo and Horto team up for antievictions vigil
July 20	Protest against evictions begins in Vila Autódromo
August 9	Mayor agrees to permanence of Vila Autódromo
September 27	Communities threatened with evictions discuss strategies
October 2	Residents prepare for meeting with mayor
October 6	Mayor meets some residents; other residents insist on attending
October 30	City sponsors protest with twenty residents who want to leave
November 7	One hundred residents protest removal tactics and city-sponsored protest
December	Popular Plan wins Deutsche Bank Urban Age Award for Vila Autódromo
December 3	Public hearing on Rio removals

2014

March 19	Mayor states no families will be forced to leave and residents demand release of plans for proposed roads
March 21	Demolitions are temporarily suspended
March 22	Phase with marked cases of City pitting residents against each other
March 25	Injunction preventing demolitions is overturned
March 26	Five families sign contracts to leave and their homes are demolished
April 28	Mayor: Residents who want to stay can stay but majority "want" to leave
May	In Vila Autódromo, 187 families confirm they want to stay
June 15	2014 Popular Committee Human Rights dossier is launched
September 24	Residents hold solidarity and protest breakfast
November 7	Vila Autódromo residents share experiences at dossier launch
November	Vila Autódromo documentary screening

2015

March 11	More houses demolished
March 19	City declares eminent domain, marks the houses of fifty-eight families for eviction
March 24	Protest and barricade at Vila Autódromo

April 2   *International Business Times* coverage

April 16   Final resident of Vila Autódromo Avenue, Tadilmarco Peixopo told his house will be demolished imminently

May 14   *O Globo*: R$95 million has been released to compensate 116 people

May   Jane Nascimento testifies to Human Rights Commission

May 20   Demolition of one house damages another

June 3   Attempted demolition leaves residents injured and draws international media coverage; Maria da Penha is injured during attempted eviction

June 8   Residents protest June 3 eviction attempt

August 15   #OcupaVilaAutódromo festival and light show

August   Neighborhood association president Altair Guimarães evicted; Jane Nascimento is evicted

August 15   *BBC*: Mayor says people who want stay can stay

September 12   Federal University of Rio de Janeiro's MediaLab presents residents with aerial map of changes taking place in Vila Autódromo

September 17   Heloisa Helena Costa Berto publishes first open letter on eviction terror

October 2   Jane Nascimento speaks at Museu da República

October 23   Lightning evictions include long-time resident Dona Mariza's home while she was out at the doctor in the early morning; she returns to find her home and all her possessions on the ground

October 25   *O Globo*: Mayor says people who want to stay can stay

November   Photographer Guilherme Imbassahy launches Evictions Have a Face campaign

November 9   Jane Nascimento speaks at Getúlio Vargas Foundation

November 14–15   Residents and supporters revitalize the community park

November 21   New leader, Sandra Maria, leads visiting groups around Vila Autódromo

November 28   Residents host second Cultural Festival

December 9   2015 Popular Committee Human Rights dossier launched

December 11   Photo coverage of eviction struggle published in *The Guardian*

December 12   Residents plan day care center

December 26   Solidarity soccer tournament

December 27   *Time* magazine coverage

2016

January 11   Heloisa Helena Costa Berto receives death threat

January 13   Municipal guard builds wall dividing community

January 14   Municipal guard removes community barricade;
              Heloisa Helena Costa Berto's house is surrounded
              by guards and bulldozers

January 19   Mayor says only one more family needs to go

January 21   Shock troops enter in force

January 21   Opening of Olympic Favela exhibition in Studio X

January 25   Screening of Olympic Favela documentary in Vila
              Autódromo

January 27   Protest march outside Olympic Park

February 6   Popular Committee and Vila Autódromo residents
              release video defending human rights dossier

February 11   Three homes are demolished behind residents
              association

February 12   Mayor confirms houses isolated in Olympic Park
              cannot remain

February 13   A burst water pipe causes flood

February 22   Residents put out SOS; suspension of residents'
              association demolition order is overturned; supporters
              camp overnight in Vila Autódromo

February 23   Heloisa Helena Costa Berto publishes second letter on
              eviction struggle

February 24   Residents' association building and Heloisa Helena
              Costa Berto's house demolished

February 24   Amnesty International highlights Vila Autódromo
              evictions as human rights abuse

February 27   Latest version of Popular Plan is launched along with
              #UrbanizaJá campaign

March 5   Former UN Special Rapporteur on Housing Raquel
              Rolnik launches book in Vila Autódromo

March 5   Former Vila Autódromo residents express discontent
              with Parque Carioca public housing

March 8   International Women's Day; Maria da Penha's house
              demolished and Penha receives award from state
              assembly; Mayor releases upgraded plan to invited press

March 15   Residents demand mayor present plan to them directly

March 23   Heloisa Helena Costa Berto writes letter to the UN
              from the United States

March 26   Olympics Poverty torch event

April 13   Residents agree to terms of upgrades with mayor

April 19   Residents announce plans for an Evictions Museum

April 23   Work on Evictions Museum begins

May 11   Heloisa Helena Costa Berto receives Dandara Award from state assembly

May 18   Evictions Museum opens

May 28   Vila Autódromo hosts Favela Literary Festival (FLUPP) workshop

May 28   Vila Autódromo mourns loss of tree coverage resulting from demolitions and destruction and reflects on Olympics Environmental Legacy

June   Construction of new homes proceeds quickly

June 25   Traditional June festivities celebrate memory of Vila Autódromo

June 27   *Vox* video released: City of Rio's project to hide the poor

June   Report of death of former Vila Autódromo resident in public housing project

July   Ten-meter banner by Pontifical Catholic University (PUC) students documenting seven years of urban transformations displayed in Vila Autódromo

July 5   Maria da Penha speaks at the United Nations in Geneva

July 25   *The Fighter* film launched about Naomy, a child who was evicted

July 26   HBO's *Real Sports with Bryant Gumbel* features Vila Autódromo's story

July 28   Heloisa Helena Costa Berto recognized by Front Line Defenders as a Front Line Defender

July 29   Remaining twenty families receive keys to new homes

August 5   Rio Olympics begins

August 11   UOL reports on the heavy psychological cost of Olympic evictions

August 12   Resident of last standing original home in Vila Autódromo tells foreign media of "terror"

August 19   Vila Autódromo "occupies" Olympic Park with celebration and protest

August 21   Rio Olympics closing ceremony

September 15 Olympic film featuring Vila Autódromo launched

September 25 Cultural occupation in Vila Autódromo celebrates memory, resistance, and hope

October 6   Vila Autódromo mother describes how children's
              education has been impacted by eviction
October 17–20 Sandra Maria represents Vila Autódromo at Habitat III
              conference in Ecuador
November 23–26 Vila Autódromo participates in UrbFavelas seminar on
              favela upgrading
December 15   Sandra Maria speaks on panel at *Favelas in the Media*
              report launch

2017
March   110 families take the City to court over just
              compensation
April 24   Reuters publishes documentary featuring Altair titled
              "One Man, One City, Three Evictions: The Human
              Cost of Rio's Growth"
May 18   Evictions Museum archive transferred to Brazil's National
              Historic Museum on International Museum Day

NOTES

1. Robert Neuwirth, *Shadow Cities: A Billion Squatters, A New Urban World* (New York: Routledge, 2006), p. 58.

2. Jane Souto de Oliveira and Maria Hortense Marcier, "A palavra é: favela," in *Um Século de Favela*, edited by Alba Zaluar and Marcos Alvito (Rio de Janeiro: Fundação Getúlio Vargas, 1999), pp. 61–114, at 65.

3. Jordana Timerman, "Is a Favela Still a Favela Once It Starts Gentrifying?" *Atlantic CityLab*, December 2, 2013 (www.citylab.com/housing/2013/12/favela-still-favela-once-it-starts-gentrifying/7726/).

4. Rio was the largest slave port in world history, and slaves constituted some 40 percent of the city's population in the nineteenth century prior to Brazil abolishing slavery in 1888; it was the last nation in the Western hemisphere to do so. Stephanie Reist, "Mapping the Slave Trade and Growing Black Awareness in Brazil," *RioOnWatch*, November 20, 2015 (www.rioonwatch.org/?p=25458); Rosana Barbosa, *Immigration and Xenophobia: Portuguese Immigrants in Early 19th Century Rio de Janeiro* (Lanham, Md.: University Press of America, 2009).

5. Bruce Douglas, "The Story of Cities #15: The Rise and Ruin of Brazil's First Favela," *The Guardian*, April 5, 2016.

6. Raquel Rolnik, "Favelas cariocas entre a montanha e o mar são patrimônio da humanidade," *Blog da Raquel Rolnik* (blog), July 2, 2012 (https://raquelrolnik.wordpress.com/2012/07/02/favelas-cariocas-entre-a-montanha-e-o-mar-sao-patrimonio-da-humanidade/).

7. Bryan McCann, *Hard Times in the Marvelous City: From Dictatorship to Democracy in the Favelas of Rio de Janeiro* (Durham, N.C.: Duke University Press, 2014), p. 2.

8. Janice Perlman, *Favela: Four Decades of Living on the Edge in Rio de Janeiro* (Oxford, U.K.: Oxford University Press, 2010), p. 333.

9. Corinne Cath, "On the Origin of 'Favela,'" *RioOnWatch*, February 14, 2012 (www.rioonwatch.org/?p=2920).

10. Alex Ferreira Magalhães, *O Direito das Favelas* (Rio de Janeiro: Letra Capital, 2013), p. 33.

11. Brodwyn Fischer, *A Poverty of Rights: Citizenship and Inequality in Twentieth-Century Rio de Janeiro*, (Stanford: Stanford University Press, 2008), p. 60; Lucas Pedretti, "Report by Rio de Janeiro Truth Commission Denounces Violence Used in Favelas During Dictatorship," *RioOnWatch*, January 27, 2016 (www.rioonwatch.org/?p=26538). Prior to Lacerda, evictions had taken place during the first decade in the century when Francisco Pereira Passos was mayor and led major urban reform initiatives, but these took out tenement houses, which hastened the settlement of favelas.

12. Catherine Osborne, "A History of Favela Upgrades Part I (1897–1988)," *RioOnWatch*, September 27, 2012 (www.rioonwatch.org/?p=5295); Catherine Osborne, "A History of Favela Upgrades Part II (1988–2008)," *RioOnWatch*, November 26, 2012 (www.rioonwatch.org/?p=5931).

13. Alex Besser, Alix Vadot, Ava Rose Hoffman, Eli Nemzer, and Nashwa Al-sharki, "Understanding Rio's Violence: The Criminalization of Poverty," *RioOnWatch*, August 1, 2016 (www.rioonwatch.org/?p=30636); Patrick Ashcroft, "Series: History of Rio de Janeiro's Military Police," *RioOnWatch*, May 1, 2014 (www.rioonwatch.org/?tag=series-history-military-police).

14. Saulo Pereira Guimarães and Bibiana Maia, "UPPs: 8 anos depois," *Vozerio*, November 30, 2016 (http://vozerio.org.br/UPPs-8-anos-depois).

15. Bryan McCann, *Hard Times in the Marvelous City: From Dictatorship to Democracy in the Favelas of Rio de Janeiro* (Durham, N.C.: Duke University Press, 2014).

16. David Robertson, "What Does the Brazilian Constitution Say About Housing Rights?" *RioOnWatch*, May 18, 2016 (www.rioonwatch.org/?p=25334).

17. Luisa Fenziola, "UrbFavelas Seminar Defends the Upgrading of Favelas and Raises Questions of Representation," *RioOnWatch*, December 9, 2016 (www.rioonwatch.org/?p=34315).

18. Rafael Galdo, "Rio é a cidade com maior população em favelas no Brasil," *O Globo*, December 21, 2011.

19. Theresa Williamson, "Rio's Favelas: The Power of Informal Urbanism," in *Perspecta 50*, edited by M. McAllister and M. Sabbagh (MIT Press, 2017).

20. Eliot Allen and Julia Jones, "Asa Branca Wins the Gold! Is a Rio Favela Greener Than the LEED-Certified Olympic Village?" *RioOnWatch*, August 3, 2016 (www.rioonwatch.org/?p=30968).

21. Renato Meirelles and Celso Athayde, *Um País Chamado Favela: A maior pesquisa já feita sobre a favela brasileira* (São Paulo, Brazil: Gente, 2014).

22. "Urban Population (Percent of Total): Brazil," *World Bank* (http://data.worldbank.org/indicator/SP.URB.TOTL.IN.ZS?locations=BR).

23. David Scott, "What Can Brazil's Favelas Teach Us About Future Cities?" *The Age*, July 14, 2014 (www.theage.com.au/national/education/voice/what-can-brazils-favelas-teach-us-about-future-cities-20140707-3bill.html).

24. Such a narrative serves in maintaining low self- and community regard in the psyche of favelados. See James Ferreira Moura, Verônica Morais Ximenes, and Jorge Castellá Sarriera, "The Oppressive Construction of Poverty in Brazil and Its Consequences in the Psyche," *Quaderns de Psicologia* 16, no. 2 (2014), pp. 85–93 (http://ddd.uab.cat/pub/quapsi/quapsi_a2014v16n2/quapsi_a2014v16n2p85ipor.pdf).

25. Juliana Barbassa, *Dancing with the Devil in the City of God* (New York: Touchstone, 2015), p. 220.

26. "Autódromo Internacional Nelson Piquet," *Wikipedia* (https://en.wikipedia.org/wiki/Aut%C3%B3dromo_Internacional_Nelson_Piquet).

27. Giselle Tanaka, "Vila Autódromo: Remoção e resistência," *Heinrich Boll Stiftung Brasil*, June 22, 2016 (https://br.boell.org/pt-br/2016/06/22/vila-autodromo-remocao-e-resistencia#_ftn1).

28. Renato Cosentino, "Barra da Tijuca e o Projeto Olímpico: A cidade do capital" (master's thesis, Federal University of Rio de Janeiro, 2015) (https://riorealblog.files.wordpress.com/2016/03/renato-cosentino-dissertac3a7c3a3o-mestrado-ippur-ufrj-2015.pdf).

29. *Adverse possession* refers to when one occupies an area for a given period without contest and is thus permitted to file to acquire the land. The Brazilian constitution stipulates this at five years in urban areas, for up to 250 square meters. Robertson, "What Does the Brazilian Constitution Say?"

30. *No Games Chicago* (https://nogames.wordpress.com/); Hugo Cotsa, "And the Electorate Has Responded! The Olympic Legacy Is Already a Failure," *RioOnWatch*, October 20, 2016 (www.rioonwatch.org/?p=33589).

31. Andréia Coutinho, Samuel Lima, and Thamyres Gonçalves, "Jane's Awakening," *RioOnWatch*, June 10, 2011 (www.rioonwatch.org/?p=1290).

32. Yet, behind the scenes Paes's administration had already been setting the public stage for the relaunch of 1960s-era eviction policies, working to

remove what he labeled "the taboo" on favela evictions. On April 12, 2009, just three months into his administration, Rio's most influential and largest newspaper, *O Globo*, firmly associated with Rio's right wing since the military regime, published the final of several articles, this one on its front page, declaring, "Since the 1980s, favela evictions were stigmatized as an authoritarian practice of the past," thus heralding the return of an evictions policy. Mario Brum, "Favelas e remocionismo ontem e hoje: Da Ditadura de 1964 aos Grandes Eventos," *O Social em Questão* 16, no. 29 (2013), pp. 179–208 (http://osocialemquestao.ser.puc-rio.br/media/8artigo29.pdf). Torrential rains on previous days had led to a number of landslides in favelas, which were used as a pretext for this campaign. "Death Toll Climbs in Rio Landslides," *New York Times*, April 9, 2010.

33. Heitor Ney Mathias da Silva, "Da Terra de Ninguém a Terra dos Fidalgos: A valorização da Barra da Tijuca e as Tentativas de Remoção da Vila Autódromo," *XII Encontro da Associação Nacional de Pós-Graduação e Pesquisa em Planejamento Urbano e Regional* 12 (2007) (http://unuhospedagem .com.br/revista/rbeur/index.php/anais/article/view/3721).

34. Jo Griffin, "One Man, One City, Three Evictions: The Human Cost of Rio's Growth," *Place*, May 2, 2017 (http://www.thisisplace.org/i /?id=c604405c-abca-456a-8611-f03f5b15d25c).

35. "Rio's City Hall Forges Resident Protest to Remove Vila Autódromo," *RioOnWatch*, October 31, 2013 (http://www.rioonwatch.org/?p =11948).

36. "Uma História de Luta," *Viva Vila Autódromo*. "O que é uma Área de Especial Interesse Social—AEIS? Para que serve? Quando apareceu? Rio de Janeiro—RJ," *Direito, Moral e Ética* (blog), April 27, 2011 (http://web-direito.blogspot.com/2011/04/o-que-e-uma-area-de-especial -interesse.html).

37. Alexandre F. Mendes and Giuseppe Cocco, *A Resistência à Remoção de Favelas no Rio de Janeiro—Instituições do comum e resistências urbanas: a história do Núcleo de Terra e Habitação e a luta contra a remoção de favelas no Rio de Janeiro (2007–2011)* (Editora Revan, 2016); Laura Bachmann, "Public Defenders Office Hosts Panel of Attorneys and Favela Leaders to Discuss Resistance to Evictions 2007–2011," *RioOnWatch*, November 3, 2016 (www.rioonwatch.org/?p=33843); "Moção pública contra a destruição do Núcleo de Terras e Habitação da Defensoria Pública do Rio de Janeiro," *Defensoria Popular*, June 3, 2011 (https://defensoriapopular .wordpress.com/2011/06/03/mocao-publica-contra-a-destruicao-do-nucleo -de-terras-e-habitacao-da-defensoria-publica-do-rio-de-janeiro/).

38. "Eviction Tactics: Divide and Conquer," *RioOnWatch* (www .rioonwatch.org/?tag=eviction-tactics-divide-and-conquer).

39. Gabriel Silvestre and Nelma Gusmão de Oliveira, "The Revanchist Logic of Mega-Events: Community Displacement in Rio de Janeiro's West End," *Visual Studies* 27, no. 2 (2012), pp. 204–10 (www.tandfonline.com /doi/abs/10.1080/1472586x.2012.677506).

40. Katie Judd, "Housing Secretary Jorge Bittar to Present Relocation Proposal to Vila Autódromo Community Sunday," *Catalytic Communities*, October 14, 2011 (http://hosted-p0.vresp.com/363276/e38ba016e2/ARCHIVE).

41. Connie Watson, "Rio's Secretary of Housing Met by Protests in Vila Autódromo," radio broadcast, CBC Radio Canada, October 16, 2011 (http://rioonwatch.org/wp-content/uploads/2011/10/2011-10-16_Canada _CBC_The_World_This_Week.m4a).

42. Yaara Bou Melhem, "Reshaping Rio," video report, *SBS Dateline*, April 9, 2013 (http://www.sbs.com.au/news/dateline/story/reshaping-rio).

43. *Plano Popular da Vila Autódromo: Plano de desenvolvimento urbano, econômico, social e cultural* (Rio de Janeiro: Associação de Moradores e Pescadores da Vila Autóromo, 2012) (https://vivaavilaautodromo .files.wordpress.com/2016/02/planopopularvilaautodromo_2012.pdf).

44. *RioOnWatchTV*, "Vila Autódromo Responds to City's Latest Threat of Eviction," video, December 7, 2011 (https://www.youtube.com/watch?v =6vI6KD41Gsw); Henrique Zizo, "Vila Autódromo/RJ—Cadastro da Prefeitura para o início do projeto de remoção," video, October 22, 2011 (www .youtube.com/watch?v=QxTE2U9IlMs&list=PLA9xC_xNGPz6Pszursu _zRZdLQkEZsTYf&index=9).

45. Simon Romero, "Slum Dwellers Are Defying Brazil's Grand Design for Olympics," *New York Times*, March 4, 2012.

46. Jonathan Watts, "The Rio Property Developer Hoping For a $1bn Olympic Legacy of His Own," *The Guardian*, August 4, 2015.

47. Lawrence Vale and Annemarie Gray, "The Displacement Decathlon: Olympian struggles for affordable housing from Atlanta to Rio de Janeiro," *Places Journal*, April 2013 (https://placesjournal.org/article/the-displacement -decathlon).

48. Yaara Bou Melhem, "Reshaping Rio," video report, *SBS Dateline*, April 9, 2013 (http://www.sbs.com.au/news/dateline/story/reshaping-rio).

49. "Depoimento de Osmarina Fernandes, Vila Autódromo," video report, *RioOnWatchTV*, October 30, 2011 (www.youtube.com/watch?v =JWReNfbiXXI&list=PLA9xC_xNGPz6Pszursu_zRZdLQkEZsTYf& index=5).

50. Kate Steiker-Ginzberg, "Vila Autódromo Under Pressure from City to Accept Resettlement Housing," *RioOnWatch*, March 22, 2013 (www .rioonwatch.org/?p=7832).

51. Catherine Osborn, "Vila Autódromo Unites in Protest Following Weeks of Pressure," *RioOnWatch*, July 23, 2013 (www.rioonwatch.org/?p=10496).

52. "Victory for Vila Autódromo! Rio's Mayor Commits to Permanence, Urbanization, and Fair Compensation," *RioOnWatch*, August 9, 2013, (www.rioonwatch.org/?p=10734).

53. Osborn, "Vila Autódromo Unites in Protest."

54. An expression arising in the early nineteenth century in Brazil reflecting the cultural tendency to engage in empty public promises—even law-making—that is not truly intended for implementation but rather to buy time, mask over true motives, or otherwise permit unpopular actions to take place, as was done with the Canudos soldiers who were promised land in Rio. Patrick Ashcroft, "Two Centuries of Conning the 'British': The History of the Expression "'É Para Inglês Ver,' or 'It's for the English to See' and Its Modern Offshoots," *RioOnWatch*, May 28, 2015 (www.rioonwatch.org/?p=21847).

55. "Vila Autódromo Meets the Mayor," *RioOnWatch*, October 10, 2013 (www.rioonwatch.org/?p=11419).

56. Mariah Queiroz, "Removidos pelo Parque Olímpico lutam por compensação mais justa," *Agência Pública*, February 20, 2017 (http://apublica .org/2017/02/removidos-pelo-parque-olimpico-lutam-por-compensacao -mais-justa/).

57. Kate Steiker-Ginzberg, "Vila Autódromo People's Plan Wins Deutsche Bank Urban Age Award," *RioOnWatch*, December 20, 2013 (www.rioonwatch.org/?p=12851).

58. "Rio's City Hall Forges Resident Protest to Remove Vila Autódromo."

59. Ruben Berta, "Apesar de indenizações milionárias, Prefeitura não consegue acabar com a Vila Autódromo," *O Globo*, May 14, 2015.

60. Comitê Popular do Rio, "Map Shows Hundreds of Vila Autódromo Residents Want to Remain," *RioOnWatch*, May 24, 2014 (www .rioonwatch.org/?p=15503).

61. Benjamin Parkin and Kate Steiker-Ginzberg, "Mayor Eduardo Paes on the 2016 Olympic Games Legacy," *RioOnWatch*, May 3, 2014 (www .rioonwatch.org/?p=14755).

62. Berta, "Apesar de indenizações milionárias."

63. "Prefeitura remove 58 imóveis na região da Vila Autódromo," *O Dia*, March 20, 2015 (http://odia.ig.com.br/noticia/rio-de-janeiro/2015-03-20 /prefeitura-remove-58-imoveis-na-regiao-da-vila-autodromo.html); Brooke Parkin, "Mayor Announces Eminent Domain in Vila Autódromo as MIT Report Criticizes City Policy," *RioOnWatch*, March 25, 2015 (www.rioonwatch .org/?p=20983).

64. Sarah Jacobs, "Tense Week Introduces New Policy of 'Lightning Evictions' Across Rio Favelas," *RioOnWatch*, June 8, 2015 (www.rioonwatch .org/?p=22402).

65. Jonathan Watts, "Forced Evictions in Rio Favela for 2016 Olympics Trigger Violent Clashes," *The Guardian*, June 3, 2015.

66. Clare Huggins, "Vila Autódromo Strengthens Resistance With 2nd Cultural 'Occupation,'" *RioOnWatch*, December 3, 2015 (www.rioonwatch .org/?p=25688).

67. Jules Boykoff, "Six Months Out from Olympics, Rich, Not Poor, Are the Big Winners," *Folha de São Paulo*, February 4, 2016 (http://frombrazil .blogfolha.uol.com.br/2016/02/04/six-months-out-from-olympics-rich-not -poor-are-the-big-winners/).

68. Heloisa Helena Costa Berto's writings for *RioOnWatch* (www .rioonwatch.org/?writer=heloisa-helena-costa-berto).

69. "Celebrating the Warrior Women of Vila Autódromo," *RioOn-Watch*, March 8, 2016 (www.rioonwatch.org/?p=27301).

70. Jefferson Puff, "Paes ataca 'dono da Barra': 'Não entendeu significado dos Jogos para o Rio,'" *BBC Brasil*, August 15, 2015 (www.bbc.com /portuguese/noticias/2015/08/150815_entrevista_eduardo_paes_hb_jp); Cerianne Robertson, "Mayor Eduardo Paes Pledges Vila Autódromo Will Remain and Claims Favela Upgrades a Success," *RioOnWatch*, January 21, 2016 (www.rioonwatch.org/?p=26453).

71. Adam Talbot and Stephanie Reist, "Rio Mayor Demolishes Home of Prize Winning 'Woman Citizen' on International Women's Day," *RioOn-Watch*, March 10, 2016 (www.rioonwatch.org/?p=27420).

72. Cerianne Robertson and Stephanie Reist, "A Tale of Two Plans: A Critique of Mayor Paes' Plan for Vila Autódromo," *RioOnWatch*, March 17, 2016 (www.rioonwatch.org/?p=27526).

73. Meg Healy and Stephanie Reist, "Vila Autódromo Residents Reach Tentative Agreement with City on Upgrades," *RioOnWatch*, April 9, 2016 (www.rioonwatch.org/?p=27988).

74. Adam Talbot, "Erasing the Favela from Vila Autódromo," *RioOn-Watch*, May 21, 2016 (www.rioonwatch.org/?p=28870).

75. "UN Human Rights Council: Sport and Human Rights," *Terre des Hommes*, July 5, 2016, (http://www.terredeshommes.org/un-human-rights -council-sport-and-human-rights/).

76. "Eduardo Paes faz balanço de seus oito anos como prefeito," *IETS*, January 2016 (www.iets.org.br/spip.php?article474).

77. Claire Lepercq and Clare Huggins, "The Fallen Trees of Vila Autó-dromo: Rio Topples Olympics Environmental Legacy," *RioOnWatch*, May 28, 2016 (www.rioonwatch.org/?p=29025).

78. Mariana Pitasse, "Museu das Remoções expõe memória de re-sistência da Vila Autódromo, no Rio," *Brasil de Fato*, May 18, 2016 (www .brasildefato.com.br/2016/05/18/museu-das-remocoes-expoe-memoria-de -resistencia-da-vila-autodromo-no-rio/).

79. Sally Jenkins, "For the Displaced of Rio, 'The Olympics Has Noth-ing to Do With Our Story,'" *Washington Post*, August 7, 2016.

80. *Plano Popular da Vila Autódromo 2016: Plano de Desenvolvimento Urbano, Econômico, Social e Cultural,* (Associação de Moradores da Vila Autódromo, 2016) (https://vivaavilaautodromo.files.wordpress.com /2016/02/ppva_2016web.pdf).

81. Alana Gandra, "Famílias de Vila Autódromo vão para o Parque Carioca," *Agência Brasil,* April 15, 2014 (http://agenciabrasil.ebc.com.br/geral /noticia/2014-04/familias-de-vila-autodromo-vao-para-o-parque-carioca).

82. Queiroz, "Residents Evicted by the 2016 Olympic Park Fight for Just Compensation."

83. "Defensoria Pública vistoria obras de urbanização da Vila Autódromo," *O Globo,* June 14, 2016.

84. Queiroz, "Residents Evicted by the 2016 Olympic Park Fight for Just Compensation."

85. Phie van Rompu, "Vila Autódromo Is Realizing Its Vocation as a Model for Resistance," *RioOnWatch,* March 24, 2017 (http://www.rioonwatch.org /?p=35336).

86. Griffin, "One Man, One City, Three Evictions."

87. Phie van Rompu, "Vila Autódromo Is Realizing Its Vocation as a Model for Resistance," *RioOnWatch,* March 24, 2017 (http://www.rioonwatch.org /?p=35336).

88. *Rio 2016 Olympics: The Exclusion Games, Mega-Events and Human Rights in Rio de Janeiro Dossier* (Popular Committee on the World Cup and Olympics, November 2015) (https://issuu.com/mantelli/docs/dossiecomiterio 2015_eng_issuu).

89. "Livro mapeia remoções de moradores na gestão de Eduardo Paes," *Estado Rio* (blog), April 24, 2015 (http://brasil.estadao.com.br/blogs/estadao -rio/livro-mapeia-remocoes-de-moradores-na-gestao-de-eduardo-paes/).

90. Jake Cummings, "Confronting Favela Chic: The Gentrification of Informal Settlements in Rio de Janeiro, Brazil," in *Global Gentrifications: Uneven Development and Displacement,* edited by Loretta Lees, Hyun Bang Shin, and Ernesto López-Morales (Bristol: Policy Press, 2015), pp. 81–99, at 84.

91. Brum, "Favelas e remocionismo ontem e hoje."

92. Information that bolstered the community included knowledge of their rights and organizing strategies, as well as the fundamental awareness to distrust what would turn out to be empty political promises, and a firm sense of the consequences and what would be lost were they to be evicted.

93. A Google News search on May 5, 2017 for "Vila Autódromo" yields more than 11,500 results.

94. "Residents of Parque Carioca Relocation Housing Express Discontent After Move from Vila Autódromo," *RioOnWatch,* May 31, 2016 (www .rioonwatch.org/?p=28110).

95. Fernanda Sanchez, Fabrício Leal de Oliveira, and Poliana Gonçalves Monteiro, "Vila Autódromo in Dispute: Subjects, Instruments and Strategies to Reinvent the Space," *Revista Brasileira de Estudos Urbanos e Regionais* 18, no. 3 (September–December 2016) (http://unuhospedagem.com .br/revista/rbeur/index.php/rbeur/issue/current).

View of Rio showing Sugarloaf Mountain, which marks the entrance to Guanabara Bay. Cleaning up the heavily polluted bay was one of the key promises in Rio's Olympic bid and one that, if accomplished, would have left a very positive legacy for the millions of citizens who live along or near its edges. Despite this promise and the fact that several Olympic events were held in its waters, the bay remains heavily polluted. (Credit: *O Estado de S. Paulo*)

A waste picker along a dirty beach with the polluted Guanabara Bay and the city of Rio de Janeiro in the background. Gross inequality in Brazil forces some citizens, such as this one, to the margins of society. (Credit: *O Estado de S. Paulo*)

Complexo do Alemão, a group of favelas where the government installed cable cars in lieu of the sewerage system residents had requested at public meetings. It is widely believed the government did this to please construction interests and because it saw the cable operation as valuable "visual" marketing of the Olympics and the city. The project cost R$210 million and was not popular among residents, although some did grow to depend on it. Operation was suspended in September 2016, however, shortly after the Paralympic Games closed. Meanwhile, the government is contemplating turning the few cable car stations into military police bases. (*O Estado de S. Paulo*)

Protest banner—Jogos da Exclusão (Exclusion Games)—at a protest organized by the Comitê Popular at Praça Sáenz Peña in August 2016. (Credit: Jules Boykoff)

Massive anti-government protest near Copacabana beach with a leading sign, "Kick Out Brazil's Money Vampires." (Credit: *O Estado de S. Paulo*)

Militarized security monitoring a protest at Praça Sáenz Peña, a public plaza close to the Maracanã stadium. Hours later the stadium would be the site of the opening ceremony for Rio 2016, August 2016. (Credit: Jules Boykoff)

Scene from violent protest outside Rio's Legislative
Assembly. (Credit: *O Estado de S. Paulo*)

Vila Autódromo before its destruction in 2012. Nearly 700 families were evicted and
relocated or compensated. Twenty families refused to negotiate and finally remained
in simple, newly built public housing units (see chapter 5, p. 108).

FIVE

Architecture and Urban Design

The Shaping of Rio 2016 Olympic Legacies

RENATA LATUF DE OLIVEIRA SANCHEZ
AND
STEPHEN ESSEX

Megaevents have become a significant driver of urban transformation and an integral part of "place marketing" strategies for host cities. Many cities have attempted to take these occasions as an opportunity to redevelop or regenerate degraded areas and consequently promote a new global image to attract international inward investment and tourism. Fundamental to securing these legacies is "good" architecture and urban design, which influences the smooth running and appearance of the event as well as the postevent utilization and image of the event sites and venues. Without the incorporation of legacy outcomes in the initial planning of the event, the potential for facilities to fail to integrate with the surrounding urban fabric, aggravate existing social problems and disparities, or become underutilized and expensive "white elephants" are considerable.

This chapter focuses on the architecture and urban design of the Rio 2016 Olympic Games and aims to assess the challenges involved in implementing the legacy master plan for Rio's Olympic park. Architecture has an undeniable impact on society, as its spatial interventions may lead to profound economic and cultural transformations. It plays an important role in shaping the city through the relationship between urban transformations and people who are associated with the built environment as residents, businesses, and visitors. By taking into consideration the much-discussed context of the Olympic Games as an opportunity for urban regeneration, this chapter evaluates the architecture and urban design of three projects: the Olympic park, the athletes' park, and the athletes' village, which are all located in Barra da Tijuca. Landscape architecture and urban theories, as well as interviews undertaken with architects in Rio de Janeiro and personal visits to the projects, serve as the main sources for this discussion. Comparisons with some former Olympics cities provide interesting insights and lessons for the legacy of such projects.

OLYMPIC LEGACIES

Hosting the Olympics has become an increasingly complex task over the years. As the event has grown in scale, with more participants (athletes, visitors, and others), competitions, sports, and sponsors, Olympics cities have had to incur the costs of much larger investments in works to prepare for the event, such as sports arenas, hotels, improvements in mobility, and general infrastructure. It is generally recognized that the growing scale of the Olympic Games from 1960 onward has required host cities to invest substantially in new urban infrastructure and facilities. Rome, host of the 1960 Games, developed a new municipal water system, built new airport facilities, and improved its public transport and street lighting, for example.[1] Barcelona, host of the 1992 Games, is regarded as a milestone in utilizing the "Olympic effect" to transform both the structure and image of the urban center. This turning point resulted from a moment when cultural and strategic planning became part of urban planning agendas so that cities might be better placed to become "global actors." Since then, the Olympics, which is also a cultural festival rather than just a sports event, have sought to foster development or regeneration to create a new global image for aspiring cities. Architecture and urban design have, as a consequence, become much more fundamental and integral to the success of the Olympic Games so that the new urban spaces fulfill their function both during and after the event.

According to Andrew Zimbalist, who has written about the economic impacts of hosting a sports megaevent, the only way the Olympic Games can prove cost-effective for their host cities is to adopt a long-term legacy perspective.[2] A host city and country is left with only a modest portion of the revenue from the Games, so it must justify the expenditure through legacy benefits. The situation is aggravated in developing countries, such as the BRICS (Brazil, Russia, India, China, and South Africa), where most of the infrastructure needed for hosting a megaevent has to be built for the Games themselves and therefore requires a much greater investment. For Zimbalist, "any justification for the investment would have to lie in a transformative long-run impact—or 'legacy,' in the PR vernacular of the IOC."[3]

One of the problems of staging a megaevent related to architecture and urban design is that of establishing the appropriate level of investment for the new facilities and infrastructure. Ever since megaevents have become part of a cultural and strategic planning agenda, politicians have sought monumental, "starchitecture" masterpieces to act as signatures for the event itself, as well as to promote a city's global image. Previous host cities like Barcelona, Beijing, and London have featured buildings by international architects, such as Arata Isozaki, Richard Meier, Santiago Calatrava, Norman Foster, Jacques Herzog and Pierre de Meuron, and Zaha Hadid. New architectural techniques and practices have also contributed to the growing extravagance of Olympics architecture: CAD/BIM (Building Information Modeling) software and "parametricism," for instance, have allowed architects to create shapes that in the past have only been possible in their minds. Peter Buchanan has argued that this turn has encouraged more complex and expensive artistic architectural forms that do not pose any lasting relevance for the urban fabric or help in facing its increasingly pressing issues.[4] This trend has not only detached architecture from real problems involved in a city, but also deflected it from one of its main purposes as an art: to attend to human needs. According to the Vitruvius triad, architecture is the art that combines *utilitas* (utility), *firmitas* (strength), and *venustas* (beauty). Megaevents-related designs can sometimes neglect future utility and therefore compromise the role of architecture in shaping urban spaces and the potential role of megaevents in creating a worthwhile legacy. Santiago Calatrava, for instance, known for his nature-inspired and highly technological buildings, was responsible for renovating Athens's Olympics Sports Complex for the 2004 Games, which has often been pointed to as a quintessential "white elephant."

A similar point can be made about the urban design of Olympics-related developments, which often ignore the established principles of creating effective public space in urban areas espoused by architects and planners such as Jan Gehl. Since the 1960s, Gehl has been an advocate of "pedestrianization," whereby quality spaces are freed from motor traffic disturbance to allow for gathering and leisure, "active façades," to create vibrancy and mixed-use urban environments, to encourage activity throughout the day. Against the modernist urbanism that prevailed throughout the 1920s until the 1950s, which segregated people and urban spaces, he severely condemns Brasília's urban planning, for which he coined the expression "Brasília Syndrome." Gehl says the Brazilian capital was planned for aerial views, not for its inhabitants, and lacks a human scale. Like Gehl, Buchanan criticizes functionalism: to him, it has proven over the years to bare devastating consequences for the urban environment, with architecture failing to relate physically, formally, and rhetorically to local history or its surroundings.[5]

The functional aspects of large-scale stadia and wide-open spaces to accommodate spectator movement in Olympic parks often oppose the creation of thriving, vibrant urban spaces in their legacy mode. Another contentious issue relates to the conversion of athletes' villages into residences. Pressures of economic viability can force developers to make related housing properties more exclusive, with higher prices and less inclusive urban design strategies. Unless the government subsidizes affordable housing schemes, there is a substantial risk of gentrification and social exclusion. This point emphasizes the importance of incorporating legacy issues into the initial planning and design of Olympics facilities. We turn now to consider Rio's Olympics and the architectural and urban design of Barra da Tijuca, with a focus on the issues related to starchitecture, gentrification, and poorly designed public spaces.

AN OLYMPIC RIO: PLANS AND IMPLEMENTATION

Brazil also tried to repeat the "Olympic urban regeneration formula" for the 2016 Games. In 2009, when Rio de Janeiro was officially announced as the 2016 Olympics city, the first host in South America in history, the whole country celebrated. The vision presented in Rio's bidding process emphasized the promotion of the city and Brazil as a safe place for investments, which suggested the building of different infrastructural works beyond those related to the staging of the Games per se. The management and sustainability plan of the 2016 Games recognized that while the legacy phase is initiated at the end of the event, "all the planning carried out in precedent phases have as reference the goal of creating positive, enduring transformations, maximizing the social, economic, sports and environmental benefit of the Games."[6]

The Games were perceived as an opportunity and catalyst for the country's economy by stimulating infrastructural, architectural, and urban planning works in the city. The world would know Rio not only as the home of Carnival but also as a global, competitive city. Along with this title, however, many promises were made, which demanded joint efforts between municipal, state, and federal governments in the seven years of preparation. The process was not always smooth, and the media released several articles pointing to delays and the prospect of imminent failure by the Brazilian host city.

Rio's Olympics investments were divided into three parts: the "Rio 2016 budget," the "Responsibility Matrix," and the "Public Policies Plan." The first involved investments directly related to the organization and delivery of the Games. The second encompassed publicly and privately financed projects exclusively related to the event, which would not have happened if Rio were not a host city (the Olympic park, for instance). The last referred to projects that anticipated or broadened government investments (municipal, state, and federal) in infrastructure and public policy, such as mobility, urban renovation, environmental, and social improvements. Among them were the Bus Rapid Transit (BRT) lines, the Light Rail Vehicle (VLT, in the Portuguese acronym) in the city center, a new subway line connecting the South Zone to Barra da Tijuca, and the regeneration of the harbor area.

A key decision about the construction of the Olympic park was that it was to be delivered through a public-private-partnership model: in the form of a fifteen-year administrative concession. The consortium created by Odebrecht Infraestrutura, Carvalho Hosken, and Andrade Gutierrez won the bidding process for the construction of the Olympic master plan. This consortium was divided into two private companies: Rio Mais, responsible for building all infrastructure (such as providing for water and sewage) and the building of some venues (Cariocas Arenas, International Broadcast Center, Main Press Center, and the media hotel), and Parque da Lagoa, responsible for the further real estate development of the area as a legacy. Ultimately, this decision has played a significant role in determining the extent and nature of the legacy outcomes, as will be demonstrated later in this paper.

The Olympic Games were staged in four areas of Rio: Deodoro, Copacabana, Maracanã, and Barra da Tijuca.[7] In addition, some soccer games were held out of the city of Rio, in former World Cup stadia in Brazil. This strategy had been adopted in Barcelona 1992, which also divided competitions among four clusters in the city in order to utilize existing infrastructure and to spread the benefits of urban transformation areas across the city. Along with the sports venues construction, there were improvement works in public transportation (especially through the BRT's corridors), as well as the construction of supporting facilities to the Games, like the athletes' park (concluded in 2011) and the athletes' village, in Barra da Tijuca. The attention given to the city has encouraged private investors to carry out restoration works in historical buildings in the city center.[8] The main event site was the Olympic park at Barra da Tijuca, which was based on an international design competition held in 2011. The analysis of this project is crucial in order to understand what the Olympic Games represent in terms of architecture and urban planning of the city.

THE OLYMPIC PARK

During the 1970s, the region of Barra da Tijuca was built as a growth axis in Rio de Janeiro, following a master plan designed by modernist master Lúcio Costa that was ordered by the municipal government in 1969. With eighty-two square kilometers of building lot, it represented 10 percent of the city's land area. During the 1980s, with the construction of many shopping malls and different high-rise building condominiums, it attracted a population that wanted to leave the high priced, already overwhelmed South Zone in search of a new, promising neighborhood. Many real estate companies invested in the region and the original 1969 master plan gradually experienced alterations in order to facilitate approvals for their new developments.

A 1981 decree increased the number of floors permitted for hotels and apartment hotels, allowing a maximum of fifteen floors, while other types of buildings had to comply with a maximum of around five. This measure led to a construction boom in the hotel and apartment-hotel sector. In 2005, another decree changed the maximum number of floors for other buildings, increasing the limit to twelve. After Rio was chosen as an Olympic city in 2009, urban laws were altered further. Through a complementary law in 2013, residential buildings could rise to eighteen floors. This increase was perfectly aligned with investors' interests for future developments in the Olympic park and surrounding areas and illustrates how the Rio Olympic Games were part of a political and economic strategy for urban renovation led by the private sector.[9]

In this sense, when Brazil bid for the Olympics in Rio de Janeiro, the most plausible place to locate the megaevent—and therefore, the main investments—was Barra da Tijuca. The region had staged the 2007 Pan American Games, so there were some sports venues that could be refurbished for the Olympics. A large open area in Barra—the former Jacarepaguá Autodrome—was chosen to accommodate most of the venues and become the new Olympic park. Nearby, an extensive privately owned area would become the athletes' village and another one, between these two, would become the athletes' park (figure 5-1).

An international design competition, held by the Municipal Olympic Company (EOM, in the Portuguese acronym) and the Brazilian Architects Institute (IAB, in the Portuguese Acronym) in Rio de Janeiro, determined the master plan for the Olympic park. The Brazilian architect, Daniel Gusmão, in a partnership with the British

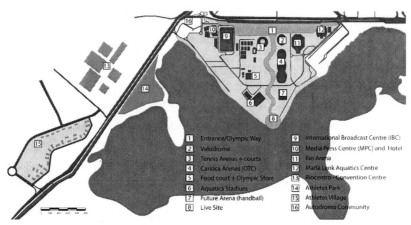

Figure 5-1. Map of Barra da Tijuca Cluster as in Games mode. Some of the locations of temporary venues were changed to benefit future real estate developments along the shore of the lagoon, like the Aquatics Stadium (6) and the Handball Arena (7) (Renata Sanchez, 2017).

Figure 5-2. The Olympic Park during the Rio Olympic Games. The large, open spaces will need substantial investments in landscaping to integrate existing and future development areas in its legacy use, August 2016 (Renata Sanchez).

branch of American consulting company AECOM, won the competition. Their proposal was different from the others, particularly regarding its legacy,[10] which envisioned the area's conversion into a high-density neighborhood. The competition demanded a three-phase project, following the model adopted previously in London 2012: Games (2016), transition period (starting in 2018), and legacy (2030) modes. The winning proposal conceived of an "urban park" (in opposition to more natural environments observed in Munich's 1972 or London's 2012 Olympic parks), outlined by a long, sinuous pedestrian path that crossed the whole site, called "Olympic Way," whose design alluded to the famous Copacabana sidewalks. Besides its aesthetic value, "the Way" facilitated logistics by strictly separating flows (visitors, staff, athletes, and others). In addition, the original proposal aimed to use some existing facilities from the 2007 Pan American Games: the Maria Lenk Aquatics Center and the HSBC Arena. A contentious issue was the dismantling of the Pan velodrome, which was not adequate for the Olympics because it did not meet the most recent technical criteria for the sport. A new velodrome had to be built and was later designated for high-performance training.

As a result of high costs and political/economic interests for legacy development, the original master plan proposal underwent several modifications during the execution of the project, including the location of some venues, their status as temporary or permanent venues, and the use of materials. Some of these modifications arguably compromised several of the intended legacy outcomes. A relevant example was the relocation of the Olympics aquatics stadium, designed by GMP Architects. This facility had originally been planned as a temporary arena at the northern main entrance to the park but was relocated to the south of the park to enable permanent arenas, such as the largest tennis arena and the new velodrome, to be relocated to this more visible position. The change also freed more valuable development sites near the lagoon shore for future real estate residential developments.

The conversion of large arenas and facilities into more ordinary uses is usually a challenge for host cities. In Rio, the mayor called the strategy of temporary arenas "nomadic architecture."[11] Besides the

Figure 5-3. *Panorama of the Tomorrow Museum, designed by Santiago Calatrava, on the renovated harbor, October 2016 (Renata Sanchez).*

aquatics stadium, the "Future Arena" (home for handball competitions) was to be dismantled and rebuilt as four different schools after the Games. Moreover, the International Broadcast Center (IBC), which has a floor space of 80,000 square meters (equivalent to four blocks of Rio's Ipanema neighborhood), was intended to become a business and educational campus after the Games, although this function has not yet been achieved. The metallic structure attached to the main building (the "Energy Center") was to be disassembled and used by the municipality to build other facilities after the Games.[12] The Olympic Way will undergo transformation in order to reduce its void spaces and to include more trees for legacy uses (figure 5-2).

If compared to former Olympics cities, Rio traced a rather modest path into "starchitecture," although it also comprised new architectural masterpieces built by important names in the field, like GMP and SBP's aquatics stadium and tennis arenas, a Danish House in Ipanema by Henning Larsen (one of the twenty-five national hospitality houses open for the general public), and the Deodoro Complex by Vigliecca and Associates. The arenas and cultural facilities in the city, however, seem to have kept a more modest character in view of the usual spectacle derived from the Olympics. The exception is the Museum of Tomorrow, by Santiago Calatrava, on the renovated harbor, the only major work by a "starchitect," which in fact was not even part of Olympics works (figure 5-3). The renovation of the harbor is part of the urban operation named Porto Maravilha (Marvelous Harbor), financed by a public-private partnership, which involves works in urban and traffic infrastructure and historical preservation. With the scale of Olympic facilities being so different from daily needs, and uncertainties regarding their maintenance, there is a fear they will be underused in the future.

The gentrification of the Olympics-related developments in Rio appears likely because the postevent transformation of the Olympic park is in the hands of the private sector. There are serious concerns about the social inclusion and diversity of the legacy use of the Olympic park. A related controversial matter regards the Vila Autódromo community, an old irregular occupation in the Olympic park area, which had been a beneficiary of land concessions during the 1990s by the State of Rio. In preparation for the Games, the government expropriated these properties and moved people to other housing complexes. However, twenty families refused to move and, after a long resistance, were accommodated in new houses within the Olympic park of questionable architectural quality. The result was a segregated community within the Olympic park, with its buildings differing completely in style and scale from the large arenas and luxury hotels nearby (figures 5-4 and 5-5). Along with several other cases of forced evictions and displacements across the city, the decimation of Vila Autódromo represents one of the negative social legacies of the Games.

The influence of private-sector concerns about economic viability is also evident in the post-Games adaptation of the Olympic park. The consortium in charge of delivering future developments is able to modify the urban design strategies of the original proposal since it is not obliged to follow the design competitions' guidelines. The original plan was aligned with contemporary, worldwide trends in architecture and urban design, such as "polycentrism" and "compact cities" (figure 5-6). The first entailed the creation of multiple centers within the city to assist traffic and mobility, while the second favored high-density, mixed-use urban spaces. The Alignment Plan, which was approved in 2012 for the urban planning of the area, outlines much larger blocks with a slightly more rigid separation between residential areas, venues, and green areas, which are likely to be detrimental to the creation of a vibrant, mixed-use neighborhood envisaged in the bid.

Figure 5-4. *The rebuilt Vila Autódromo community—with low-rise residential properties in the foreground and the towering Media Press Center and Hotel in the background, October 2016. Only some 2 percent of former residents were able to return (O Estado de S. Paulo).*

Figure 5-5. *In order for the Vila Autódromo community (right middle ground) to gain some long-term coherence, the huge supporting areas needed during the Games, such as the parking lots shown here, will need to be transformed into embracing urban units that dialogue both with large-scale venues and the simpler typologies observed in the village, August 2016 (Renata Sanchez).*

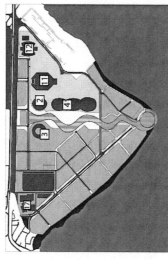

1. Entrance/Olympic Way
2. Velodrome
3. Tennis Arenas + courts
4. Carioca Arenas (OTC)
5. Retail Hub
6. Waterside Park + Wetlands
7. School
8. Live Site
9. Sewage Treatment Plant
10. Commercial/Educational Campus
11. Rio Arena
12. Maria Lenk Aquatics Center
13. Residential Area
14. Commercial Area
15. Recreation and Leisure Hub
16. Autodromo Community
17. Media Hotel

Figure 5-6. Winning proposal for the Olympic Park on the left (redrawn from original Legacy Master Plan for 2016 Olympics) and the actual Alignment Plan approved by the Municipality of Rio de Janeiro in November 2012 (redrawn from original). The new neighborhood will have bigger, straighter blocks (Renata Sanchez, 2017).

THE ATHLETES' VILLAGE: ILHA PURA

Another development compromised by private-sector-led urban design ideas is the athletes' village, which was built as the residential complex called Ilha Pura by contractors Carvalho Hosken and Odebrecht. Ilha Pura is composed of 3,604 high-profile apartment units distributed among thirty-one towers that are seventeen stories tall. The units vary from seventy-seven square meters to 230 square meters, spread across more than ten kinds of buildings, with eleven different apartment plans. Until August 2016, 600 units had been offered for sale, from which 40 percent were sold.[13] The other units will be available from 2017 onward.[14] According to the developers, the 820,000-square-meter area follows a mixed-use concept of urban planning. As a new neighborhood, Ilha Pura was intended to include all commercial and service facilities in one place, as well as a public park and leisure areas. Nonetheless, a visit to the site reveals a different reality: instead of mixing residential buildings with commercial activities on the street level, a big shopping mall is intended to occupy a plot near the prominent high-rise residential towers, excluding the possibility of a real mixed-use urban environment. Moreover, the towers are arranged as a concrete belt around the park that, despite advertised as a public one, has gated access. As informed during a visit to the sales stand, developers intend to build a business campus close to Ilha Pura's plot. No schools, clinics, or day cares are part of the project. It is estimated that contractors Carvalho Hosken and Odebrecht assumed a R$2.9 billion debt to build the entire area, R$2.3 billion of which came from a state bank at subsidized interest rates (the Caixa Econômica Federal).[15] With sales trailing badly behind plans, many wonder whether the loan will ever be repaid.[16]

From the 820,000-square-meter total area, approximately 206,000 square meters was used by the athletes' village, lodging around 18,000 people during the Games, including 11,000 athletes. The Olympic village should have been completed by the end of February 2016, but, as in other Olympics works in Rio, delays occurred and the apartments were finally delivered in July, weeks before the start of the Games.[17] Nonetheless, several media articles pointed to the infrastructural problems encountered by athletes in the complex, such as poor gas and electricity installations.

The development has been the first one in Latin America to receive the Leadership in Energy and Environmental Design (LEED) Neighborhood Development certification. However, the character of the Ilha Pura development appears more as that of a condominium rather than as a neighborhood. Despite being promoted as incorporating a public park and as a sustainable community, the complex is completely gated and lacks a dynamic urban environment. Ilha Pura is the complete opposite of the traditional, gradually consolidated types of neighborhoods (like Copacabana or Ipanema in Rio's South Zone) that include different typologies, active façades, lively public spaces, and diversity of people and social backgrounds. Its model of high-rise, isolated towers reiterates the ongoing model of development in Barra da Tijuca, which focuses on cars instead of pedestrians and on individualism instead of the community. Moreover, this model is part of a process that has exemplified altered zoning laws, changed building heights, and implemented plot utilization coefficients favored by private developers.

Former Olympics villages have presented approaches that are far more interesting in terms of urban and architectural design. For the 1972 Games in Munich, two kinds of lodging were built: high-rise buildings designed by world-known Heinle, Wischer und Partner, and the students' "bungalows," built in 1971 by the organization Studentenwerk and used during the Games to lodge women athletes. Heinle, Wischer und Partner's project foresaw separated paths for automobiles, leaving the surface free for people to walk and cycle in a safer environment. The complex represents around 255,000 square meters of floor space within nine twelve-story buildings containing 3,100 units. At the beginning, the project was much criticized, since landscaping was not yet completed (trees were not fully grown, for instance), making the whole scenario rather arid and grey. However, as landscape evolved, the area eventually became a very valuable asset, based upon its privileged location and the sense of "community" that formed there. After the Games, in 1972, the bungalows were utilized to lodge students, who reinvented the sober architectural style by drawing graffiti on their walls. After a big renovation held between 2007 and 2010, the colorful, customized architecture was again turned into grey concrete blocks but were soon repainted by students, continuing the tradition with diverse drawings and pop art. Nowadays, these bungalows represent a much-sought-after and fashionable location: it has become a "place" in the sense of being appropriated by its inhabitants.

London also presented an interesting model of housing legacy for the 2012 Games, although many of the developments intended for the Olympic park were still not ready in early 2017. The adaptation of the athletes' village as a residential legacy created the East Village, the first neighborhood within the park, which mixes private and social housing. According to London's Olympic Delivery Authority (ODA) annual report 2013–14, the adaptation of the village included the construction of a health center, a day care for eighty children, a school for 2,000 students (opened in 2013), and new public infrastructure, such as new parking areas, twenty-five acres of green areas, new bus stops, bicycle stands, hundreds of benches, and a new road system. Regarding the urban layout chosen for the athletes' village project, its buildings follow a "perimeter block" development principle, which is a traditional urban form in many European cities, including London. In contrast to the Brazilian's athletes' village for Rio 2016, East Village preserves a closer relation between environment and building through lower heights and the exploration of the inner courts of a block formed by this perimeter block occupation. Recent openings of retail and commercial activities on the ground floor of buildings have helped the area to become livelier, with the concept of "active façades" by Jan Gehl beginning to take shape. By increasing urban density, the model encourages a more dynamic urban life. Different architects have designed each complex, which has contributed to a broader range of styles and approaches while at the same time not losing sight of the whole.

THE ATHLETES' PARK

Confirming a "pedestrian-unfriendly" character of Barra da Tijuca's projects is the athletes' park, which lies next to the Olympic park and the athletes' village in Rio. The park was laid out in 2011 and covers 150,000 square meters. It was claimed as the first legacy of the Olympics 2016 and was used for training and leisure by athletes during the

Games. It is a large events venue, but it is more of a concrete urban square than a park. Designed to host the music festival Rock in Rio, which attracts millions of people, the space is very distant from a more humane concept of a park.

For landscape architects such as Samuel Parsons or the more contemporary, Olympics-commissioned Günther Grzimek, it is of utmost importance to create park landscapes that relate deeply to human affections and feelings. This effect can be achieved in a park through a good design, which includes an interesting set of masses of trees, lawns, water, paths, and banks,[18] as well as offering different reliefs, fauna, climate zones, and activities.[19] Grzimek, who designed Munich's Olympic park in 1972, also defended a democratization of open public spaces and a more human-centered architectural/landscape design. Munich's Olympic park has been widely recognized for the legacy of public space that it created.

Rio's athletes' park, on the contrary, seems to have been designed without any landscape architecture concerns, and the absence of trees contradicts the first requirement of a landscape. For Parsons, a tree should be a holy thing and a crucial element in determining a good relation between man and nature.[20] At the pedestrian level, the public space of the athletes' park seems empty and alien, which is worsened by the absence of trees. In such a warm city as Rio, this absence of vegetation might dissuade people from using this public space. Sculptural elements have replaced trees (figure 5-7) and almost half of the park area is covered by geometrically laid synthetic grass beds, punctuated by paved paths that converge into a focal point as a semicircle. The complex seems to be a good example of what Gehl has described as the 'Brasília Syndrome,' as it only makes sense when viewed as a pictorial element from above. The park disregards existing urban fabric and flows and incorporates nature only by its proximity to the shore of Jacarepagua's lagoon.

Two personal visits to the "park" in May 2014 and December 2015 revealed a strange urban area, disconnected from its surroundings. On the first visit, there were some children riding their bicycles around, although there were already signs that the space was underused as a public leisure area. In December 2015, the place was closed, with many metal pieces stacked and synthetic grass tiles

Figure 5-7. The arid athletes' park and the sculptural white elements along its entrance, May 2014 (Renata Sanchez).

damaged or removed—probably awaiting transformations for the Games. During the Olympics, large temporary structures were built there, eliminating any possibility of an open, enjoyable space for athletes. In November 2016, Rock in Rio organizers announced the relocation of the music festival to the Olympic park in 2017,[21] which means the athletes' park will lose one of its main temporary activities.

CONCLUSIONS

All the projects presented, although just a part of Rio Olympics infrastructure, have one characteristic in common: the distance between them and the city's inhabitants. Although architects and urban planners, like Gehl, have pointed to the importance of lively urban spaces, the urban planning model adopted in the Rio Olympic park and village in Barra da Tijuca continues to reproduce the same mod-

Figure 5-8. *One of the artistic interventions on the façades of otherwise derelict buildings along the new harbor promenade during the Olympics in August 2016. The intention of this treatment was to create a sense of animation and vitality in what otherwise might have appeared a derelict and deprived scene and was likely to detract from a festival atmosphere (Renata Sanchez).*

ernist design criticized in several other cities around the world. Although world-acclaimed architectural offices were involved in the design of Rio's Olympics works, the projects seem to neglect their users. The legacy of the built environment created by the Rio Olympics appears to be counter to the creation of a sustainable, mixed-use community, and the area is poorly connected and integrated with the rest of the city. The infrastructural transportation works have proven themselves to be insufficient on a short-term basis, with completely full BRTs from day one and a new subway line awaited for more than three decades with only one stop in Barra da Tijuca. For the Games, the experience might have been mitigated because the government declared school holidays for the whole period of competitions as well

Figure 5-9. The same façades (on the left) after the Olympics in October 2016. The promenade has a good landscape architecture project but needs time for vegetation to grow (Renata Sanchez).

as holidays on specific days, and the new subway line could be used only by those holding a ticket for the event.

The renovated harbor is often presented as a real legacy from the Olympics, as it was included in the Olympic Public Policy Plan. However, the site did not host any sporting venues and many parts were only façade decorations for the period of the event itself (figures 5-8 and 5-9). The future of the linear warehouses that hosted the U.S. National Basketball Association (NBA) house and the Coca-Cola stop during the megaevent, for instance, is still uncertain. A good quality landscape architecture is, nevertheless, observed throughout the promenade, along with the provision of public transport in the form of the VLT (whose functionality is still in doubt). However, since this project is not strictly an Olympics one, the true legacy of the 2016 Games in architecture and urban planning is still questionable, especially in the main cluster—Barra da Tijuca.

It is clear that for the Games to be more sustainable not only must changes related to the environment be taken (less fossil fuels, LEED certifications, and so on) but changes related to the way in which cities are shaped by these events must be made. Large arenas, if not planned concurrently with the development of their surroundings and their future uses, will become white elephants. Unilateral processes of planning will always result in painful evictions and removals, negating any social legacy. More participatory design processes and open debates, although time consuming, offer more benefits in the long term. These public engagement exercises should be part of a new agenda for Brazilian architecture and urban planning as in other parts of the world. It would avoid criticisms of social exclusion as one of the main negative legacies of megaprojects, as appears to have been the case in the redevelopment of the Vila Autódromo favela in the Olympic park.

Olympic parks must be planned with their legacy uses in mind from the outset—rather than as an afterthought. A better balance between investors' interests and those of the local community and residents must be found through state regulation and intervention. When Rio assigned the building of the athletes' village to private investors, it might have imposed rules that guaranteed that the new neighborhood would present favorable conditions for all segments of society, such as requiring a certain percentage of social housing. Moreover, when approving the alignment plan for the future development of the Olympic park, the municipality might have followed the outlines drawn by the original winning proposal, which foresaw smaller blocks to encourage a more mixed environment. To have the Olympic park legacy designed by the same private investors that have shaped Barra da Tijuca over the past decades represents a retreat in urban design and architectural terms. A change in federal legislation and in the Brazilian bidding law is necessary in order to secure compliance of design competition proposals by the consortia in charge of their implementation. Yet, economic conditions over the seven to ten years between the initial bid plans and the eventual legacy transformation can be volatile and change considerably. The ability of developers to be able to respond flexibly to these changing external pressures acts to ensure the economic viability of Olympics-related developments in their postevent mode. Strict regulation to ensure compliance with the original urban design and planning visions of bid documents might actually be counterproductive and create many more negative and wasteful legacies. Nevertheless, modifications to Olympics master plans should not be allowed to completely alter the original conception of Olympics infrastructures. This issue of changing economic viability over the course of an Olympiad encapsulates one of the main planning dilemmas for securing legacy outcomes from Olympics-related regeneration, which cannot be easily regulated.

Finally, it must be said that Rio has still much to reveal in terms of the legacy of the Olympic Games of 2016, which might only be observable in fifty years' time. Nonetheless, architecture and urban design must work together in the process to ensure that "spaces" will become "places" and that the city will not only be attractive to tourists but will become an inclusive, renovated urbanity for its inhabitants.

NOTES

1. Brian Chalkley and Stephen Essex, "Urban Development through Hosting International Events: A History of the Olympic Games, *Planning Perspectives* 14 (1999), pp. 369–94.

2. Andrew Zimbalist, *Circus Maximus: The Economic Gamble behind Hosting the Olympics and the World Cup* (Brookings Institution Press, 2015).

3. Ibid., p. 24.

4. Peter Buchanan, "Empty Gestures: Starchitecture's Swan Song," *Architectural Review*, February 27, 2015 (www.architectural-review.com /archive/viewpoints/empty-gestures-starchitectures-swan-song/8679010 .article).

5. Peter Buchanan, "Monumente für eine klassizistisch-konstruktivistische Stadt," in *Barcelona Architektur und Städtebau zur Olympiade 1992* (Stuttgart, Ger.: Karl Krämer Verlag, 1991), pp. 20–25.

6. *Plano de Gestão da Sustentabilidade dos Jogos Rio 2016*, March 2013, version 1, p. 9.

7. Although Copacabana is actually one neighborhood of Rio's South Zone, in the Olympics the nomenclature embraced all of the South Zone, reaching close to the city center, with sports being held on Copacabana Beach, the Rodrigo de Freitas Lagoon, Guanabara Bay, Flamengo Park, and Marina da Glória. The same applied to the "Maracanã" cluster, which had competitions at Engenhão Stadium (Olympic Stadium) and the Sambódromo in addition to the Maracanã Stadium itself.

8. One example is the Moinho Fluminense, a historical building complex (mill) from the end of the nineteenth century, located in the recently regenerated harbor area to be renovated and converted into a multipurpose conglomerate with a hotel, retail and commercial spaces, residences, a corporate tower, and a medical center.

9. Developments planned included, for instance, the luxurious high-rise development near the Olympics golf course by real estate company Cyrela.

10. According to the competition's public notice, the ratio between sports venues and urban legacy should be forty to sixty. The winning project accomplished a thirty to seventy ratio.

11. Eduardo Paes and Washington Fajardo, "Arquitetura nômade," *PMDB*, April 20, 2012 (http://pmdb.org.br/artigos/arquitetura-nomade/).

12. Information obtained during a visit to the Olympic park construction site in December 2015 with an architect from AECOM.

13. Marcela Sorosini and Nelson Lima Neto, "Vila dos atletas da Rio-2016 tem apenas 7% dos imóveis vendidos; preço mínimo supera R$ 800 mil," *Extra Globo*, August 28, 2016 (http://extra.globo.com/noticias/economia/vila-dos-atletas-da-rio-2016-tem-apenas-7-dos-imoveis-vendidos-preco-minimo-supera-800-mil-20003067.html).

14. According to an article from February 2017, current mayor of Rio, Marcelo Crivella, has attempted to close a deal with Caixa Econômica Federal in order to sell the units to public servants under special conditions. There is a fear that the apartments will not be sold due to the current economic crisis in Brazil, and pressure to increase tax collection from the municipality of Rio and from Caixa to recover its 2.3 billion reais construction loan lent to the private contractors. Since March 2016, the Organizing Committee of Rio 2016 has paid the monthly installments. From 2018 onward, Carvalho Hosken will be responsible to pay the debt. See Gabriela Valente and Luis Ernesto Magalhães, "Prefeitura negocia venda de imóveis na Vila dos Atletas para servidores," *O Globo*, February 1, 2017 (http://oglobo.globo.com/rio/prefeitura-negocia-venda-de-imoveis-na-vila-dos-atletas-para-servidores-20853503).

15. See "Transparência–Rio 2016," *Portal do Governo Brasileiro* (www.portaldatransparencia.gov.br/rio2016/barra/viladosatletas/index.asp).

16. Samantha Lima, "Carlos Carvalho, o dono da Barra da Tijuca," *Exame*, June 15, 2012 (http://exame.abril.com.br/revista-exame/carlos-carvalho-o-dono-da-barra-da-tijuca/).

17. Lucas Altino, "A um ano de prazo para entrega, Vila Olímpica está 70% pronta," *Jornal O Globo*, February 19, 2015 (http://oglobo.globo.com/rio/bairros/a-um-ano-de-prazo-para-entrega-vila-olimpica-esta-70-pronta-15334840).

18. Samuel Parsons Jr., *The Art of Landscape Architecture* (1915; repr., New York: The Knickerbocker Press, 2009).

19. Günther Grzimek, "Gedanken zur Stadt- und Landschaftsarchitektur seit Friedrich Ludwig von Sckell," (1973), in *Demokratisches Grün Olympiapark*, ed. Stefanie Hennecke, Regine Keller, Juliane Schneegans (München: Jovis, 2013), pp. 118–119.

20. Parsons, *The Art of Landscape Architecture*, p. 200.

21. "Rock in Rio anuncia que Cidade do Rock será no Parque Olím-pico," *G1 Rio*, April 11, 2016 (http://g1.globo.com/musica/rock-in-rio/2017/noticia/2016/11/rock-rio-anuncia-que-cidade-do-rock-sera-no-parque-olimpico.html).

SIX

Strictly Confidential

Access to Information and the Media in Rio

JAMIL CHADE

With their hands up in the air, ministers, four-star generals, and IOC officials danced to some of the most famous samba tunes at the closing ceremony of the Olympics in Rio. While carnival was taking over the Maracanã Stadium and the entire world was watching the party, politicians hugged each other in the VIP area. It was a true moment of relief after seven years of tensions, controversies, and scandals. The confetti falling over their heads was like a curtain, closing the Rio Games of 2016 on a high note.

But the drums could not hush some very legitimate questions: Who will actually pay for the event? Who made money from it? Who actually got the real gold? Already authorities in Brazil had declared that, some days before the Olympics' end, a bailout program was being drawn up to sort out the finances of the organizing committee and thus cover part of the bill for the Paralympic Games, held traditionally after the Olympic Games with disabled athletes.

For the IOC, the party was worth it. The organization ended 2016 with over $5.6 billion in revenues[1]—a record. Most of the money came from broadcasters, who paid a fortune to be able to show the event in their home countries. When buying the rights to the biggest event on earth, they also became partners of the Games and not just broadcasters covering the Olympics.

If you pay, you expect benefits. So, as soon as Olympics gold medalists Usain Bolt, Michael Phelps, or Neymar Jr. stepped out of the arena, they gave their first interviews to those companies that paid millions of dollars. The rest of the press would have to fight for the crumbs, with journalists battling to get their microphones close to the legends.

These asymmetries beg the question, what is the role of journalism when broadcast networks are actually financing the event they need to cover? And, most important, what was the media strategy of organizers and politicians in order to show the world only one side of the medal?

During the seven years of Rio's preparations for the Olympics, the reality was that the so-called "Olympic values" do not always sync with transparency, press freedom, or access to information. Over the years confidential documents have shown the crisis inside the organizing committee, the financial problems, and the major work delays. While these assessments were under internal scrutiny, the official line was that everything was on track and that no crisis would undermine the "good relationship" among local organizers, politicians, and the IOC.

Even if it meant the suppression of access to information and manipulation of data, no one wanted to experience a repetition of what had happened at the World Cup in Brazil two years earlier, when the country was beset by protests and FIFA was in the spotlight. The soccer tournament had become a turning point for mega sports events in the world. If the so-called mecca of soccer—Brazil—was ready to question and protest the event coming back home after sixty-four years, nothing would be spared elsewhere in the world.

For local politicians, the World Cup was planned to be an event where votes and popularity could be enhanced. But this aspiration was radically affected by the unexpected reaction of the masses in stadia that were, ironically, built with public funds. The lies told to citizens, voters, and fans in Brazil were largely imploded even before the World Cup began, obliging the politicians to hide during the event in 2014, from the government as well as from the opposition parties. No one was immune.

The "surprise" reaction from citizens began even before the party was actually ready. In 2013 the country hosted the Confederations

Cup, a test event for the World Cup itself, which was scheduled a year later. But soccer was the least of the preoccupations of the organizing committees.

It was, actually, what happened outside the arenas that became part of the history of soccer in the fifteen days that shook the structures of FIFA and surprised the government of Brazil. The incidents and protests in 2013 led to concrete questioning about the capacity of the country to take the tournament to its end. Those were two weeks—from June 15 to 30—that started to send a clear warning to FIFA and other sports organizations that fans and citizens would not tolerate having their demands ignored any longer.

On the streets, students, medical doctors, and regular citizens brought signs and banners proclaiming that the World Cup had serious difficulties. Both the government and FIFA were astonished. A few days after the inaugural game, FIFA still thought what it saw in the streets was an isolated incident with no consequences. I met FIFA President Sepp Blatter on the third day of the competition. At that point in time his tone was still one detached from reality. "Football is stronger than the anger of people," he said.

But the height of the demonstrations was still to come. On the night of June 20 the country stopped and one million people took to the streets. The luxurious Copacabana Palace was a mirror of the crisis. In a sophisticated ballroom of the hotel, FIFA had set up a lounge where sponsors, officials, and politicians could meet in peace. Huge sofas, palm trees, champagne, and some of the best chefs of Rio de Janeiro were serving those VIP guests. But in the face of the turbulence, the lounge overlooking the Atlantic Ocean was empty while a giant screen placed in the VIP room showed images that no one was expecting: demonstrations, not soccer.

The decision on June 21, 2013, was to go ahead with the event and to transform the stadiums into bunkers. FIFA made it clear to the government: if security in the games were not guaranteed, the Confederations Cup would be suspended. This would have threatened the World Cup, generated an unprecedented loss to the government, and turned years of preparation for an international event into a global embarrassment.

If a cancellation would be disastrous for Brazil, the suspension of the tournament would unleash a profound crisis at FIFA too. One concern in Zurich was that the protests in Brazil would open a Pandora's box for new demonstrations at all their events around the world. After all, if the "soccer country" questioned the World Cup, why wouldn't others do the same? If the World Cup and FIFA were being questioned, why not other events, such as the Olympic Games?

"STRICTLY CONFIDENTIAL"

The IOC, based in the Swiss city of Lausanne, well knew that it could not follow in FIFA's footsteps, even though they had been dealing with the same group of Brazilian politicians and the same construction companies, many of which had already been under investigation beginning in 2014.

The strategy for politicians, IOC delegates, and the Rio 2016 Organizing Committee was established that an eventual crises would never be made public, and in the same way, debates about how the event would be financed should also not leak to the press. In shielding the Games, the main goal was to avoid a repetition of what had happened with FIFA, an institution that had been accused of using Brazil as a way to make a handsome profit without leaving any kind of legacy. The tone to be adopted would be cordial, and the Brazilian organizers would never be criticized in public. But to be able to set such a positive tone, transparency would be consistently put aside.

Away from the spotlight, the crisis was very deep, and a glimpse of that came to light on August 31, 2013, when I first published a set of confidential documents that had been leaked by a high-ranking official.[2] These reports began to unveil to Brazilians the scale of information manipulation behind the scenes. These were documents of the task force within the IOC that was closely monitoring everything that unfolded in Rio de Janeiro. The conclusions were worrying, with clear evidence of conflicts between the state and the organizers.

The preparation of the 2016 Summer Olympic Games in Rio de Janeiro and its funding was at serious risk. Unfinished stadiums and infrastructure work, sport modalities without a clear definition of the venue, general lack of cash, shortage of sponsors, and a chronic shortage of hotel accommodation, these were just some of the problems that the city had to tackle.

Considered to be "strictly confidential," the report showed, in stark reality, a city that was utterly unprepared for an event of this magnitude—and with massive financial problems to boot. The technical document color-coded its forty-four chapters according to the degree of Rio's preparation using three different colors: green for those areas in which work was running to schedule, yellow for those that presented a certain degree of threat, and red for those cases where the delays already jeopardized the Games themselves. Only half of the preparations work was on time.

A point of much concern to the IOC was infrastructure, a chapter in the report classified throughout in red. Regarding transportation, the IOC advised that there should be "a closer and more thorough monitoring" of Line 4 (Yellow Line) of the Rio de Janeiro Underground (specifically the work between the South Zone and the neighborhood of Barra da Tijuca), as well as the Transolímpica and Transbrasil Bus Rapid Transit (BRT) projects, all of which were running behind schedule.[3]

The institution also mentioned the risk that there would not be enough buses in the fleet and suggested that an alternative plan should be developed in the event that Line 4 should fail. Several projects were pushed back from May to the end of 2013, including a study that would establish the real demand for transport in the city. The IOC also requested that there should be "careful monitoring" of infrastructure projects for supply of water and electricity.

Accommodation was yet another point that ran the risk of generating serious problems and therefore received a red classification in the report. Up until that moment, the number of hotel rooms available was only 19,200. But the IOC estimated that the event would need around 45,000 hotel rooms.

The report also showed the postponement of contracts with ships that would be used as hotels in the port of Rio de Janeiro. The original time frame stated that these contracts should have been finalized in March 2013. However, they were put off until the end of that year. According to the IOC, "the interest shown by shipping lines fell short of what was expected."[4]

But the main concern shown by the delegates was the sporting venues, which were running far behind schedule. "The master plan for sporting venues needs to be frozen right now," warned the IOC, in a clear reference to the organizers' constant changes of plans.[5] "There are still many frequent changes of venues or uncertainty about the location and specifications of the venues," they criticised.[6] Delays at venues for water sports, canoeing, those at the Maracanã Stadium, and others were among the uncertainties that hovered over the event. "These changes and uncertainties have, or could have, a significant negative impact on operations," the document said.[7]

In the case of the Maracanã Stadium, the IOC warned that legal wrangles could also have a negative impact on the plans for the adaptation of the sports complex, which could effectively paralyze the preparation of the stadium for 2016.

A barrage of harsh criticism was also aimed at the Deodoro cluster, which had shown "further delays in the tender process. This jeopardises the capacity of having these venues ready in time for the test events and, more globally, has a negative impact on the effective completion of the whole development of this zone."[8] The IOC thus requested "extreme urgency" with regard to planning, tenders, and construction of the Deodoro site.

The João Havelange Stadium—later called Engenhão—was also included in a list of issues to be tackled. "An integrated calendar for construction is urgently needed," the IOC said. "This would have to assure not only the work for correction of the roof, but other requirements for the installations already in place," it pointed out.[9] The IOC made demands to the city of Rio so that the city could "accurately demonstrate" the calendar for the João Havelange Stadium and also "guarantee that time frames and schedules shall be strictly followed, without any further postponements."[10]

It was confirmed that Rio was behind schedule in all aspects of the Olympic Games and that the final definition of the number of events, their size, and an agenda would be "very challenging, in the light of the delays that have been shown in the time frames for construction."[11]

The IOC also asked the government to adopt laws to reduce the risk of appeals being made in the courts by companies that did not come out winners in the tender processes, as this would avoid any further delays. These law changes only compounded the risk of construction payoffs and bribery. Another demand made to the authorities in Brazil and to the Local Organizing Committee was that of guaranteeing that there would be no lack of materials, cement, or sand for the work.

But, above all, the document showed a terrifying financial reality that would have a direct bearing on the Brazilian taxpayer: the preparations for the Olympic Games in Rio de Janeiro were beset with serious financial problems that could put the event at risk if not quickly overcome. Part of the costs had to be transferred to the government— in a clear sign that the organizers preferred to seek a larger participation of public funding—to assure the timely delivery of the venues and infrastructure.

At that point in time the city had not even managed to reach its sponsorship targets for the event. The IOC, in light of the crisis, recommended that Rio start to prepare an alternative plan, should it not be possible to finance the budget that had been planned for the work projects. In sum, the crisis was well known much before the country entered its worst recession in decades.

"So far, Rio 2016 has reached about 60% (of sponsor contracts)," with regard to an ambitious sponsorship target," warned the IOC in 2013. "Rio should study its activity plan for total generation of income (sponsorship, licensing and ticket sales), faced with a general budget for the Olympic Games, to understand the sheer impact of the deficit on the delivery of the Games and their operations."[12]

According to the IOC, the contract for the financing of the Olympic village was running behind schedule. There was also a delay in the program of insurance for this event. In sports venues, there would be a delay in the hiring of specialists to plan electricity aspects, "owing to financial pressures."[13]

If the internal rules of the IOC were based on absolute silence about what was in fact going on, with press access to such evaluations being seriously restricted, these very same documents prepared by the IOC in 2013 suggested that the government should be called upon to give some assistance for the event—with public funds. All this was done amid an Olympics opaqueness. Far from any public oversight, the IOC admitted that a "change of financial responsibilities and work projects for the Governments" had to be made.[14]

But the internal crisis was also accompanied by a strategy to stop such information from being leaked to the public and even a campaign to make sure that the general feeling about the World Cup was not repeated in the Olympics. In a war, how the facts are revealed (if ever) is just as important as the facts themselves.

In an excerpt from the documents prepared by the IOC, officials made a recommendation to organizers, suggesting that the communications department should monitor what was happening in terms of protests. "Protest demonstrations linked to major sporting events in Brazil need to be closely monitored,"[15] the IOC warned. One of the strategies was to reduce the opposition to the event by insisting that the Games would leave a real "legacy" for the development of the city.

But the leakage of these documents in 2013 did not make the IOC or Rio 2016 any more transparent. To the contrary: because of the information I published, the organization set up a system in which a leaked document would lead investigators straight to the leak, the person who had released the secrets to the public. There was only one information strategy: that of suppressing any attempts to disclose the true situation of the Games, especially in terms of finance. This strategy was kept up for the next three years, with the help of an army of press officers who took full advantage of social media to disseminate the messages they wanted the world to take as the truth.

The use of imagination to fight facts in the post-truth world, as Katharine Viner would write,[16] was a reality that had lingered in the sporting world for years. The misguided throngs had to be taken into a sphere of patriotism and emotion. Therefore, this strategy had to include diminishing the status of truth, even if this would force a democracy to avoid telling its citizens how they would pay for the party.

The reasoning used in Lausanne was quite clear: the IOC is a private entity and, as such, it does not need to follow the same transparency rules as governments do.

Three years after this first document leaked, once again the IOC and Rio 2016 were confronted by a new internal document being brought to light.[17] Five months before the Games, the evaluation was dramatic once again.

At the beginning of March 2016, after a meeting of the IOC Executive Board, IOC President Thomas Bach used a press conference in Lausanne to praise Rio's preparations for the Olympic Games and show his entire and utter confidence in the smooth progress of the project. Once again, the public discourse could not have been further from reality. In the technical reports used for those same meetings, the tone adopted by Bach to explain the situation to other delegates revealed some serious challenges.[18]

One of the documents used at that meeting was the "President's Report," a confidential activity report. On explaining a meeting with European Olympic committees, Bach described how he "invited" the group to "work in close solidarity with the organizers of the Games, in relation to the deep and serious crisis that Brazil is going through."[19]

The report of the IOC's administrative activities listed in detail the problems that were still being faced in Rio with only five months to go before the start of the event.[20] In a section entitled "concerns related to sports," the IOC was quite clear in mentioning that there were shortcomings in several areas. Problems had been identified in the "completion of the premises for rowing and canoeing (including the stands for the spectators by the Rodrigo de Freitas Lagoon), water polo and diving, cycling, volleyball, equestrian sports, and the Olympic Stadium itself."[21]

In the document dated February 29, 2016, the technology and information department of the IOC also warned of power problems in Rio de Janeiro. "The project, and temporary electricity supply, still poses a high risk," the report observed.[22] Elsewhere in the same document, the IOC mentioned the "tight time frames"[23] to ensure that the delivery of these services would be done by July 2016.

In an assessment never intended to reach the press, the IOC inspectors also made it clear that the problems and the delays in Rio de Janeiro were closely linked to budget cuts: "The main problems are related to current budget cuts, with possible impact on the levels of technology services and also risks connected with the late delivery of Olympic layouts and also the temporary system for electricity supply, and upon the Olympic venues."[24]

In the aftermath of a further meeting about the financial situation, held in Lausanne on February 2, 2016, with the participation of the IOC, the city of Rio de Janeiro, and twenty-eight international sports federations, it also became clear that the Olympics movement requested to be informed about any further cuts the organizers in

Brazil would have to make in the general budget for the Games. The document said the impact on athletes was indeed a grave and real concern, even though the federations had agreed to reduce their demands.

According to the document, eight federations had another meeting on the very same day to specifically address the situation at the Deodoro cluster (used for sports such as equestrian, cycling [BMX and mountain bike], modern pentathlon, shooting, slalom canoeing, and field hockey). According to the document: "The main result of these meetings was an increased concern with the planning of the spectators' experience and, as a result, a special Task Force was established, to make sure that the experience of athletes and spectators alike were in line with the standards expected in the Olympic Games."[25]

In the final months before the event, the IOC decided to move part of its staff to Rio de Janeiro. Special task forces were also created to handle specific issues. The crisis was deep and an intervention was needed.

OVERCOMING OBSTACLES

The reality could not be hidden any further. But, in a skillful manner, the IOC and Rio decided on a radical change in their tone, in part to prepare for possible chaos. Once again, manipulation of facts was the main focus of its communications strategy. The idea was to show that the challenges Rio was facing had nothing to do with lack of planning or corruption; instead, the country's economic and political crisis was deemed the culprit. Ignoring that Rio had had seven years to prepare for the Games and that most of this preparation was in fact during Brazil's boom years, the communications strategy insisted that it was these financial uncertainties, which erupted in 2015, that threatened the entire event and, thus, opened the door to the request for a bailout.

The message conveyed to the world was that the Games were victims of a crisis that could not have been avoided by the IOC or by their Brazilian counterparts. Rio would also show the world that, despite the difficulties imposed by politicians, sports had prevailed in the end, together with the capacity of officials who organized and delivered the event.

In April 2016, in a speech given in Lausanne during a congress attended by businesspeople, investors, and broadcasters, Bach made sure this was the tone to be used. "We well know that the political and economic situation of Brazil will mean that the final preparation will still be a challenge," said the IOC president. "Despite the challenges that have been faced, I am still firmly convinced that the 2016 Summer Games in Rio de Janeiro shall be a real inspiring spectacle. . . . Faced with this unprecedented situation, it is important that we all come together. The Games shall be a signal of hope in a moment of turbulence. This message of hope could be the most important legacy that this event could bring to the city of Rio, to Brazil and to the world."[26] The promised legacy for citizens had been transformed into a semispiritual legacy for the world.

At that point Rio 2016 was not even sure about how it would finance the costs to be incurred. At the same meeting in Lausanne, sports federations brought together by the Association of Summer Olympic International Federations (ASOIF) produced a sobering evaluation of the Games. Confidential documents showed that there was indeed a risk of casting into doubt the organizers' ability to erect some of the venues to be used in the event and also to ensure the athletes' security.

The list of concerns was in fact quite frightening, even for officials who had kept tabs on the preparation of about a dozen editions of the Games. The document stated, "the finance issue at federal, state and municipal levels dominated the preparation," in addition to other equally serious issues like "the mediocre quality of the water, affecting several federations, the general capacity of sustaining the Games, the reduction in the number of employees allocated to the Local Organising Committee, and the delay in operational planning."[27]

The confidential document also contradicted the official version released by Rio 2016, which stated that there had been no budget cuts, as had been declared by Carlos Arthur Nuzman, the president of the organizing committee. "The Organizing Committee has announced a 30% saving in the remaining expenses, and several sports federations have already started to feel the pinch," according to the document.[28] In the opinion of the ASOIF, corruption in Brazil was also partly to blame for the situation.

In another confidential document sent by the International Federation of Gymnastics (IFG) on April 18, 2016 to the ASOIF, the institution said that the test event that had been held in Rio over the previous days had received scathing criticism from the officials. With budget cuts, one result was precarious lighting. In a section with the suggestive title of "important problems," the IFG warned that five power cuts occurred, harming the Omega data—which maintains the accounts of the competitors.[29] The report added that one of the power outages occurred while the athletes were participating in competitions, putting the athletes' safety at risk.

The IFG also asserted that Rio 2016 did not carry out its promises regarding the lighting of the training center: "The minimum requirement of 1500 lux in the competition venue and 800 lux in the training centre were not complied with, as a result of cost-cutting, a move detrimental to the athletes and also to television production."[30]

BURNING QUESTIONS

In the three months leading up to the Games, the operation to play down problems was further boosted with marketing campaigns and with the transformation of some of the television broadcasters that had bought the right to show the event into a publicity arm for the event. At the center of the new push was the Olympics torch and its route within Brazil. The flame was used to win hearts and minds, creating a feeling that the event that was about to occur could be a way to "bring together" a deeply divided country.

This struggle for a positive image also included the invitation to me and other journalists to carry the Olympics torch, hence bringing us on to the same "side" at the event. I declined the "honor." But many others did seize the opportunity. Throughout the country they wore the official uniform and displayed the main symbol of the Games. From that moment on, the hope of the organizers was that the torchbearers would become part of the Olympics family, not only professionals covering the event but also actors in the Olympics drama itself.

Although public opinion can indeed be manipulated with excessive patriotic feeling, emotional stories, and the explicit use of partners within the press to avoid questions, sports officials in the rest of the world are not so easily manipulated. This became evident only a few days before the gala opening of the main event. The IOC dedicated part of its 120th annual session on August 4, 2016, to hearing the last reports and updates from Rio 2016 about the event. But the crisis could not be hidden any longer. When Bach opened the meeting for members' comments, he looked concerned when faced with the long list of delegates wishing to speak. "Oh no," he groaned into a hot microphone.

During the IOC congress, the Rio 2016 Organizing Committee was the subject of intense criticism, with the most important delegates of the Olympics movement attacking the local plans in areas such as transport, security, access to event venues, decoration, finances, and pollution and also stressing that parts of the construction work were running behind schedule. According to them, the athletes were "nervous" in light of the problems.

A microphone went around the room, and one by one the members of the IOC criticized Rio 2016. For Pierre Beckers, a Belgian member of the group, the main problem was access to the Olympic park. "Long queues, very long in fact, have been formed, with waiting time up to 45 minutes, and the event has not even started. This can breed a lot of frustration," the delegate warned.[31]

Transportation was also criticized. "The traffic is a mess, and this has made athletes and coaches nervous. They need to arrive on time for training sessions and events," Beckers announced. In the opinion of Denis Oswald, a prominent IOC member, the access issue needed to be solved urgently. "We have had great difficulty in getting to the venues. Traffic is terrible," Oswald said.

There was also plenty of criticism related to the delays in venue preparation. "Only 15 percent of signs and posters have been installed," said Camiel Eurlings, another IOC member. "When will this be completed?" he asked. The list of delegates who were worried about the event also included Prince Albert of Monaco, who made demands about water quality.

In all these complaints, it was clear that the crisis was financial more than anything else. Sidney Levy, the CEO of Rio 2016, admitted that, due to problems at the athletes' village, contingency plans had to be established and cuts had to be made in certain services. "It has been very difficult to strike a balance," the CEO admitted. "We have also had to make cuts in several other areas," he said.

Upon leaving the meeting, Nuzman refused to talk about financial issues and deferred the issue to Levy. However, the executive quite literally fled from the journalists, also refusing to explain the problems that had been faced. "Save me, save me in the name of the Lord," he said, with his hands raised high, as if he were being mugged. Levy was stopped by his own communications director for Rio 2016, Mario Andrada, who warned him in front of the journalists: "This is not a circus. Let's stop and answer." Levy did stop. But he never replied, and he snuck out of the location without giving any explanations for the crisis.

CRISIS MANAGEMENT OR ACCESS TO INFORMATION?

Once the Games got under way, the management of the information simply proved to be a summary of seven years of lack of transparency. With each new outbreak of a crisis, the order was to apologize, play it down, and claim that things were being resolved, even if they weren't.

A daily briefing for journalists was held by the IOC and the Rio 2016 organizing team—but the difference between communications and information has rarely been so stark. This became clear when I asked a question about how a particular company had been chosen for a contract with Rio 2016. A very high-ranking official inside the organizing committee came to my desk at the media center after the briefing and asked to talk to me. While we were walking he only made one remark: questions such as the one I had just asked should not be made in public.

He told me that, even though in the past he was willing to take calls from me on his mobile phone, if I chose to ask questions like that in public, he would only talk to me at press conferences. This was a very clear threat about which questions were "acceptable" in a public forum and which ones would be considered a declaration of war.

This same official, five months before the Games started, had admitted to me that the information war they fought did include some misinformation tactics. The media gurus of Rio 2016, he alleged, actually fed the controversy of the polluted waters of Guanabara Bay in order to distract the press from more pressing problems, such as the shortage of funding and the widespread corruption.

So, while the Games were actually taking place, similar tactics would not come as a surprise. Indeed, the misinformation strategy took a fast track when, on August 9, 2016, only four days after the Games had begun, the swimming pool had turned green—a clear statement about the lack of testing.

For the next five days Rio 2016 would give different answers about what they were doing to clean the water, from joking about the fact that it had the Brazilian colors to promising that the problem would be righted "very soon." At one point, the official line was that "chemistry was not an exact science." Then, when athletes complained about itching eyes, the response given by Mario Andrada, head of communications, was even more astonishing: it all depends on how long you keep your eyes open in the water.

For journalists following the daily news briefing, the credibility of the information given deteriorated by the day. In the case of the pool, telling the simple—and embarrassing—truth that preparations were not carried out properly did not seem to be an option for the organizers. While searching for a new excuse every day, press conferences became a collection of empty phrases, turning the communication strategy into a symbol of how a group of officials, who for seven years never attempted to tell the truth about the event itself, operated. At the end, however, the water had to be replaced, proving that words and journalists can indeed be manipulated but science cannot.

Manipulation, however, was not the only instrument. Three days before the end of the Games, I published the salaries of the eight executive directors of the Rio 2016 Organizing Committee, based on official financial statements that had just been released. In total, they earned over R$26 million ($8 million) over four years.[32] Moreover, this did not even include the money to be paid out in 2016, when payments were to be even larger.

Earning high salaries is not the problem. The real issue was that the salaries were paid at a time when the organizers' official line was that Brazil was in a recession, that they were obliged to make important cuts that would affect athletes, and, of course, that they needed public money to bail out the event. The truth is that, while some were actually getting richer, it was up to the people to pay for part of the bill in the event of a deficit.

Late on the night when I published the executives' salaries, I received a message on my phone from a senior executive on the organizing committee. Using again a threatening tone, he asked me if I thought this was the "appropriate moment" to publish a "cheap sensationalist" story. He was right. It was not an appropriate time. It was actually too late, and information such as that should have been made known to the public many years before.

Payments to executives grew in each successive year leading up to the Games, as if in lockstep with the growing Rio 2016 Organizing Committee of the Olympic and Paralympic Games (ROCOG) and public deficits. In 2011 a total of R$2.7 million was paid to the eight executive directors. The following year, the total payout to the executives had edged up to R$3.1 million. This upward trend continued in 2013 (R$5 million), 2014 (R$7.3 million), and 2015 (R$8.3 million). The sums paid out in 2016 were scheduled to exceed those of 2015. Rio 2016 also spent R$24 million (approximately $9.2 million at the time) a year on executive travel between 2014 and 2015.[33]

Some days before I received the alert from the senior executive, Pat Hickey, the president of the European Olympic Committee, was arrested in a five-star hotel in Rio that also served as the bunker for the Olympics family. He was charged with selling tickets on the black market, in a scandal that would put the IOC in the spotlight.

I was one of the few journalists who had access to the hotel, with the IOC giving a special pass to just a handful of media representatives. But on that day my pass was no longer valid. When I was at the hotel while the arrest was taking place, a military guard told me he would have to take my documents for verification. Five minutes later, he came back with just my passport and informed me that my accreditation had been withdrawn until further notice.

The reason? No official reason. I asked to speak to those who had made the decision. This request was repeatedly denied. After insisting that I needed to know the reason for the suspension of the valid pass, the only answer I got was that it "was an IOC decision." When it was clear that I had to leave, one of the security officers came to me and said that he knew who I was from my reporting. In a very cordial way, he explained that they had been told "above all" that they were not to allow me on the premises. "When they saw your name in the documents we brought to them, they went crazy," he claimed. "Sorry, I am only doing my job," he apologized.

Fighting alone against the powerful IOC would not result in any positive outcome. So I decided to appeal to a larger audience. After using social media to denounce the decision to withdraw my accreditation for no clear reason, I received an e-mail from the IOC saying it was a "misunderstanding" and that my pass was going to be given back. By the time the accreditation was reissued, the story of Hickey's arrest was over.

The strategy adopted by the Olympics movement was to isolate the Hickey crisis and insist that it would be up to the Irish Olympic Committee to come up with an answer and not the international institution. For many days the official response that the IOC gave to the press was that the case did not have any involvement in the Lausanne group. This meant that any investigation would have to be conducted by the Irish rather than by Thomas Bach.

As the investigations progressed, it became evident that the IOC did indeed know about Hickey's interest in acquiring tickets. On arresting the Irishman, the Rio de Janeiro police ended up discovering a string of contacts between the suspect and the top management at the IOC. Some e-mails, for example, showed that Hickey had requested more tickets directly from the IOC president, Thomas Bach. On April 10, 2015, Hickey had requested that the IOC allow the Irish committee to be appointed as a partner for selling tickets. If that were agreed, the Irish would choose the company THG as their "sub-agents" to operate the sales. This company was accused of being part of the ticket scam.

In an e-mail message that was also sent to the CEO of the Games, Brazilian Sidney Levy, Hickey showed the plan and even went as far as getting Bach involved. "I also had a conversation yesterday, with

Bach, and explained the strategy to him. He then confirmed that he would accept the plan," Hickey wrote. In the same message, Hickey explained that "over the last few weeks" he had been in contact with Pere Miró, the vice director general of the IOC.

In an e-mail sent April 16, 2015, Howard Stupp presented what would be the draft of the agreement and suggested to Hickey himself that an e-mail should be drawn up by IOC executive director Christophe Dubi. The message would indeed propose a solution for the request made by Hickey, accepting the proposal of the executive who had been indicted in Rio. "I suggest that the IOC should write the following letter to Pat," explained Stupp. "It could be in the name of CHD." CHD are Christophe Dubi's initials.

The e-mails and evidence collected by the police do not implicate Bach personally but were considered in the inquiry to be elements pointing to the fact that the IOC did know about the interest of Hickey regarding tickets.

I approached the IOC in this regard, and they refused to make any comment when asked about the e-mails mentioning two of their top executives. "We have no comments, as the issue is the subject of an investigation," said Mark Adams, the spokesperson of the IOC. Some hours later, on finding out that the same news report would be published in an important German newspaper, with a direct repercussion on public opinion in Thomas Bach's own country, Adams sent by e-mail to me a long explanation, denying any kind of involvement.

Brazilian authorities had hoped that Bach would have given some explanation about these e-mails when he came to Brazil for the Paralympic Games. However, for the first time since 1984, an IOC president decided not to attend the event. Officially, Bach would miss the opening of the event because of a funeral that he needed to attend in Europe. The IOC did not explain why the president was absent during the rest of the Paralympic event; he has not been to Brazil since.

COST OVERRUNS AND GOVERNMENT BANKRUPTCY

One area where media cover-ups and spin were most necessary was in regard to financing the Games. The government had claimed from the outset that no public money would be used. Over time it became increasingly obvious that billions of dollars of public funds were being deployed to enable the Games and the government had to use various ruses and subterfuges to allow monies to flow to the Olympics effort. By the final accounting, more than R$17 billion came directly from government funding to host the Games, surpassing by nearly 50 percent the R$12 billion the city of Rio spends on education and health services in a typical year.[34]

To ensure sufficient funds for infrastructure work connected to the Games, government authorities decided to simply delay the payment of active civil servant wages, as well as payments to retirees and pensioners of the executive branch. Without any cash in hand to pay the salaries for May 2016 in full, the state of Rio de Janeiro announced that only 70 percent of the payroll would effectively be paid on the 14th, with a financial outlay of some R$1.1 billion. The delay in the payment of wages that month affected a total of 393,000 civil servants in administration, hospitals, and public schools.

Seven weeks prior to the opening of the Games the state of Rio declared a "state of calamity." This sly move assured that the state of Rio would immediately receive a sum of R$2.9 billion from the federal government for expenses brought about by the Olympic and Paralympic Games and also for the payment of salaries. In addition, these funds would also be used to pay for security and for the completion of Line 4 of the Rio de Janeiro Underground, which would connect the upmarket neighborhood of Barra da Tijuca (West Zone) to the neighborhood of Ipanema (South Zone). This was considered an essential work project for the Games to proceed.

Three months after the Olympics circus had closed the tent and left the country, the state of Rio de Janeiro gave clear evidence that it was bankrupt. In November 2016, the state government would come up with a proposal that showed the sheer extent of the crisis, as well as who would have to foot the bill. Pensions started to be taxed, social programs were cut, and salary increases were canceled.

Social programs simply disappeared. Salaries would also be cut, according to the proposal, and salary readjustments that had been granted in 2014 to law enforcement workers, firefighters, and tax auditors were postponed.

The population of Rio de Janeiro would also pay the price for uncontrolled spending over the last few years. The plan also proposed increases in consumer taxes and higher taxes for items such as electricity, communications services, petrol, tobacco products, beer, and soft drinks. At that moment, the total debt of the state stood at R$17.5 billion, without any forecast as to when the debt would be settled.

It was not only the state of Rio that suffered. The skyrocketing Olympics costs, delays in deliveries, and lack of planning ended up making expenditures go well above budget. Without any clear way of increasing revenue, the Rio 2016 Organizing Committee had to slash R$900 million from the Games' operational budget of R$7 billion, with less than three months to go before the event got under way. The main cuts were in areas such as sports arenas and elimination of temporary buildings, which made several sports organizations angry at Rio 2016 for the breaking of promises compared to what was outlined in the city's bid back in 2009.

At the soccer stadium in Itaquera, for example, the cuts affected some structures that were to be assembled exclusively for the ten soccer games of the Olympics tournament. One of the most-awaited projects, the floating stands for the rowing competition on Rodrigo de Freitas Lagoon, was ruled out. For the International Rowing Federation, the impact of the reduction in the number of people watching the races was significant. The initial project mentioned stands for 14,000 spectators, which ended up being reduced to only 6,000. (In London, during the 2012 Olympic Games, there were 25,000 seats at the rowing events.) Jean-Christophe Rolland, president of the International Rowing Federation, told me he "understood" the crisis in Brazil. However, he did criticize the fact that the decision was made without consulting the group. In his opinion, the institution would have had some options to propose if they had been informed earlier.

The people responsible for water sports also showed anger with what happened in Rio. In London there were three swimming pools, while only two were available in Rio. In theory, the competitions would not have been affected. However, the main cause for concern was the training agenda for the diving, synchronised swimming, and water polo competitions. The result was that one of the swimming pools did not withstand the intensity of its use and ended up taking on a green color.

For days, specialists could not understand the reaction of the water and one of the theories was that the chemical agents used to allow the intensive use had created the situation.

Despite the severe cuts, the organizers never stopped meeting the needs of the most interested party: Brazilian politicians. Days before the event started, the organizing committee offered 1,188 tickets to the 594 Brazilian members of parliament and their partners. This meant that the committee would forsake potential revenue of some R$1.6 million. About 150 Brazilian members of Congress accepted the invitation. ROCOG justified this gesture, saying that congressmen and congresswomen and senators are "personalities who represent Brazil."

The inability to get higher revenue from ticket sales and publicity led the organizers to press the federal government to allow expenses to be paid with government funding, once again breaking one of the vows that the Games would occur without having to use taxpayers' money. Within the IOC, delegates were also of the opinion that the government had to do its part. In June, one of the IOC vice presidents, Yu Zaiqing from China, declared to me that what was in play for the government was a matter of "reputation." Francesco Ricci Bitti, one of the most influential executives in the Olympics world, confirmed that, with only a few days to go before the start of the Games, the target now was no longer that of balancing the accounts but rather that of paying for the event: "Now we need to make the Olympics work. Only then comes the budget."

One of the ideas was that state companies would pay for the opening ceremony by signing sponsorship deals, at an estimated cost of R$280 million. This would mean that the money used for the event would be released so that the organizers could break even in other segments. However, after weeks of discussions, this option ran adrift. The organizers insisted that there would be no way of changing the opening ceremony program to meet the requirements of the government or to include publicity in exchange for sponsorship money. For the people in Brasília, this would make it more difficult to seek justification for the public expense of the event.

A second strategy was to promote a kind of "barter." Without any money, the government opened the possibility of subsidizing the supply of some items, without needing to give money to the organizers of the 2016 Games.

Two rounds of negotiations were carried out: a search for a supply of petrol for the 4,000 cars used in the event, for a total value of R$60 million, and the supply of energy for the Olympic village and for the competition venues. Thus, companies such as Petrobras could become sponsors of the event without actually sending cash to Rio 2016. However, this option also failed before the Games started.

The option to have sponsors was of particular interest to the organizers. The sending of money for the event by the federal government meant that the Games could be targeted by a control sting by the federal audit court, demanding transparency of accounts. This would not happen with sponsorship, where state companies would give money in exchange for the promotion of their brands.

However, there was one serious obstacle for the rescue of the event by the government: the judicial system. For months on end, federal prosecutors had warned that the Rio 2016 committee needed to make their accounts and contracts public if they wanted to have access to public funding. However, the organizers made a point of ignoring these pleas.

On July 20, 2016, with only fifteen days left before the Games and with an important deficit in Rio 2016's accounts, the federal prosecution office in Rio de Janeiro lodged an appeal and gave a period of twenty days for Rio 2016 to open their financial black box. The penalty to be applied if the black box were not opened would be a fine of R$10,000 per day.[35]

The case reached the federal judges who, during the event, decided to forbid public transfers of funds to the committee until the presentation of accounts on the expenses of the Games, attending to a request made by the government Prosecution Office (MPF, acronym in Portuguese) in Rio de Janeiro. In the decision, made on August 12, 2016, judge Márcia Nunes de Barros said, "as well observed by the representatives of the MPF . . . there is justified doubt that the due publicity and transparency has indeed been given to the sums transferred" to the committee.[36] The judge reminded everyone that the funds, after being deposited into the account of the Rio 2016 committee, "can be spent without any type of control, and it will be difficult for the funds to be recovered by any of the government organizations in a difficult financial situation, as is generally known."

The Rio 2016 Organizing Committee and IOC claim that the deficit was caused by Brazil's economic crisis held no sway with the prosecutors. Documents that are part of the investigations of the federal prosecution office showed that the shortfall in the accounts of the event was already very high in 2010 and 2012 and increased at an alarming rate. The study showed that, over the years and even at a moment when the general Brazilian economy was expanding, Rio 2016 did not manage to break even. In 2010, the shortfall was R\$22.6 million, a figure that had soared to R\$90.6 million by 2012. In those years, the Brazilian GDP actually grew by as much as 7.5 percent.

During the Olympics, funds that were earmarked to be used in the Paralympics ended up being used to cover shortfalls in the hope that new public funds would come weeks later. The shrinking of the financial allocation of the Paralympics, however, triggered a second crisis: the possibility that the Paralympics would simply be abandoned, also with the cost cuts and defaults that threatened the athletes.

The strategy of the organizers was to remind the press that there had never been a Paralympics without public funding. "To hold the Paralympic Games the way we want to, we need financial backing. All the Games have had support from countries," was how Mario Andrada, the communications director of Rio 2016, justified the funding.

In fact, the directors of the International Paralympic Committee went to Brasília in August to meet with the Brazilian chief of staff, Eliseu Padilha, and request solutions in light of the financial crisis the event was facing. The executives were assured that support would come, with the injection of some R\$100 million. That same day the institution also received, from Rio de Janeiro Mayor Eduardo Paes, further assurance that they would receive an additional R\$150 million in the form of sponsorships.

However, for the funds to be released, Nuzman needed to show all the accounts to the judicial system. "Clearly, the simplest and easiest way round this is for the Rio 2016 Organizing Committee to be open and transparent with its financial records in order to allow this additional funding to come in," said the president of the International

Paralympic Committee (IPC), Sir Philip Craven, in an effort to put pressure on the Brazilian official.[37]

The opening of the accounts, however, would not be necessary. An appeal was lodged by the organizing committee, and close to the end of the Games the Regional Federal Appellate Court of Rio de Janeiro suspended the injunction that forbade the transfer of funding from the Brazilian federal government and from Rio de Janeiro city hall to the organizing committee of the Games.

So the Games were saved, the Paralympics were saved, and Nuzman's accounts would never be made public. The only party who would never know the extent of his or her participation in the budget of the Olympic Games would be the Brazilian taxpayers.

In the end, neither the sham sponsorship deals nor the help from the state nor the breaking of promises nor the accounting maneuvers would ensure that the accounts would break even. Two months after the event finished, the unpaid electricity bill of the Olympic and Paralympic Games was more than R$22 million. This debt was owed by the Rio 2016 Organizing Committee to Light, the electricity company in Rio.

Just for the energy used in the International Broadcasting Center (IBC), the organizers owed R$4.3 million. The IBC was the communications center for the event, where dozens of television networks broadcast the Games around the globe. In November, it was in a penumbra, with the power having been cut off and the future use of the facility in doubt.

In stadiums and arenas, debt also mounted. At the iconic Maracanã Stadium, the energy bill came to R$1.2 million by the end of October, with no funds to pay it. At the Engenhão Stadium where Usain Bolt showed off his athletic prowess, the debt had broken the R$1 million mark, and the power was also cut.

The golf course constructed for the event had also suffered. The payment of the energy bill by Rio 2016 was in arrears at the end of November 2016, and the risk was that without electricity the irrigation pumps would stop working. One week without power would be enough to deeply affect the grass that took months of work to be shaped.

The energy supply, at the end of 2016, accounted for about 10 percent of the whole debt of Rio 2016, which has been estimated at R$200 million. The organizers had reached an agreement to receive a R$250 million transfer from Rio city hall and the Brazilian federal government. However, in November about R$100 million of the part to be paid by local government had not yet been deposited.

The outcome was late payments to suppliers, especially food companies, security companies, cleaners who worked at the Paralympics, and hundreds of unpaid workers, both domestic and international. Rio 2016 was forced to negotiate with creditors and even managed to obtain some discounts.

One of these was the cleaning company Sunplus, which revealed it had not received payments from the Rio 2016 Organizing Committee, affecting its ability to pay the salaries of the company's staff in September. The next month, the employees took to the streets to protest, even surrounding the building that was the headquarters of the Rio 2016 committee. Sunplus was far from being the only company affected. In all, 20,000 suppliers had still not been paid or had payments in arrears in November 2016 for services that had been provided in August. The organizers had assured that everyone would be paid—but they just didn't know when.

The Prosecution Office suspects that Rio 2016 has attempted to cover up public funds in their accounts by clinching a sponsorship deal with government companies and the Agency for Promotion of Exports and Investments (Apex, acronym in Portuguese) days before the Games started. The suspicion of the prosecutors is that the contract would not actually be a sponsorship deal but just a way of assuring public funding for the event. "If there was a cover-up of these contracts, then this could be a case of administrative corruption," the prosecutor said, also adding that he has no assurance that other contracts with state companies are not being designed in the same manner.[38]

Apex, in order to justify the sponsorship, used the closing ceremony of the Olympics to promote its campaign. On the floor of the Maracanã, the projection that lasted a few seconds showed the brand "Be Brasil" and thus became in theory a part of the general theme of the event. But hardly anyone realized that this was an advertisement of the state. The projection was so quick that not even all the employees of Apex became aware of the fact that the campaign was being inserted on the agenda of the closing ceremony.

The president of the Brazilian Agency for the Promotion of Exports and Investments (Apex-Brasil), Roberto Jaguaribe, denied that the agreement for the payment for Rio 2016 had been clinched with public funding. "Apex is an independent social service, and does not receive any money from the budget," he declared to reporters on that same day. Jaguaribe only told half the story.

This is because, according to the Apex statutes, the company did not receive any funds directly from the general federal budget but rather from contracts signed bilaterally between the "independent" agency and the Brazilian Ministry of Development, Industry and Foreign Trade. In documents signed on May 9, 2016, Apex received from the ministry total funding of about R$553 million to carry out its mission up to 2019. The ministry, like any other, was funded by the federal budget.[39]

Part of the funds used for the construction work on the Deodoro cluster was blocked after a federal police investigation saw signs of massive fraud. The operation known as Operação Bota-Fora (Operation Throw-Away), together with the Brazilian federal police, the Brazilian prosecution office, and the Brazilian Inland Revenue, the agency responsible for collecting taxes, noted that the losses incurred in the construction of the complex could be as high as R$85 million to public coffers. An investigation into possible bribery by the construction companies Queiroz Galvão and OAS was also launched.[40]

THE CEREMONIAL BEGINNING AND ENDING

Given the country's political turmoil, its budgetary crisis, its violence, its corruption, and the dubious preparations and contracting for the Summer Olympics, it should come as no surprise that world leaders stayed away from the opening and closing ceremonies of Rio 2016. After London 2012 had received a total of ninety heads of state at its opening ceremony, Beijing 2008 seventy heads of state, Athens 2004 forty-eight, and Sydney 2000 twenty-four, the Olympic Games in Rio received but eighteen. The remaining representatives of foreign governments consisted of vice prime ministers, governors, and other second-level authorities. I was the only journalist to enter the presidential boxes on that festive day. I was able to confirm that many of the VIP locations remained empty, while ministers and authorities would walk around without any commitment.

On the official list of heads of state, the government also included dignitaries who, in essence, were members of the IOC, such as those of Luxembourg and Monaco, and who therefore were required to attend their own event. Still, the list was significantly different from what the government had announced back in May, which included fifty such people confirmed, with plans to get as high as seventy VIP guests. Their absence was well noted in the internal corridors of the stadium, which were often empty, with food, employees, and security staff in excess.

Among the delegations, one could see former Rio de Janeiro State Governor Sérgio Cabral talking with São Paulo Governor Geraldo Alckmin at one of the tables. Less than three months later, Cabral would be jailed after being charged with taking bribes for the works done in that same stadium. The Brazilian finance minister, Henrique Meirelles, also walked calmly around, looking for something to drink at the empty counters of the bars that had been installed at this location.

The Brazilian government tried to invite the few foreign leaders to stay in the main box alongside interim Brazilian president Michel Temer. Without any success, the box instead was filled with federal government ministers and state and municipal authorities.

Before the event had even finished, and soon after the parade of the French delegation, French President François Hollande snuck out of the Maracanã. He had not come to Brazil to meet Temer or to honor the country with his presence. His agenda was to show the IOC that he was firmly engaged with the Olympics cause, in a move to take the Olympics to Paris in 2024.

Temer, with his ministers and also a group of local politicians, had received extra protection to avoid popular protests. If the ceremony was marked by a call to the world for tolerance, the fact is that neither the politicians nor the IOC managed to stop the Maracanã once again from becoming a protest venue, repeating what had already happened to Brazilian heads of state at the 2007 Pan American Games, at the 2013 FIFA Confederations Cup, and the 2014 FIFA World Cup.

At the "Olympics à la Brasil," as the IOC called them, the opening ceremony of the Games was broadcast to an estimated three billion people and was intended to transmit a political and social message to the world. Because of this global impact, the organizers used measures to avoid protests against Temer. The only time he spoke publicly, Temer was loudly jeered. "I hereby declare the Olympic Games of Rio de Janeiro open," he said, and he quickly stepped down.

During the four hours of the event, however, Temer was forgotten by the organizers, and he stayed distant from the other guests. His name was not announced at the start of the event, and the loudspeakers only mentioned the presence of Bach. In the official program the organizers eliminated any reference to the Brazilian president. In his speech, Bach mentioned the president of the Rio 2016 Organizing Committee, Carlos Arthur Nuzman, and also Ban Ki-moon. However, Temer's name was left out altogether, and there was only a general reference to "Brazilian authorities."

Similarly, Carlos Arthur Nuzman did not mention Temer by name during his speech. Like others, Nuzman was booed when he mentioned the federal, state, and municipal governments. The Brazilian presidential palace maintained that as the event was organized by the IOC the program was also organized by this institution. In Rio, IOC sources confirmed that this omission was "negotiated."

Protocol was also under intense observation. With one hour to go to the start of the event, Bach visited the VIP stands of Maracanã to check where each of the heads of state would sit and make sure there would be no problems of any kind and no political enemies sitting next to each other. Considering the political situation of the country, any missteps could lead to trouble.

In the stands, one group started to belt out a chorus of "Temer Out," but this ended up muffled by another group of supporters who booed the political demonstration. Members of the national security forces said that some 500 police agents were mixed with the supporters and scattered around the stadium to identify possible threats and also political protests.

The same protection was seen at the closing ceremony. On that occasion Temer decided not to go to the Maracanã, and all the jeers were aimed at Rio de Janeiro Mayor Eduardo Paes. As required by protocol, the Rio de Janeiro politician was obliged to step onto the podium to pass the Olympics flag to Tokyo. Paes had been profusely praised by Bach, dubbing him "a great leader." Nonetheless, at the Maracanã the mayor of Rio was targeted by boos on at least four occasions.

As in the case of the opening ceremony, the IOC and Rio 2016 tried to avoid the exposure of politicians as much as possible. At the start of the event, only Bach was announced to the public. Beside him was Rodrigo Maia, the president of the Brazilian parliament and a representative of the Temer government.

The Brazilian politicians only got up at the end of the event, when samba music took over at the Maracanã. With index fingers pointing upward, the top leaders of the Brazilian military and ministers such as Alexandre de Moraes (justice) and Raul Jungmann (defense) danced and hugged each other while confetti cascaded from above and the loudspeakers played some famous Brazilian samba tunes, like "Me dá um dinheiro aí" ("Give Me Some Money Now").

Largely deflated in the stands and in the political boxes, the closing ceremony only had the presence of eight heads of state, of which at least three were IOC members, meaning that they had to be there and that they received a $900 per diem allowance from the IOC for their troubles.

The good news was that with massive media manipulation, backroom deals, furtive public money transfers, and a large dose of good fortune, Rio 2016 was pulled off. For some of the politicians involved in its preparations, however, the closing ceremony was not the end of the story. Over the next seven months, former governor of Rio, Sergio Cabral, was arrested and accused of receiving alleged bribes for the works at Maracanã Stadium. Eduardo Paes, former mayor of Rio, was investigated by the Supreme Court of Brazil for also receiving bribes regarding the event. Judges and sport officials were also indicted. The full extent of payoffs and bribes connected to Rio 2016 will likely not be known for years.

NOTES

1. *The IOC Annual Report 2015: Credibility, Sustainability and Youth* (Lausanne, Switz.: International Olympics Committee, 2015) (https://www.olympic.org/documents/ioc-annual-report).

2. Jamil Chade, "Jogos do Rio correm risco, diz Comitê Olímpico International," *Estadão Esportes*, August 31, 2013 (http://esportes.estadao.com .br/noticias/geral,jogos-do-rio-correm-risco-diz-comite-olimpico -internacional,1069679).

3. International Olympic Committee (IOC), "Status of Progress," report delivered to the fifth meeting of the IOC Coordination Commission for the Games of the Olympiad, Rio 2016, Lausanne, Switzerland, August 26, 2013.

4. Ibid.

5. Ibid.

6. Ibid.

7. Ibid.

8. Ibid.

9. Ibid.

10. Ibid.

11. Ibid

12. Ibid.

13. Ibid.

14. Ibid.

15. Ibid.

16. Katharine Viner, "How Technology Disrupted the Truth," *The Guardian*, July 12, 2016.

17. "President's Report and the Report of Administrative Activities," IOC, Lausanne, Switzerland, February 29, 2016.

18. Ibid.

19. Ibid.

20. Ibid.

21. Ibid.

22. Ibid.

23. Ibid.

24. Ibid.

25. Ibid.

26. Speech delivered by Thomas Bach, president of the IOC, on April 19, 2016, at the SportAccord Convention in Lausanne, Switzerland.

27. Report of the ASOIF Council at the fortieth General Assembly, Lausanne, Switzerland, April 19, 2016. Document distributed to sports federations and delegate members of the ASOIF.

28. Ibid.

29. Document sent by the International Federation of Gymnastics (IFG) on April 18, 2016, to the ASOIF.

30. Ibid.

31. 120th annual session of the IOC, August 4, 2016, Rio de Janeiro.

32. "The Organisation," *Olympic.org* (www.rio2016.com/transparencia /sites/default/files/fnc_demonstracoes_financeiras_2015_2016_portugues _07042016.pdf).

33. www.rio2016.com/transparencia/sites/default/files/rio2016 _demonstracoes_financeiras2014_201504_port_vfinal_0.pdf.

34. These numbers are not readily converted into U.S. dollars because the expenditures took place over at least a seven-year period and the exchange rate of the Brazilian currency fluctuated significantly over this time. See chapter 9 in this volume for a fuller discussion of this issue and an estimation of the actual costs in U.S. dollars.

35. Even though Rio 2016 insisted on saying that they used no government funds for the event, the organizers benefited from laws that allowed the suspension of taxes. Rio 2016 was freed from paying R$5.3 million of the Industrialized Products Tax (IPI), R$155.9 million in the Social Security Financing Contribution (Cofins, acronym in Portuguese), and R$33.8 million to the Social Integration Programme (PIS). Of course, billions of dollars of public funds were also spent. See chapter 9 for a full discussion.

36. https://cdn.oantagonista.net/uploads%2F1471105410626 -decisão+justiça+olimp%C3%ADada.pdf.

37. "The IPC's Update on the Rio 2016 Organising Committee's Financial Situation," *Rio 2016 Paralympic Games*, August 15, 2016 (www.paralympic .org/news/ipcs-update-rio-2016-organising-committee-s-financial -situation).

38. Interview with the author, Rio de Janeiro, August 14, 2016.

39. www.apexbrasil.com.br/uploads/Contrato%20de%20Gestão%20 MDIC%20e%20Apex-Brasil%202016-2019_de%2006.05.2016_Anexos %20Assinados.pdf.

40. "Operação Bota-fora desarticula esquema de desvio de recurso em obra olímpica," *Ministério da Transparência, Fiscalização, e Controladoria-Geral da União*, July 6, 2016 (www.cgu.gov.br/noticias/2016/06/operacao -bota-fora-desarticula-esquema-de-desvio-de-recurso-em-obra-olimpica).

SEVEN

Safety for Whom?

Securing Rio for the Olympics

JULIANA BARBASSA

The video is grainy, typical of cell phone footage, but there is no doubt as to what it shows: a sheer granite cliff. Bullets fired from police helicopters hovering just outside the frame ping off the rock, raising puffs of dust. A man falls from the ledge into the abyss. He is shirtless, wearing only board shorts, like so many young men in Rio de Janeiro. Out of control, he bangs against the vertical granite wall on his way down. His blue backpack remains stranded on the rock face as he plummets. It isn't clear if he died before falling or if he perished upon impact. What is certain is that he did not survive.

Versions of this video, taken by residents of nearby buildings on October 10, 2016, were beamed from cell phone to cell phone as Rio natives, known as cariocas, discussed the daylong shoot-out between police and gang members that shut down the subway and several main thoroughfares in the Copacabana and Ipanema neighborhoods.[1] What gripped the attention of locals was not just the graphic horror of the death of a young man police later described as a suspected drug dealer or the fact that two other suspects died and three officers were injured that day. Deaths at the hands of the police happen in Rio every day. In 2015, 644 people were killed by officers on duty,

153

according to Rio de Janeiro state's Instituto de Segurança Pública (ISP), or Institute for Public Safety, charged with gathering and analyzing public security data.[2] What made this gun battle stand out was its location and timing; together, these factors sent a clear and worrisome signal of a broader failure.

The gunfire exchange was in Pavão-Pavãozinho and Cantagalo, conjoined favelas that straddle the peaks crowning the tony neighborhoods of Ipanema, Lagoa, and Copacabana. During the previous two months, in August and September, crowds of Olympic and Paralympic visitors had surged through these posh streets on their way to canoeing, rowing, swimming, and other sporting competitions. These favelas were among the first to benefit from an ambitious security program launched in December 2008 and became showcases for the program. Known by its Portuguese acronym, UPP, for Unidades de Policia Pacificadora, or Units of Pacification Police, it was the flagship security program during the years Rio prepared for the World Cup and the Olympics, when it had raised public expectations of a policing paradigm shift and garnered widespread media attention.

The UPP program was striking in that it did not promise to crack down on drug trafficking in Rio. Its goal was narrower, and, perhaps, attainable: to take control of favelas that had been under the influence of drug trafficking gangs and, in doing so, reduce violence in these communities and their surrounding areas. It would do this by bringing specially trained police into favelas and establishing regular patrols. Officers and residents would, theoretically, develop relationships that over time could reverse the animosity and lethal violence that had long characterized relations between law enforcement and favela residents.[3]

Expectations in Rio were high; no policing program on this scale had ever been attempted and certainly none that proposed to leave behind the old, lethal policing methods. But cariocas were also deeply skeptical—none more so than the favela residents. Drug gangs had been occupying favelas, largely unchallenged by the state, for decades. While living under the control of heavily armed drug dealers was undesirable, few felt any allegiance to the police, whom they knew from violent, spasmodic incursions that left bodies in their wake. Despite this legacy, positive results in the first two and one-half years had raised hopes among cariocas and even among favela residents. These included a reduction in the rate of violent deaths in favelas with UPPs by nearly 75 percent and a reduction in the rate of death at the hands of police.[4] By late 2010, 92 percent of residents of UPP favelas and 77 percent of residents of favelas without UPPs approved of the program.[5]

So when cariocas heard the gunfire exchange and witnessed the police kill a young man in broad daylight—less than two weeks after the 2016 Paralympics' closing ceremony—in the relatively privileged Pavão-Pavãozinho and Cantagalo, they knew the UPP program was in trouble. It was a signal that Rio had apparently failed to curb violence and gang control of favelas and to change the police force's approach to patrolling favelas. In a coincidence that nevertheless exacerbated Rio residents' fear and uncertainty regarding the future, the man who had masterminded the UPP program and headed state security for nearly a decade, José Mariano Beltrame, announced his resignation the following day.[6]

What happened to the program? What role did Rio's megaevents play in its development? This chapter will attempt to answer these questions by examining the course of Rio state's UPP program in the years leading up to the World Cup and Olympics and exploring how it was captured by the megasporting event's agenda, schedule, and priorities, which strained the program, expanded it beyond capacity, and helped undermine its chances of success, with tragic consequences.

SECURITY AND BRAZIL'S MEGAEVENT STRATEGY

When Brazilian President Luis Inácio Lula da Silva flew to Copenhagen in October 2009 to defend Rio de Janeiro's bid to host the 2016 Olympic Games, it wasn't the country's first try. Brazil had made two previous attempts and lost. But this run was different. Brazil was different. The economy was stable and growing. Lula, as he is known to Brazilians, was first elected in 2002 then reelected for a second term in 2006. During his first seven years in office, poverty decreased by more than 50 percent as millions joined the middle class.[7] A significant oil discovery just beyond Rio de Janeiro's coastline attracted investment, generated jobs, and suggested there would be funding to salve historical deficits in areas like health and education well into the future. The president himself was a powerful symbol of what could be achieved in this new Brazil. He had left the impoverished northeast to become a steel worker in São Paulo's industrial heartland, only to rise as a union leader into politics and, ultimately, into the presidency. The message—one welcomed by many Brazilians, who gave him popularity ratings above 80 percent—was that if he could overcome seemingly insurmountable barriers, then so could Brazil.

There were other elements that made Rio's bid for the 2016 Games—Brazil's bid, as the president's presence made clear—more promising than the previous attempts. By 2009, Rio was not just a candidate city. Its bid was the culmination of a multiyear development strategy in which municipal, state, and federal interests aligned to attract major sporting events: "Politically, hosting the Games was a key part of then-President Lula da Silva's strategy to re-brand Brazil on a global stage, and offered a form of soft power to advance Brazil's political weight regionally and within the international community. For the state, hosting the Games was understood as an opportunity to showcase Brazilian modernity through displays of initiative, civility, organization, and urban growth."[8] This strategy included the successful hosting of the 2002 South American Games following a relocation from Colombia, Rio's victorious candidacy for the 2007 Pan American Games, and Brazil's securing in May 2007 of the 2011 World Military Games. Three months after the closure of a successful Pan American Games, FIFA awarded the 2014 World Cup to Brazil.[9] Rio entered the dispute for the 2016 Games against Chicago, Tokyo, and Madrid as the declared gateway into an up-and-coming nation on its way to becoming the world's sixth largest economy—a nation that had already proved its mettle as the host of prominent international sporting events and was the chosen host of the world's premiere soccer championship.

Despite the surfeit of good economic news, Brazil's success in securing other global sporting events, and president Lula's charisma, Rio's victory was not guaranteed. The city would have to build venues from scratch and overhaul major infrastructure, including airports and public transportation. The biggest concern, however, was security—one of the major weaknesses in previous bids.[10] Rio's 2016 Olympic bid specifically promised "a safe and agreeable environment for the Games."[11] Cariocas were well aware of the challenge this posed. An analysis of the bid book found the word *security* was used 230 times—more than any other noun.[12] It was, arguably, Rio's single biggest obstacle—not only to hosting a major international event but also to drawing the investment and assuming the greater international prominence desired by elected authorities. This was a multifaceted effort, involving more than sporting megaevents. Rio state's marketing budget, for example, would nearly double from $69.4 million in 2008 to $115.1 million in 2010.[13]

A closer look at the security situation in Rio as it prepared to host the Pan American Games reveals why the International Olympic Committee needed so much reassurance on this front. The Pan, as Brazilians called it, was expected to draw 5,000 athletes and approximately 60,000 tourists when it opened in July 2007. It would be the largest international tournament held in Brazil in forty-four years and the largest in Rio de Janeiro since the 1950 World Cup. Hosting an event of this magnitude raised a number of challenges, but its success was crucial. Not only would it raise the city's profile and demonstrate its capacity to welcome the Olympics, the most notorious and prestigious international sporting event.[14] It would create opportunities for tremendous investment and send a clear signal that Rio—like Brazil—was a global player.

But first, Rio would have to curb the violence that marred its image, discouraged visitors, and imposed such a heavy burden on its population: between 2000 and 2006 the city averaged one murder every 3.5 hours, according to Rio de Janeiro state's ISP,[15] charged with gathering and analyzing public security data. During the last week of 2006, when cariocas settled in to celebrate Christmas and New Year's, a dispute among gangs and police flooded the nightly news with gruesome images of burning buses and police raids in favelas that left eighteen dead.[16] On January 1, 2007, a new governor, Sérgio Cabral, took the oath of office, promising a regime of law and order.[17]

One of Cabral's first acts was to appoint Beltrame as head of state security. Beltrame was a native of southern Brazil, an outsider to Rio de Janeiro state's notoriously corrupt police force. Few knew what to expect when he took office with a public security crisis on his hands and seven months until the start of the 2007 Pan—an event that would put Rio under unprecedented scrutiny.

Beltrame took immediate action to mitigate the influence of gang leaders, transferring those suspected of ordering attacks in Rio from local prisons to maximum-security federal penitentiaries in the far south of the country. Then, on June 27, 2007, with sixteen days to go until the Pan American Games, with a mandate from the governor and support from a federal task force, Beltrame ordered the invasion of the Complexo do Alemão.[18] This ensemble of favelas with a population of approximately 70,000 was the headquarters of Rio's most powerful criminal organization, the Comando Vermelho, or Red Command. The operation was bloody: nineteen people were killed that day. Human rights organizations denounced the massacre; independent investigations later found widespread evidence of extrajudicial executions.[19]

Over the following two weeks, 8,000 National Force and Federal Police officers poured into Rio to secure it during the Pan American Games. This made for a tense month, but one in which there were no incidents involving the national sports delegations and in which "the feeling of safety was great," according to the head of National Public Security, Luiz Fernando Corrêa.[20] The effort had the desired effect. Two months later, on September 13, 2007, Rio de Janeiro officially submitted its bid for the 2016 Olympics, with promised security improvements heavily emphasized. A month after that, FIFA gave Brazil the 2014 World Cup and another security challenge.

The Pan might have been pulled off without any attacks on tourists or athletes, as the head of national public security noted, but the heavy-handed approach to selectively ensure safety for some at the expense of others made for denunciations from human rights groups: "Murder is not an acceptable or effective crime-control technique," wrote Philip Alston, the United Nations special rapporteur on extrajudicial executions, in a report.[21] Rio would need another solution. The goal was not only to secure Rio for the Games but also to shed the image of a bloody gangland where a lethal and corrupt police force was part of the problem. The task was substantial: in 2007 active-duty police officers killed

1,330 people in the state; 902 of those deaths were in the city of Rio, according to ISP.[22]

In his first four months as governor, Cabral sought inspiration abroad. The month after he took office, he visited Bogotá and Medellín to see and hear firsthand the results of the *Plan de Convivencia y Seguridad Ciudadana*, or Plan for Coexistence and Citizen Security, developed by Hugo Acero. Built on the pillars of *mano dura* (heavy hand) and public works, the program was credited with reducing violence precipitously: during Acero's nine years as head of Bogotá's public security department (1993–2005), the city's homicide rate dropped from eighty to eighteen per 100,000. During Cabral's visit, Acero explained that it was necessary to connect public safety and citizenship, a process that started by taking back territory controlled by criminal organizations then winning over the population with social programs.[23] In April 2007, Cabral visited Rudy Giuliani, crediting the former New York mayor's "zero tolerance" approach to law enforcement with a drop in crime rates and calling his tenure "a success."[24]

THE UPP AS SOLUTION

The first opportunity to implement some of these ideas came by chance, according to Beltrame.[25] On November 18, 2008, during a torrential downpour, Rio police staged an operation in the favela of Santa Marta—a community of around 10,000 residents perched on a steep hillside in the middle-class neighborhood of Botafogo. The community was controlled by the Red Command, but internal disputes had removed its leader; one hundred officers easily occupied the favela. Only once they were in place did Beltrame call the governor and say he intended to keep them there and try something new. That was the first time he used the word *pacification*. The base established in Santa Marta would become the first in Rio state's new public security initiative.[26]

From the beginning, the implementation of the UPP intended to highlight the differences of this new approach. The Santa Marta incursion and occupation happened without a shot being fired. Once the base was established, the person appointed to command it was a charismatic woman—Captain Pricilla Azevedo. The officers recruited for the twenty-four-hour patrols were young, in a conscious decision to avoid older officers steeped in the culture of confrontation, corruption, and animosity toward favela residents.[27]

The program started without an official name or even a publicly stipulated structure, budget, or objective. The state laws that officially created the UPP, establishing it under the authority of the military police, and the one that set UPP officers aside from other military police personnel, stating that they would need differentiated training, were not signed by the governor until January 21 and 22, 2009, respectively.[28]

Despite the very basic legal parameters and the lack of any officially designated structure, objectives, or officer training specifications, the police occupied five favelas under the program's guise in its first year. The communities added immediately following Santa Marta had significant symbolic value. The second UPP was in Cidade de Deus, or City of God, which had its takeover by criminal networks portrayed by a blockbuster Brazilian film of the same name. The third one was in Jardim Batan, where in 2008 a newspaper photographer had been kidnapped and tortured by members of a militia—one of various groups of armed, off-duty state agents who abuse their access to arms to control low-income areas.[29] The other UPP units created that year were, like Santa Marta, relatively small communities nestled in Rio's touristy beachside neighborhoods: Babilônia/Chapéu Mangueira in Copacabana, and Cantagalo/Pavão-Pavãozinho, between Ipanema, Copacabana, and Lagoa.

Municipal, state, and federal authorities promoted the UPP widely within Rio, Brazil, and beyond as evidence of security improvements. Positive headlines followed as the program gathered support from the media and public opinion. Series like the award-winning *Democracia nas Favelas*, or *Democracy in Favelas*, by Rio's largest newspaper, *O Globo*, played a major role in promoting UPPs. The articles portrayed the police as a victorious force with a positive influence on the community, and the discourse about favelas was framed in terms of citizenship and participation, in contrast to traditional mainstream media approaches that had historically portrayed the communities as the source of crime or the site of violent clashes.[30] Brazil's conservative news magazine, *Veja*, awarded the head of Santa Marta's UPP, Pricilla Azevedo, its Carioca of the Year award.[31]

Most significantly, when the Brazilian delegation went to Copenhagen at the end of 2009 to argue before the International Olympic Committee (IOC) that Rio was fit to host the Olympics, Azevedo was included in the delegation. Much like the 230 repetitions of the word *security* in Rio's bid book, her presence on the podium next to the mayor of Rio, Eduardo Paes, Governor Cabral, and President Lula was a clear message to the members of the IOC: safety will not be a problem.

Indeed, Rio's presentation in Copenhagen embraced the IOC's vision of the Olympic Games as a global platform that could burnish the city's image and provide impetus for it to renew its infrastructure and overcome social problems; Azevedo's presence on the stage cast the UPP program as part of this renewal, spurred even by Rio's candidacy. As academics Darnell and Millington summarized, "The state has positioned the Games in support of economic and social development, urbanization and industrialization, environmentalism, improved security, and tourism, all of which are understood to create a secure and modern Brazil, albeit in terms commensurate with the current dominant political economy."[32]

In his speech to the IOC, Paes highlighted this aspect of Rio's proposal, telling members that the Games would "accelerate my vision for the city." More than that, he said, "the Games' master plan is the city's master plan. They are one and the same."[33] In Brazil, the security infrastructure, including the military and the civil police forces, is under the control of the state, not the city; but no matter: all three levels of government were backing the city's claim with political and financial capital.

IOC members responded to this message, choosing Rio as host of the 2016 Games, prompting an emotional celebration among the Brazilians in Copenhagen, including tears from President Lula and a raucous party along Copacabana beach.[34] Once authorities returned home, however, they had a sobering reminder of the challenges ahead.

EXPANSION

Two weeks after the IOC vote, war broke out between rival gangs for control of a favela called Morro dos Macacos, near the Maracanã Stadium, which was slated to host seven World Cup games in 2014

and Olympic events two years later. Drug traffickers shot down a police helicopter; nearly three dozen people died in the ensuing firefight,
including two officers. Ten buses were set on fire. The image of a man's
body stuffed into a shopping cart and left by the side of a road made
national and international news. The headlines that followed spread
just the kind of image that Rio de Janeiro authorities feared and were
trying to eradicate: "Twelve dead and helicopter downed as Rio de
Janeiro drug gangs go to war," in *The Guardian*,[35] and "Rio police
kill 7; total of 33 dead in drug war," in *Reuters*.[36] *The New Yorker*'s
October 2009 issue carried an article entitled, "Gangland: Who controls the streets of Rio de Janeiro?"[37]

State authorities responded by rapidly expanding the UPP program.
It went from five units with a total of 712 officers at the end of 2009 to
13 units with a total of 1,279 officers by the end of 2010—including
one unit in Morro dos Macacos.[38] In November 2010, after attacks in
which gang members torched dozens of cars and buses in retaliation
for the law enforcement offensive into their territory, a force of 2,700
police and military personnel invaded the Complexo do Alemão.[39]
This time they went in to stay, establishing UPP bases within it.

This was the largest, most complex, and most symbolic police operation to date under the UPP program. Police had not entered Alemão
since the bloodbath that preceded the Pan American Games in 2007.
Once inside, officers planted a Brazilian flag on its highest peak—a
ritual crafted to convey a strong message about state control of territory. This image was widely reproduced by local and foreign media.[40]

According to André Rodrigues, a political scientist at the Rio-
based think tank Instituto de Estudos da Religião (ISER), the Alemão
invasion generated tremendous expectations among the population.
But it was also the moment when a narrow policing program that held
some promise as a way to curb violence and heavily armed drug traffic
when deployed in a handful of smaller favelas was definitively pushed
too far: "There was a need to consolidate gains and structure the program before continuing. This didn't happen. This was the most significant factor in its later degradation."[41]

After its initial occupation in November 2010, the Complexo do
Alemão continued under army control until June 2012. Its five UPP
units required 2,000 officers, and there were simply not enough UPP
police prepared for the job.[42] However, soldiers are not trained as

police and certainly not trained in the proximity policing methods theoretically employed by the UPP program. Conflicts escalated between soldiers and local residents; in their first five months in Alemão, soldiers arrested seventy-five people for disobedience, disrespect, threatening behavior, or resistance.[43] Most significantly, the program became, in Alemão, simply an occupying force. The repercussions of this for the community and for the program's credibility would take time to unfold but would prove disastrous.

The program's growth had even outpaced the development of the regulations outlining its basic structure and establishing its goals. This only happened two months after the Alemão invasion, when state decree #42,787 was signed by the governor and published in the state register on January 7, 2011.[44] This was the first decree to institutionalize what previously had only been suggested in Beltrame's speeches and interviews. Among its measures, these were particularly noteworthy:

Article 1 laid out the program's philosophy as inspired by the principles of "proximity policing" and stipulated the criteria for targeting communities: "poor communities, with weak presence of government institutions and a high degree of informality" and "the opportunistic installation of overtly armed criminal groups." It also laid out the program's goals: "To consolidate state control of communities under strong influence of armed criminal organizations. To return to the local population the peace and tranquility needed for the full exercise of citizenship, guaranteeing social and economic development."[45]

Article 2 laid out the four steps of the program's deployment within a community: the entrance into the community; the security situation's stabilization; the UPP's implementation within the community; and, finally, evaluation and monitoring of the impact of police actions.[46]

Articles 5 and 6 established the minimum number of UPP officers per community, according to size, and specified that the UPP officers' training would have an emphasis on "human rights and in the doctrine of community policing."[47]

Essentially, the program proposed to occupy territory controlled by criminal gangs and reduce armed confrontations. According to Ignácio Cano, coordinator of the Laboratório de Análise da Violência, or Laboratory for the Analysis of Violence, at the Universidade do Estado do Rio de Janeiro (UERJ), the state university of Rio de Janeiro, this statement represented a very important paradigm shift in how the police force defined its work:

> The traditional public security policy in Rio de Janeiro consisted in periodical invasions of the slums by the police, in which they shot and killed a few members of the drug dealing groups. They left and returned a few months later to start the cycle again. It was a very detrimental policy, which killed lots of people, caused a lot of insecurity, and never dismantled any criminal circle. . . . Officers had never seen anything different. The UPP was an alternative. . . . Entering, shooting and killing was not the only way.[48]

Five new UPP units were inaugurated in 2010. By the end of 2011, after three full years of existence, the UPP program had delivered significant positive results. There were problems in Alemão, where the population chaffed under army control and alleged rights abuses during a public audience with federal prosecutors,[49] but the news elsewhere was largely positive. The most dramatic evidence of provisional success was a reduction in lethal violence: there were sixty fewer violent deaths per 100,000 residents in favelas with UPPs, according to a study coordinated by Cano.[50] A later study, which looked at different UPP favelas through 2013, found specifically that there were twenty-nine fewer police killings per 100,000 residents: a startling 60 percent reduction in lethal violence by police.[51] The dissemination of these initial results meant the UPP program had a "very strong social and political impact, with widespread and generally very positive media, eliciting great interest not only locally, but also nationally and internationally," Cano's report concludes.

INSTRUMENTALIZATION

The political acclaim and positive media coverage that followed, however merited, largely obscured the program's flaws, its narrow scope, and its reduced potential for expansion in the interest of casting its initial success as evidence of broader public security and socioeconomic development fueled by the city's embrace of megaevents. The program's promise and potential, degraded as it was, pushed into fast-paced expansion to meet a time frame and agenda that were set by the need to make the city appear safe in time for the World Cup and the Olympics. This link was established early on, during Rio's candidacy for hosting the 2016 Games. It was strengthened as the program was widely used in billboards and television advertisements by Governor Cabral and even by then candidate for president Dilma Rousseff, who said she would expand it to other states.[52]

The accelerated pace it set left little room for consolidating gains, learning from mistakes, or correcting midcourse, said Col. Robson Rodrigues, the UPP's commander until 2011: "The UPP started without a plan and laid-out objectives. We had to learn and correct the course along the way. There were positive results. But there were also political appeals, demands. It became a political platform. We fell into traps."[53]

In order to better understand how this happened, it is worth examining several factors that contributed to the discrepancy between the rhetoric and the reality of the program's expansion. First, the UPP's scope: although it was presented in the media and in political discourses as a solution for the complex security challenges in the city and state of Rio, it was never a security policy, but something much more focused: a favela policing program. Even within the universe of Rio's favelas, it was extremely restricted. The city of Rio has between 600 and 946 favelas or complexes of favelas, depending upon the definition used.[54] The state of Rio has far more. The UPP program's explicit goal was to reach forty units by 2014—a very small fraction of them.

Second, the units' locations were clearly selective. Although Beltrame repeatedly said in interviews and speeches that the program was meant to benefit locals, not Rio's preparations to host megaevents, their siting suggested otherwise: all but two of the first seventeen were in the city's affluent south side or in the part of the north side that formed a belt around the Maracanã Stadium. These would be the areas of greatest visibility and circulation during the megaevents, but they were not the areas with the greatest need. The highest homicide rates were in the outskirts of metropolitan Rio, in a region known as the Baixada Fluminense.[55] But the Baixada, far from beaches, stadiums, and Olympic venues, was largely overlooked. The Baixada region eventually got one UPP, the Mangueirinha unit, in 2014.

Third, the UPP's high cost also ruled out its expansion to the rest of the city and certainly to the remainder of the state. UPP officers required special training and unique infrastructure. One of the program's defining characteristics was the high ratio of officers to residents. Whereas the state had an average of 2.3 military police officers per 1,000 residents, the UPP program averaged sixteen officers per 1,000 residents.[56] Maintaining one hundred UPP officers cost the state about R$6 million a year ($4 million at 2011 conversion rates).[57] By the end of 2011, 3,494 UPP officers were in the field. Although Rio state's total security budget had shot up from R$2.6 billion in 2007 to R$3.7 billion in 2011 and would increase to R$5 billion in 2013, with fully 88 percent of the total going to payroll (numbers corrected for inflation), it was clear the UPP program was consuming a disproportionate amount of the security budget.[58] Expansion at this rate was clearly unsustainable.

Fourth, surveys indicated that from the start the people at the core of the program—UPP police and residents—tempered any expectations with heavy doses of skepticism about the program, its intended beneficiaries, and its future. Direct exposure to factors such as the ones mentioned above, among many others, meant UPP officers did not universally embrace the UPP program and that significant tensions remained between them and favela residents. A 2010 survey of UPP police found that despite the fact that 66 percent felt residents welcomed them, 70 percent would prefer another assignment within the police force.[59] The survey also revealed the underlying difficulties in resolving Rio's historically situated security problem. In particular, officers believed that the program's focus was ensuring safety during the World Cup and the Olympics (70 percent); that the unit locations were intended to reassure the middle class (68 percent); that the program was intended to win votes (65 percent). This was terrible for morale and performance and made for cracks in the UPP program that would widen as the program expanded.

The favela residents surveyed in 2010 placed their hopes in the UPP program even as they shared police cynicism. Although 87 percent agreed UPPs were important to reduce violence and 80 percent wanted the program to remain in their community indefinitely, 54 percent thought the program would remain in place only through the Olympics. Only 35 percent believed traffickers would not return to their community. Moreover, 80 percent recognized that there were tensions between the officers and residents, with one-fourth of youth between sixteen to twenty-five reporting police aggression during the frequent frisking to which they were subjected. Subsequent attitude surveys of UPP police and favela residents reflected deteriorating conditions, relationships, and expectations.[60]

Fifth, there was a significant delay or an outright failure, depending on the community and the specific service, to follow police intervention with the resources, civic engagement, and urban improvements that were supposed to go hand in hand with the policing effort. Despite Beltrame's repeated emphasis on the importance of social investment following police incursion into a community,[61] the UPP Social, billed as the social counterpart of the policing program, was only created in August 2010. It was implemented under the Secretaría de Estado de Assistência Social e Direitos Humanos, or the State Social Welfare and Human Rights department, then under the leadership of the economist Ricardo Henriques.[62]

This new institution's goals were to gather information about community needs, articulate connections with public and private services and civil society, and improve access to resources and services. The ultimate objective, Henriques wrote, would be to provide services and access within these communities on par with those available in any other neighborhood in Rio, thus integrating favelas served by UPPs into the urban fabric. This, in turn, would consolidate the state's territorial control.[63]

However, very soon after its creation and immediately following the 2010 state and federal elections, the UPP Social program was transferred from the authority of the state into the hands of a city planning think tank, the Instituto Pereira Passos (IPP). This weakened the link between the policing and social aspects of the program and reduced its reach. The IPP had the resources and know-how to map needs but lacked (by design) the capacity to deliver services.

Furthermore, observers repeatedly found that much like in the UPP program itself, there was a gap between discourse and reality in the workings of the UPP Social. Observers related little effective popular participation in meetings, with residents generally disbelieving the program would take their thoughts and needs into consideration.[64] IPP president Eduarda LaRocque, in a candid commentary, seemingly confirmed this perspective. Asked about the opposition of Rocinha residents to a proposed cable car project—they preferred improvements to basic sanitation—she said, "the priorities are those of the city of Rio de Janeiro as a whole. We are paying taxes to invest R$1.8 billion in Rocinha, so society as a whole has to identify the priority. (We do not) have to cater to what the favela wants."[65]

Later, then mayor Paes would sever the only remaining tie between the social program and the policing effort—the name—by rebranding it as Rio Mais Social in August 2014. The change did little to improve expectations among experts who said the city had largely failed to invest in social programs in UPP favelas. According to Ignácio Cano, of UERJ, "The UPP today is a police program. The social part is a decoration that hasn't changed the quality of life in communities."[66]

This reinforced the feeling among favela residents that the UPP was not principally a means to integrate their community into the city and connect it to resources and services, but largely a police occupation intended to serve needs that were not their own. Surveys reflect this. In 2010, 66 percent of UPP officers felt welcomed by residents; by 2012 that number dropped to 44 percent; and by 2014, to 25 percent. Officers surveyed in 2014 said residents manifested most frequently: hate/anger/hostility (36 percent); mistrust/resistance (17 percent); indifference (10 percent). This shift in attitudes came alongside the increasingly frequent evidence of drug trafficking in the community (70 percent of officers said this was very frequent by 2014) and illegal bearing of arms (35 percent said this was very frequent in 2014).[67]

Despite the growing dissociation and the perception of dissociation between the UPP's stated objectives and its reality by residents of UPP favelas and UPP officers, nine new units were created in 2012—including, finally, the ones in Alemão. Seven more were inaugurated in 2013. This expansion included the largest favela in Rio, Rocinha, and raised the number of UPP officers in the field to 5,280. As the program grew, allegations of corruption, human rights abuses, and killings by police officers, including UPP officers, mounted. In 2013 the number of people killed by Rio state police officers started to tick up again, after decreasing for six years straight. The number of deaths at the hands of police had dipped significantly, from 1,330 in 2007 to 416 in 2013. By 2014, the year of the World Cup, that number went up to 582. By 2015 it reached 644, according to ISP.[68]

One emblematic case was the disappearance of the construction worker Amarildo de Souza. He was last seen going into a UPP base in his home community of Rocinha in July 2013. Twelve UPP officers were later sentenced in connection to his torture and death. This case and a growing number of documented police abuses were a blow to the police's and specifically to the program's credibility. As Human Rights Watch's July 7, 2016, report on police violence states in its conclusion, "UPPs led to a decrease in crime and police killings initially but unlawful killings and other police abuses have played a central role in the unraveling of the project."[69]

CRISIS

The UPP program reached its breaking point in 2014. During the first semester, as Brazil geared up to welcome World Cup visitors, two UPP units were inaugurated, and police backed by the Armed Forces invaded the Maré Complex, conjoined favelas with a population of 130,000. It was a violent operation that left sixteen dead. Soldiers patrolled Maré throughout the World Cup.[70] Beltrame's promise was that the community would have its own UPP units before the Olympics. That never happened. By December 2016 there were not enough resources or trained officers to accomplish the task.

In early 2015, with shoot-outs regularly interrupting daily life in UPP favelas, governor Luiz Fernando de Souza (who succeeded Cabral in the post after serving as his vice governor) signed decree 2015/45,146 institutionalizing the UPP program and creating an executive commission to oversee it, so it would not be extinguished by a subsequent administration. Nevertheless, to favela residents the program remained firmly identified with the megaevent cycle that was coming to a close in the city: a survey of residents in twenty UPP favelas between 2014 and 2016 revealed that most believed the UPPs would end after the Olympic Games.[71]

They might be right. Independent of the program's official status and the intentions of elected officials, the finances of the state of Rio de Janeiro were so dire by 2016 that the acting governor decreed a state of financial emergency and appealed to the federal government for financial help in meeting Olympic obligations.[72] There were budget cuts across the board, with a one-third reduction for the security department.[73] Although Rio state's investment in security was more than double the investment in health and one quarter greater than the investment in education between 2008–15,[74] Beltrame's successor, Roberto Sá, took over in October 2016 a department with an estimated debt of R$500 million and a widening credibility gap.[75]

Distrust in the program, its objectives, and in the intentions of elected authorities was highest among those who ideally should have been most involved in its success, such as community leader Raull Santiago, a lifelong resident of Alemão and founder of the Papo Reto, or Straight Talk, a youth collective: "The only thing that changed with us with UPP and the Olympics was the discourse. We had interventions, we had more police, more violence, more segregation. The reality we see is the opposite of the official discourse. Public policy has to involve more than guns."[76]

CONCLUSION

By the time the 2016 Olympics opened in Rio, what started as a small, focused favela policing program that broke from existing law enforcement paradigms and had some positive initial results was largely denatured. This process took place as its laudable, if initially poorly articulated, goals and methods were subsumed under city, state, and national officials' overarching desire to present an image of Rio de Janeiro and, by extension, an image of Brazil as safe for some—tourists, investors, athletes—even if that safety came at the expense of the welfare of others—favela residents themselves. The need to control favelas and to present an image of favelas under control, that is, under law enforcement or if necessary military control, through national and international media was prioritized over the more difficult and long-term process of training officers in a new way of policing and thereby winning their confidence in the program and the trust of favela residents.

This was also true of the social aspect of the program. When long-term needs of the communities and their residents clashed with the short-term needs linked to the hosting of megaevents (as in the case of Rocinha residents who wanted basic sanitation, not an expensive but high-profile and tourist-friendly cable car to the top), the short-term, megaevent-driven objective was prioritized, even at the cost of the community's engagement and allegiance. Any long-term improvement in security within favelas would have to be linked to an improvement in standards of living within these communities. This should have meant an extension of public services such as mail delivery and trash collection on the same standards as are available in other city neighborhoods and, more than that, equal access to civil and human rights. The violence that burdens Rio and Brazil extrapolates differences in income or access to resources; it also lays in the differentiated treatment of rich and poor, even by state agents and institutions such as the police. The incorporation of favelas into the urban fabric required a different way of policing, certainly, but it also demanded much more than effective policing. The UPP Social, later renamed Rio Mais Social, failed in this role.

It is impossible to know if the UPP program would have had another, slower, and possibly more positive trajectory had the city not been chosen to host the 2016 Olympics. But by looking at the program's evolution, starting with its inception on December 2008, its rapid escalation, and its subsequent exhaustion, it is clear that the program's promise helped secure its capture and subjection to the broader political objectives that also drove Rio's candidacy: the need to improve the city's, and consequently Brazil's, image and attract investment.

Its unraveling comes at great cost in opportunities and in lives. As the UPP lost credibility, gangs began openly bearing arms again. They also began targeting UPP officers, and all officers, directly. Deaths of military police ticked up: twenty-three died on duty and sixty-five off duty in 2015; in the first ten months of 2016 alone, twenty-nine died on duty and eighty-seven off duty.[77] Scenes like the confrontation in Pavão-Pavãozinho were once again regular features in the lives of cariocas. By October 2016, 846 people had been injured or killed by stray bullets resulting from shoot-outs in Rio state, according to the police.[78]

Despite the institutionalization of the UPP program, a look at the state's finances suggests its post-Olympic future is uncertain. This is no longer a problem for the men responsible for Rio's candidacy, its preparation for the Olympics, or the UPP's escalation—Mayor Paes, Governor Cabral, President Lula, and state secretary for security Beltrame. They have all left office. One officer who remains is Maj. Pricilla Azevedo, who once went to Copenhagen to help reassure IOC officials that Rio would be a safe and agreeable place for the Games. She's now head of the program and has a daunting task ahead.

NOTES

1. Nicolás Satriano, "Tiroteio Deixa 3 Mortos E Comandante Da UPP Pavão-Pavãozinho É Ferido," *G1*, October 10, 2016 (http://g1.globo.com /rio-de-janeiro/noticia/2016/10/tiroteio-no-pavao-pavaozinho-faz-comercio -fechar-em-ipanema.html).

2. Instituto de Segurança Pública (www.isp.rj.gov.br/).

3. Ignácio Cano, Doriam Borges, and Eduardo Ribeiro, eds. *Os Donos Do Morro: Uma Avaliação Exploratória Do Impacto Das Unidades de Polícia Pacificadora (UPPs) No Rio de Janeiro*, São Paulo, Brazil (Rio de Janeiro, Brazil: Heinrich Böll Stiftung, 2012).

4. Ibid.

5. Fábio Vasconcellos, "Pesquisa Mostra Alta Aprovação Das UPPs Em Favelas, Sejam Pacificadas Ou Não," *O Globo*, December 11, 2010, (http:// oglobo.globo.com/rio/pesquisa-mostra-alta-aprovacao-das-upps-em -favelas-sejam-pacificadas-ou-nao-2911694).

6. David Biller, "Rio de Janeiro's Top Cop Resigns as Firefights Roil City," *Bloomberg*, October 11, 2016 (www.bloomberg.com/news/articles /2016-10-11/rio-de-janeiro-s-top-cop-resigns-as-firefights-roil-city).

7. Marcelo Cortes Neri, *Income Inequality on the Decade in Brazil* (Rio de Janeiro, Brazil: Fundação Getúio Vargas, May 3, 2011) (www.cps.fgv.br /cps/bd/dd/dd_eng/dd_texto_eng_MONTAGEM_2.pdf).

8. Simon Darnell and Rob Millington, "Modernization, Neoliberalism and Sports Mega-Events: Evolving Discourses in Latin America," in *Mega-*

Events and Globalization: Capital and Spectacle in a Changing World Order (Abingdon: Routledge, 2016), pp. 65–80.

9. Nelma Gusmão de Oliveira, *O Poder Dos Jogos E Os Jogos de Poder: Interesses Em Campo Na Produção Da Cidade Para O Espetáculo Esportivo* (Rio de Janeiro, Brazil: Editora UFRJ, 2015), pp. 173–96.

10. Samantha McRoskey, "Security and the Olympic Games: Making Rio an Example," *Yale Journal 5*, no. 2 (June 10, 2010) (http://yalejournal.org/article _post/security-and-the-olympic-games-making-rio-an-example/).

11. Official Rio Olympics website, question no. 23, on security at the Games.

12. Christopher Gaffney, "Between Discourse and Reality: The Un-Sustainability of Mega-Event Planning," *Sustainability 5* (2013), pp. 3926–40.

13. Juliana Barbassa, *Dancing with the Devil in the City of God: Rio de Janeiro on the Brink* (New York: Simon & Schuster, 2015), p. 81.

14. M. Curi, J. Knijnik, and G. Mascarenhas, "The Pan American Games in Rio de Janeiro 2007: Consequences of a Sport Mega-Event on a BRIC Country," *International Review for the Sociology of Sport 46*, no. 2 (June 1, 2011), pp. 140–56, doi:10.1177/1012690210388461.

15. Instituto de Segurança Pública (www.isp.rj.gov.br/).

16. "Ataques Criminosos Deixam 18 Mortos No Rio de Janeiro," *G1*, December 28, 2006 (http://g1.globo.com/Noticias/Rio/0,,AA1402220 -5606,00.html).

17. Emani Alves, "Esses Covardes Terão Uma Resposta, Diz Cabral," *Terra*, January 1, 2007.

18. Personal interview with José Mariano Beltrame, August 1, 2013.

19. Philip Alston, "Report by the Special Rapporteur on Extrajudicial, Summary or Arbitrary Executions, Philip Alston, Addendum MISSION TO BRAZIL (4-14 November 2007)," Human Rights Council, General Assembly United Nations, April 14, 2008.

20. José Carlos Mattedi, "Preparação Dos Jogos Reduziu Número de Homicídios No Rio Em 40%," *EBC*, July 26, 2007.

21. Alston, "Report by the Special Rapporteur."

22. Instituto de Segurança Pública: (www.isp.rj.gov.br/).

23. Cristina Tardáguila, "Polícia, Câmera, Ação," *Revista Piauí*, August 2010 (http://piaui.folha.uol.com.br/materia/policia-camera-acao/).

24. Bruno Garcez, "Cabral Vai a NY 'Aprender' Lições de Segurança Com Giuliani," *BBC Brasil*, April 7, 2007 (www.bbc.com/portuguese/reporterbbc /story/2007/04/070425_cabralgiulianibg.shtml).

25. Personal interview with José Mariano Beltrame.

26. Ibid.

27. Ibid.

28. Cano, Borges, and Ribeiro, *Os Donos Do Morro*.

29. Nilton Claudino, "Minha Dor Não Sai No Jornal," *Revista Piauí*, August 2011 (http://piaui.folha.uol.com.br/materia/minha-dor-nao-sai-no-jornal/).

30. César Tartáglia, "Há Democracia Nas Favelas?" *O Globo*, August 2009 (http://memoria.oglobo.globo.com/jornalismo/premios-jornalisticos/haacute -democracia-nas-favelas-9216055).

31. "Os Cariocas Do Ano de 2009," *Veja*, November 27, 2012 (http:// vejario.abril.com.br/cidades/cariocas-do-ano-2009/).

32. Darnell and Millington, "Modernization, Neoliberalism and Sports Mega-Events."

33. McRoskey, "Security and the Olympic Games."

34. Juliet Macur, "Rio de Janeiro Is Awarded 2016 Olympics," *New York Times*, October 2, 2009.

35. Tom Phillips, "Twelve Dead and Helicopter Downed as Rio de Janeiro Drug Gangs Go to War," *The Guardian*, October 17, 2009.

36. Pedro Fonseca, "Rio Police Kill 7; Total of 33 Dead in Drug War," *Reuters*, October 22, 2009 (www.reuters.com/article/us-brazil-violence -idUSTRE59K5JE20091022).

37. Jon Lee Anderson, "Gangland: Who Controls the Streets of Rio de Janeiro?" *The New Yorker*, May 10, 2009 (www.newyorker.com/magazine /2009/10/05/gangland).

38. Data compiled from Secretaria de Segurança do Estado do Rio de Janeiro (www.rj.gov.br/web/seseg/exibeconteudo?article-id=1349728).

39. Fabio Grellet, "Prisões No Alemão Ficam Aquém Do Esperado," *Último Segundo*, November 28, 2010 (http://ultimosegundo.ig.com.br/brasil /rj/prisoes-no-alemao-ficam-aquem-do-esperado/n1237841795311.html).

40. Ana Cluadia Costa, "Polícia Invade Complexo Do Alemão," *O Globo*, November 28, 2010 (http://oglobo.globo.com/rio/policia-invade-complexo -do-alemao-2919504).

41. Personal interview with André Rodrigues, June 11, 2015.

42. "Exército Continua No Alemão E Na Penha Até Junho de 2012, Diz Governo," *G1*, August 30, 2011 (http://g1.globo.com/rio-de-janeiro/noticia /2011/08/exercito-continua-no-alemao-e-na-penha-ate-junho-de-2012-diz -governo.html).

43. Sergio Vieira, "Moradores Dos Complexos Do Alemão E Penha Acusam Exército de Abuso de Poder," *R7*, November 18, 2011 (http://noticias.r7.com /rio-de-janeiro/noticias/moradores-dos-complexos-do-alemao-e-penha -acusam-exercito-de-abuso-de-poder-20111118.html).

44. Sérgio Cabral, "Decréto No 42.787 de 06 de Janeiro de 2011. Dispõe Sobre a Implantaçao, Estrutura, Atuação e Funcionamento Das Unidades de Polícia Pacificadora (UPP) No Estado Do Rio de Janeiro E Dá Outras Providências," *Diário Oficial Do Estado Do Rio de Janeiro*, July 1, 2011.

45. Ibid., p. 2.

46. Ibid.

47. Ibid.

48. Personal interview with Ignácio Cano, August 23, 2016.

49. "Permanência Do Exército No Complexo Do Alemão Causa Polêmica Entre Moradores," *BBC Brasil*, November 18, 2011 (www.bbc.com /portuguese/ultimas_noticias/2011/11/111118_alemao_rio_exercito_rn .shtml?print=1).

50. Cano, Borges, and Ribeiro, *Os Donos Do Morro*.

51. Beatriz Magaloni, Vanessa Melo, and Edgar Franco, "Killing in the Slums: An Impact Evaluation of Police Reform in Rio de Janeiro," Working paper (Stanford, Calif.: Center on Democracy, Development, and the Rule of Law, December 2015) (https://cddrl.fsi.stanford.edu/publication/killing -slums-impact-evaluation-police-reform-rio-de-janeiro).

52. "UPP Vira Marca Da Campanha de Dilma E Cabral No Rio," *Estado de São Paulo*, August 11, 2010.

53. Personal interview with Robson Rodrigues, June 11, 2015.

54. Luciana Nunes Leal, "Ninguém Sabe Quantas Favelas Existem No Rio," *Estado de São Paulo*, December 11, 2011 (http://sao-paulo.estadao .com.br/noticias/geral,ninguem-sabe-quantas-favelas-existem-no-rio-imp -,809440).

55. Cano, Borges, and Ribeiro, *Os Donos Do Morro*.

56. Ibid.

57. André Paino, "Governo Gasta R$60 Mil Por Ano Por Cada Policial de UPP, Diz Beltrame," *R7*, June 21, 2011 (http://noticias.r7.com/rio-de -janeiro/noticias/governo-gasta-r-60-mil-por-ano-para-cada-policial-de -upp-diz-beltrame-20110621.html).

58. Vinícius Matos Alves, "The Cost of Violence: The Case of Rio de Janeiro," Paper for The Institute of Brazilian Business & Public Management Issues, The Minerva Program (Washington, D.C.: The George Washington University, n.d.) (www2.gwu.edu/~ibi/minerva/Fall2014/Vinicius_Alves.pdf).

59. Julita Lemgruber et al., "O Que Pensam Os Policiais Das UPPs," *Ciência Hoje* 49, no. 294 (July 2012), pp. 34–39.

60. Ibid.

61. Elenilce Bottari and Liane Gonçalves, "Beltrame Quer Pressa Em Investimentos Sociais Pós-UPPs: 'Nada Sobrevive Só Com Segurança,' " *O Globo*, May 28, 2011 (http://oglobo.globo.com/rio/beltrame-quer-pressa-em -investimentos-sociais-pos-upps-nada-sobrevive-so-com-seguranca-2764060).

62. Ricardo Henriques and Silvia Ramos, *UPP Social: Açõs Sociais Para a Consolidação Da Pacificação* (Rio de Janeiro, Brazil: Instituto de Economia, Universidade Federal do Rio de Janeiro, 2011) (www.ie.ufrj.br/datacenterie /pdfs/seminarios/pesquisa/texto3008.pdf).

63. Ibid.

64. Tom Smith, "UPP Social and Participation: How Not to Integrate Rio," *RioOnWatch*, December 6, 2011 (www.rioonwatch.org/?p=2592).

65. Ed Bentsi-Enchill, Jessica Goodenough, and Michel Berger, "The Death of UPP Social: Failing to Make Participation Work," *RioOnWatch*. March 30, 2015 (www.rioonwatch.org/?p=17660).

66. Geoffrey Ramsey, "Making Rio's Pacification Work: The Limits of 'UPP Social,'" *InSight Crime*, August 22, 2014 (www.insightcrime.org/news -analysis/rio-pacification-limits-upp-social).

67. Leonarda Musumeci, "'Eles Nos detestam.' Tropeços Do Policiamento de Proximidade Em Favelas. Resultados Da Pesquisa UPP: O Que Pensam Os Policias, 2014," *Boletim de Segurança E Cidadania*, November 2015.

68. Instituto de Segurança Pública, or Institute for Public Safety (www .isp.rj.gov).

69. "'Good Cops Are Afraid,'" *Human Rights Watch*, July 7, 2016 (www .hrw.org/report/2016/07/07/good-cops-are-afraid/toll-unchecked-police -violence-rio-de-janeiro).

70. Gustavo Maia, "Após Polícia Matar 16 Em 15 Dias, Exército Ocupa Complexo Da Maré, No Rio," *UOL Noticias*, April 5, 2014 (http://noticias .uol.com.br/cotidiano/ultimas-noticias/2014/04/05/exercito-inicia -patrulhamento-na-mare-na-manha-deste-sabado.htm).

71. Márcio Grijo Vilarouca and Ludmila Ribeiro, "Dimensionamento Dos Impactos Sociais Das UPPs Em Favelas Cariocas," *FGV and UFMG*, June 21, 2016.

72. Carina Bacelar, "Dornelles, Governador Interino Do Rio, Decreta Estado de Calamidade Pública," *O Globo*, June 17, 2016 (http://oglobo.globo .com/rio/dornelles-governador-interino-do-rio-decreta-estado-de-calamidade -publica-19529791).

73. Flávia Villela, "Beltrame Diz Que Investimento Na Segurança Do Rio É 'Praticamente Zero,'" *Agência Brasil*, March 21, 2016 (http://agenciabrasil .ebc.com.br/geral/noticia/2016-03/investimentos-na-seguranca-do-rio -chegam-praticamente-zero-diz-beltrame).

74. For the investment figures, see http://br.transparencia.gov.br/tem/ ?estado=RJ.

75. Marco Antônio Martins, "Sucessor de Beltrame Assume Seseg Com Dívida de R$100 Milhões," *G1*, October 17, 2016 (http://g1.globo.com/rio -de-janeiro/noticia/2016/10/sucessor-de-beltrame-assume-seseg-com-divida -de-r-100-milhoes.html).

76. Personal interview with Raull Santiago, July 28, 2016.

77. Number of on-duty military police deaths comes from the Instituto de Segurança Pública, or Institute for Public Safety (www.isp.rj.gov.br); the number of off-duty military police deaths comes from the Fórum Brasileiro

de Segurança Pública, or Brazilian Forum for Public Safety (www.forumse
guranca.org.br).

78. "Segundo Polícia Civil, Rio Teve 846 Vítimas de Bala Perdida Só
Este Ano," *O Globo*, October 27, 2016 (http://oglobo.globo.com/rio/segundo
-policia-civil-rio-teve-846-vitimas-de-bala-perdida-so-este-ano-20373021).

EIGHT

Green Games

The Olympics, Sustainability, and Rio 2016

JULES BOYKOFF

In November 2015 Brazilian President Dilma Rousseff appeared at the Rio 2016 Organizing Committee's headquarters brandishing a plaque with the "10 Commandments of the Rio 2016 Games." Members of the media were on hand to capture the moment, cameras snapping and flashing. The plaque was a gift from Rio's mediagenic mayor Eduardo Paes, a politician well versed in the art of the photo-op. The list of "commandments" was noticeably fuzzy, promising to "deliver a better city after the Games" and to "deliver more than you promised." The list also lacked any mention of environmental upgrades.[1] To many, this was puzzling. After all, creating a positive environmental legacy was a significant element in Rio de Janeiro's original Olympic bid as well as a well-traveled mantra of the International Olympic Committee (IOC).

In an opening letter to then IOC President Jacques Rogge, Brazilian aspirants vowed that their Olympic plan "covers all aspects of the Games preparation and delivery plan as well as the all-important pre- and post-Games legacies. These legacies will strengthen the social and environmental fabric of Rio and of Brazil as well as developing sport throughout South America." The letter, which was signed by Brazil's President Luiz Inácio Lula da Silva, State of Rio de Janeiro Governor Sérgio Cabral, Rio Mayor Eduardo Paes, and Carlos Nuzman, the president of the Brazilian Olympic Committee, vowed that "Even in the current difficult global economic climate, we can guarantee that funding for Rio 2016 is secure and that the Brazilian economy is stable."[2] Little did they know that the Brazilian economy would falter in 2015, suffering its worst recession in more than a century, and that a political maelstrom would slam the country less than six months before the Games commenced. This sharp economic downturn would affect Rio 2016 organizers' ability to follow through on their bold environmental promises, and they were already far behind schedule. The political mayhem, in which Brazil's democracy was at stake as President Rousseff faced impeachment, would pull attention away from the Games, with the Olympics and its ecological pledges sliding down the priority list.

The Olympic movement's concern with ecological issues stretches back at least as far as the Sapporo 1972 Winter Games in Japan. The official report from those Olympics mentioned that organizers afforded special consideration to "environmental conditions" and "environmental development."[3] By the 1990s, the IOC began to concertedly fold ecological concerns into its official rhetoric. In the twenty-first century, vowing to hold sustainable Games has become de rigueur for aspiring host cities. This article charts the evolution of environmental argot vis-à-vis the Olympic Games before offering an examination of sustainability promises made ahead of the 2016 Summer Olympics in Rio de Janeiro. How much has ecological rhetoric lived up to reality in Rio?

ENVIRONMENTAL SUSTAINABILITY
AND THE OLYMPICS

With ecological considerations in mind, organizers of the Sapporo 1972 Games gestured in a green direction when they decided to construct ski jumps in ways that minimized their environmental impact: "In order that the jump site be in harmonious balance with the beautiful natural environment of the Miyanomori area, the alteration of terrain features was kept to a minimal necessity."[4] Yet, construction of the downhill ski course—and its concomitant ecological destruction—gave rise to public outcry. As the Sapporo 1972 final report noted:

> Since the downhill courses were to be located on the slopes of Mt. Eniwa, which commands a panoramic view of Lake Shikotsu and is situated in Shikotsu-Toya National Park, the clearing of virgin forest and the alteration of the original geographical features came into question, a matter which also gave rise to not a little objection from the public. It was recognized, however, that Mt. Eniwa was the only mountain within easy access of Sapporo which could meet the conditions required for the downhill courses. Consequently, the government offices concerned, with the consent of the Natural Park Council, granted their permission for the course, on the condition that all the related course facilities be removed and that the terrain in the affected area be permanently restored to its original state.[5]

This account affords a glimpse at the tension and complexities that Olympics organizing committees face when trying to carry out green Games. The demands for Olympics-standard facilities can clash with environmental conservation. An awareness of environmentalism does not automatically translate to meaningful material policies with positive environmental outcomes. The state of exception that the Olympics inherently bring can give rise to practices that slice against publicly proclaimed rhetoric.

In the wake of Sapporo 1972, the environment became contentious political terrain in the context of the Olympic Games. The possibility of environmental destruction in the area around Denver, Colorado, led citizens of that city to rise up and challenge the IOC in the early 1970s after the sport body awarded Denver the right to host the 1976 Winter Olympics. Organizations like the Rocky Mountain Center on Environment and Protect Our Mountain Environment spearheaded an activist campaign that pressured IOC officials to relocate the Games. These groups helped start a petition drive that demanded a state referendum on a $5 million bond issue that would fund the

Denver Olympics. They eventually emerged victorious in a public vote in November 1972, winning convincingly with 60 percent support. With taxpayer funding undercut, the IOC had no choice but to move the 1976 Winter Games to Innsbruck, Austria. This made Denver the first city to rebuff the Games after having been granted them.[6] Environmental awareness sat at the core of the political fightback.

In 1987, the World Commission on Environment and Development—known as the Brundtland Commission—published a report that injected new lingo into the environmental debate: sustainable development. The commission defined the concept as "development that meets the needs of the present without compromising the ability of future generations to meet their own needs."[7] Five years later, the United Nations (UN) took the baton from the Brundtland Commission when it came together for the "Earth Summit" in Rio de Janeiro. The conference culminated with the UN publishing the "Rio Declaration on Environment and Development," which adumbrated future collaboration on sustainability issues. The document advocated the idea that economic development should not proceed full-steam ahead without serious environmental consideration.[8]

Meanwhile, the IOC was firming up its emergent links with the UN. Less than two months after the "Rio Earth Summit" the IOC advanced a symbolic "Earth Pledge" that gingerly charged Olympic officials with "making the Earth a safe place."[9] But the 1992 Winter Olympics in Albertville, France, would put even that tepid principle to the test. Olympics scholars across the board have dubbed those Games an ecological debacle. In creating an Olympics-standard bobsled track, Nordic ski runs, and other Olympic structures, significant environmental degradation occurred.[10]

The 1994 Lillehammer Winter Games served as an antidote to the Albertville calamity. Spearheaded by local environmental activists, a fruitful collaboration emerged between Norwegian elected officials, Olympics planners, and environmentalists to forge a specific sustainability plan. The Norwegian Ministry of the Environment took a lead role, hoping to convert the ideas of the Brundtland Commission into meaningful policies. Activists from the Lillehammer chapter of the Norwegian Environmental Organization jumpstarted an initiative called Project Environmental Olympics. They pushed the Lillehammer Organizing Committee to adopt a more active role.[11] But even with this success story, Jon Helge Lesjø argues, "the slogan of an 'environmental Olympics' did not change the IOC in any substantive fashion." Rather, "The IOC simply deployed the marketing strategy of 'corporate environmentalism.'"[12] "Moreover," Lesjø continues, "the environmental 'shift' at Lillehammer came after the most important decisions affecting local surroundings had already been made."[13] Ecological victory was largely symbolic, he argues.

After the Lillehammer Games, the IOC sniffed opportunity. President Juan Antonio Samaranch proclaimed his wish to put "the Olympic Games at the service of the quest for excellence, solidarity and respect of the environment." He added, "United by and for sport, the Olympic Movement can and must mobilize itself to make its contribution to the protection of the planet Earth and the wellbeing of mankind."[14] Such broad-brush edicts would soon become firmly embedded in IOC rhetoric. At the IOC's 1994 Olympic Congress it proclaimed the environment as "an essential component of Olympism."[15] In 1995, the IOC adapted the *Olympic Charter* so that "the Olympic Games are held in conditions which demonstrate a responsible concern for environmental issues."[16] That year the IOC also inaugurated a Sport and Environment Commission that would meet each year to discuss environmental themes, programs, and procedures; this built from a 1994 cooperative agreement with the UN Environment Programme (UNEP).[17] Since 2009 the IOC has been a Permanent Observer at the UN.[18]

In October 1999, the IOC established "Agenda 21," echoing the program of the same name put forth by the UN in 1992 after the "Earth Summit." In doing so, the IOC aspired "to integrate sustainable development into their policies and activities" and "encourage all individuals . . . to behave in such a way as to ensure that their sporting activities and their lifestyles play a part in sustainable development."[19] Eventually the IOC made sustainability "the third pillar of Olympism," astride sport and culture.[20] Sport scholars Graeme Hayes and John Karamichas assert that despite bumps along the green road, "the Olympics now generally operates as an international showcase for the development and dissemination of environmental and sustainable best practice."[21] Yet, they also point out that while knowledge transfer may flourish, the megaevent-driven brand of environmentalism "rarely addresses, in any systemic way, one of the fundamental principles of sustainable development: the inclusion of civic publics in deliberative or participatory forms of decision-making."[22] The Games remain a top-down, elite-driven affair, with little meaningful input from everyday people in the host city when it comes to environmental planning.

The Sydney Summer Olympics of 2000 was a primetime testing ground for the IOC's proclaimed environmental concerns. The Sydney Organizing Committee partnered with Green Games Watch and Greenpeace Australia, which were to serve as ecological watchdogs.[23] Mass media generally proclaimed the Games to be a smashing green success. The Sydney Games official report echoed the media consensus: "The environment record of the Sydney 2000 organisations was one of the shining achievements of the Sydney 2000 Olympic Games. From the earliest days, commitment to the highest standards of environmental achievement were a hallmark of Sydney's Games."[24] The Sydney Games galvanized the improvement of local waterways, tree planting to offset carbon emissions, and the implementation of solar power within the Olympic village. Still, as the Games approached, the Wilderness Society of Australia's national campaign director, Kevin Parker, categorized Olympics organizers' efforts as "sophisticated greenwashing"—publicly voicing concern for the environment and claiming credit for providing solutions while in reality doing very little, if anything at all. He added, "It is breathtakingly hypocritical of Australia to portray itself to the rest of the world as environmentally sensitive when our environment is under a greater threat than ever."[25] And when Greenpeace issued its Sydney 2000 report card, organizers were only awarded a bronze medal, scoring six on a scale of ten points. After all, Sydney organizers had staged the beach volleyball competition at Bondi Beach, an ecologically sensitive area.[26] In any case, the Sydney Olympics led to the institution of the now-familiar trope whereby Olympics organizers claim their event "the greenest Games to date."

Critics maintain that the IOC has rhetorically proclaimed the ecological word while doing little by way of green deed. Post-Games accountability has been a significant issue. The IOC tends to move on to the next Olympic Games while local officials, with the Olympics in the rearview mirror, tend to move on to other priorities. Lawyer Marc Zemel has argued that the IOC "has not used its power to impose specific binding requirements or regulations to achieve its objectives" even though theoretically the group "has the power to impose legally binding environmental requirements."[27] This dearth of postevent environmental accountability has facilitated the practice of greenwashing. Academic researchers examining the 2006 Winter Games in Turin found a similar pattern. The "negative impact on the environment" was a consistent concern among Torino 2006 participants they interviewed. This included "the negative change of the landscape associated with the construction of the sports facilities" as well as "the lack of real attention to environmental issues by local administrators" and Torino's Olympic organizing committee.[28]

This slippage between rhetoric and reality featured at the 2008 Beijing Summer Olympics. Beijing bid organizers launched their campaign with a decidedly green slogan: "Green Olympics, High-tech Olympics, the People's Olympics." Yet Beijing painted a mixed picture in regard to ecological follow-through. On one hand, the Chinese government built several wastewater treatment plants, constructed brand-new public transportation lines, improved vehicle emission standards, and introduced water conservation methods. Chinese officials also relocated approximately two hundred heavily polluting industries before the Games opened.[29] Still, air quality was a real concern. In the weeks prior to the Games, the government imposed drastic measures to improve air quality; it closed down factories, made power plants use alternative fuels, assigned cars to an every-other-day schedule, and forbade heavily polluting vehicles from entering Beijing. These policies helped reduce pollutants during the Olympic Games, with harmful concentrates of carbon monoxide (CO), nitrogen oxides (NOx), and sulfur dioxide (SO_2), black carbon, and benzene decreasing significantly.[30] This led to higher birth weights for babies born to mothers pregnant during the Beijing Games.[31] However, these measures were repealed after the Games, with some pollutant levels returning to their previous—and dangerous—levels.[32] Such political decisions gave greenwashing grist to critics.

After the 2010 Vancouver Olympics, Games supporters once again proclaimed the event to be "the greenest Games ever." On one hand, one group of scholars argued that the Games' purported sustainability values were a "social leveraging" opportunity that helped Vancouver with its subsequent "Greenest City" branding initiative, which was "an effort to capitalize on the Olympic moment."[33] On the other hand, greenhouse gas emissions rose sharply during the Olympics. Also, an expansion of the Sea-to-Sky highway that connected the City of Vancouver to venues in Whistler endangered animal life, such as the red-legged frog, as well as nesting locations for the bald eagle and many other protected migratory bird species. When local people raised serious questions about these issues, "the government of British Columbia rode roughshod over citizen opposition."[34]

At the 2012 Summer Olympics in London, the issue of greenwashing once again slid to the fore when organizers conceived of "sustainability partners," a new category of sponsor for the Games. Six sponsors were named: BP, BMW, BT, Cisco, EDF Energy, and GE. This raised eyebrows since BP had inadvertently spilled massive amounts of oil into the U.S. Gulf Coast in 2010.[35] The Commission for a Sustainable London 2012, an independent watchdog group set up to monitor London 2012 sustainability practices, revealed that becoming a "sustainability sponsor" required no special credentials.[36] It was a pay-to-play partnership. Numerous activist groups carried out public actions challenging London 2012 on environmental grounds.[37]

As the 2014 Winter Olympics in Sochi, Russia, commenced, UN Secretary-General Ban Ki-moon publicly stated that the UN and IOC were "a team" that was "joining forces for our shared ideals. Sustainability. Universality. Solidarity. Non-discrimination. The fundamental equality of all people."[38] Yet, according to environmentalists, the Sochi Games were notable for their ecological destruction: Olympics construction projects disregarded environmental regulations and flouted the environmental impact assessment process. Further, venue and infrastructure construction damaged the sensitive mountain landscape around Sochi, diminishing biodiversity. By 2010, Greenpeace and the World Wildlife Fund were asserting that Russia's state-owned construction firm Olympstroi was responsible for dumping heavy metals and industrial waste into local waterways. In February 2013, the Russia-based group Environmental Watch on North Caucasus notified the IOC that deforestation and the discharge of toxic effluents had degraded the natural landscape.[39]

In December 2014, the IOC unanimously passed "Olympic Agenda 2020," a collection of forty recommendations (that is, 20+20). These recommendations—not to be confused with full-force policies— were a concerted effort to rekindle interest in hosting the Olympics and burnish the Olympic brand. At the 2014 Sochi Winter Olympics, Games organizers spent at least $51 billion, which was more than all previous Winter Olympics combined. By some estimates around $30 billion was siphoned off through corruption.[40] The Olympics had taken a reputational hit, and the IOC sprung into action, focusing on cutting spending and increasing transparency. Olympic Agenda 2020 also aspired to "include sustainability in all aspects of the Olympic Games" and to "include sustainability within the Olympic Movement's daily operations."[41] Since passing the recommendations, the IOC has begun implementing a few, though it has been sluggish to translate general sustainability principles into specific, toothy policies. Critiques of the Olympic movement's sustainability policies would emerge again in the lead-up to the Summer Olympics in Rio de Janeiro, where environmental themes were woven thickly through the city's initial bid.

RIO 2016 SUMMER OLYMPICS: GREEN GAMES?

Rio de Janeiro has a long history of backing environmentalism. As mentioned, the city hosted the 1992 UN Earth Summit and another iteration of the conference in 2012, Rio+20. In November 2015 the Pew Research Center found that 86 percent of Brazilians said that climate change is a very serious problem deserving of concern; this was more than any of the forty countries polled, including France, India, Japan, Germany, and the United States.[42] Would the Rio Olympics, which took place from August 5–21, 2016, follow in this eco-minded tradition?

Rio's bid documents asserted that this would certainly be the case. After all, the directive from the top was clear. An IOC questionnaire distributed to cities bidding on the Olympics to help them organize their plans and pitches directly encouraged environmental planning. The document mentioned the environment more than seventy times and included "Environment and Meteorology" as an explicit theme. A "key message" in the questionnaire stated, "As a responsible organisation, the IOC wants to ensure that host cities and residents are left with the best possible legacy in terms of venues, infrastructure, environment, expertise and experience."[43] In the twenty-first century, every Olympic host-city aspirant is expected to enumerate a bold list of "legacy" projects that will remain after the Games: policies, programs, and infrastructure that will benefit residents of the host city for many years into the future. Modern bids come chockfull of "legacy" projects that gleam green.

The Rio 2016 candidature file, submitted to the IOC in 2009, made environmental legacy a primary selling point. In order to secure public support (the IOC reviews polling numbers of would-be host cities), Rio 2016 bidders anted up more than twenty-five legacies; approximately half of them were directly or indirectly related to environmental issues.[44] In describing their vision and legacy plans, bidders wrote that the Games would "accelerate the implementation, and in some cases the initiation, of major sustainability projects, including those related to environmentally sensitive sites, air quality and waterways."[45]

A critical discourse analysis of the Rio 2016 bid books carried out by urban geographer Christopher Gaffney found that *environment* (and derivative words such as *environmental*) was the second-most frequently used term, behind only *security*. (The prevalence of *security* made sense, since in 2004 and 2012 when Rio applied for the Olympics it was criticized for lacking a proper security infrastructure.) Gaffney found that the bidders also featured the word *sustainability*; it appeared three times as often as *education* and eleven times more often than *citizen*.[46] Rio boosters reinforced its green message throughout the bid: "The 2016 Games will accelerate several important environmental projects bringing direct benefits to local communities including regeneration of urban areas, air quality improvement and reduced consumption of non-renewable natural resources."[47] Bidders also hailed Brazil's "excellent legal and regulatory instruments" related to the environment.[48] They vowed that the local, state, and federal governments would work effectively together to ensure that "the Rio 2016 Games in Rio will catalyze the environmental policies and programs" related to "the Rio 2016's Sustainability Management Plan" replete with its "three pillars" of "planet, people, [and] prosperity." The basic idea was to "integrate economic, environmental and social elements into the 'Green Games for a Blue Planet' vision for the Rio Games."[49]

Rio was vying with Chicago, Madrid, and Tokyo for the 2016 Games. After receiving the bids, the IOC Evaluation Commission visited each aspiring host city to assess the feasibility of each candidature and to issue a technical report that compared the plans of each candidate city. The commission visited Rio de Janeiro from April 29 through May 2, 2009, and walked away from the experience impressed with Rio's environmental vision. The commission reported, "A feature of Rio's plans is the cleaning and regeneration of Rio's waterways and lakes through government projects for major new water treatment and sewerage works and education campaigns." It further noted, "Other Games legacies would include the reforestation of areas of the city, improved air quality standards and public transport systems."[50] The commission's summary of the Rio bid asserted that the Rio 2016 plans were "closely aligned with general development plans and the social needs of the city" and hammered home the point that the city's waterways would be a major beneficiary of the Games. The presentations and documentation provided by Rio 2016 bidders were deemed "detailed and of a very high quality."[51]

Despite the IOC Evaluation Commission's enthusiasm, implementing Rio's sustainability plans proved problematic. While there were some modest positive strides made in the environmental field, especially in regard to public transport upgrades, a significant gap emerged between bid rhetoric and empirical reality. The broken promises were especially distressing for cariocas experiencing a sense of megaevent déjà vu: when Rio hosted the Pan American Games in 2007, promoters promised water cleanup and improved living conditions. However, the waterways were not remediated and organizers made the mistake of constructing the athlete village on ecologically sensitive peat land.[52]

The Rio 2016 bid documents made the construction of a "High Performance Transport Ring" a predominant post-Games legacy with important environmental implications. Transport was a prime element in the plans for "technical excellence," one of four "key principles of the Rio 2016 Games concept." Bidders promised to plunge $5 billion dollars into big transportation improvements "to be completed by 2015, with a dedicated Olympic Lane network at Games time, enabling significantly reduced travel times for all Games clients."[53] (This alluded to special, VIP driving lanes that recent hosts—for example, London 2012—have set up to transport IOC members, athletes, medics, and corporate sponsors. Under this regime, everyday people were barred. Thus, critics in London called them "Zil lanes" in honor of Soviet-era fast-lanes exclusively for Politburo elite).[54]

The bid described how the four Olympic pods where the sports events would take place would be linked via mass transit routes and with "critical city areas," which would create a "sustainable transport legacy."[55] It also promised an airport upgrade, an extension of the Metro line that would stretch service from the South Zone's General Osorio Station to Barra de Tijuca in the western zone where many Olympic venues were to be located, and the creation of three Bus Rapid Transit (BRT) systems. An idea that originated in Brazil, the BRT is, according to the bid, "an innovative, environmentally-friendly, high capacity mass transit system operating on exclusive right-of-way lanes that transfers the strengths of a rail system to road transport."[56] The Metro extension—known as Linha 4, or Line 4—would be a significant stride forward; with traffic between the tourist-friendly *Zona Sul* and the Olympic epicenter in Barra da Tijuca perpetually snarled, the metro promised thirteen-minute rides when trips by car could take up to two hours. After the Games Linha 4 would remain in place for all to use. This is precisely what bidders meant when they heralded a "sustainable transport legacy."[57]

Despite ambitious transportation plans, construction lagged behind schedule. In fall 2015 the opening date for Linha 4 was pushed back to early July 2016, merely a month before the Games commenced.[58]

Then, less than six months before the Games were scheduled to begin, Brazilian media behemoth *O Globo* reported that Mayor Paes was warning the IOC that there was a "high risk" that the new metro line to Barra da Tijuca might not be ready in time for the Olympics and that he was proposing a provisional bus system as a second-best alternative.[59] In the end, Linha 4 opened less than a week before the Games. It was only available to Olympics ticket holders who also bought a special R$25 Olympics day pass. Everyday residents of Rio were out of luck.

Beyond the delayed construction schedule, the transport upgrades entailed widespread eviction of Rio residents as well as fare hikes and the deletion of bus lines that served low-income populations, as the Rio-based activist group *Comitê Popular da Copa do Mundo e das Olimpíadas* (Popular Committee for the World Cup and Olympics) pointed out in a research dossier.[60] Rio bid documents optimistically stated, "All 2016 spectators and workforce will enjoy free travel to Games events and workplaces by public transport."[61] But by January 2016, in the throes of economic crisis, organizers reneged on this promise, announcing that metro travel during peak hours would require a special Olympics pass, selling for $6 a day, $17 for three days, or $39 for a week.[62] Ordinary cariocas would also have to pay, after MetrôRio announced a fare hike from R$3.70 to R$4.10, set for April 2016.[63]

Additional environmental promises were also appearing quixotic. In order to offset carbon emissions, the Rio 2016 bid vowed to plant twenty-four million trees by Games time.[64] The secretary for the environment for the state of Rio de Janeiro proceeded to raise the stakes in 2012, promising thirty-four million trees. However, by 2014, the official "Rio 2016 Sustainability Report" conspicuously neglected to mention tree-planting progress. This did not stop Rio organizers from launching an "Embrace Sustainability" program; Dow—the "official chemistry company of the Olympic Games"—became the first sponsor.[65] Eventually Rio 2016 named additional sustainability "partners"—Cisco, Coca-Cola, Embratel, Estácio, and EY—although, like London 2012, it was never clear what these corporations actually did, other than pay the requisite dues, in order to earn the environmental moniker.[66] In May 2015, Brazil's state secretary for the environment admitted that fewer than six million saplings had been planted. On that pace, Rio 2016 would only plant around eight million trees by the time the Games opened, fewer than one-fourth of the promised amount.[67]

Then there were Rio de Janeiro's waterways. As with plans for the 2007 Pan American Games, the Rio Olympic bid pledged to clean up Guanabara Bay, host of the sailing event, and the Lagoa Rodrigo de Freitas, slated to host rowing as well as some canoeing and kayaking events. The bid stated that two sanitation upgrade systems—one installed at Barra-Jacarepaguá in western Rio and the other at Guanabara Bay—would "result in more than 80% of overall sewage collected and treated by 2016."[68] However, Luiz Fernando Pezão, the governor of the state of Rio de Janeiro, pushed back the goal for Guanabara Bay to 2035.[69] River Treatment Units (RTUs) vital to the recovery of Jacarepaguá basin were simply not installed.[70]

In July 2015, only a year before the Games commenced, the Associated Press (AP) produced an investigative report in conjunction with Brazilian virologist Fernando Spilki of Feevale University that determined every Olympics water venue unsafe. Spilki's scientific testing found astronomical levels of human waste in the water that contributed to "dangerously high levels of viruses and bacteria." Rio residents put their health at risk. So did athletes who would participate at the Games. Everyone was susceptible to "explosive diarrhea, violent vomiting, respiratory trouble and other illnesses." Imbibing three teaspoons of the polluted water afforded a 99 percent chance of infection by virus, although that did not necessarily mean that individual would fall ill.[71]

In December 2015, AP released results from a second round of testing, which found the Olympics venues were "as rife with pathogens far offshore as they are nearer land." This had direct implications for Olympic athletes: the water in which they would compete—even if far from the polluted shoreline—would not be diluted of dangerous pathogens. The risks to everyday residents of Rio were more long-term—once the athletes vacated their city after the Games, cariocas would remain—and were thus even more grim. AP found no improvement from the tests it ran in July, where virus-inducing human sewage was found "at levels up to 1.7 million times what would be considered highly alarming in the U.S. or Europe." The lack of progress did not bode well for swift improvement prior to the Olympic Games. Plus, Rio organizers and the IOC refused to carry out viral testing for athletes, citing World Health Organization (WHO) standards that only required bacterial testing for water quality. Rio's Olympics venues sometimes fell within the safe range for fecal bacterial levels even while viral contamination spiked to astronomical levels.[72]

Meanwhile, Mario Moscatelli, a Brazilian biologist and professor at the Central University of the City of Rio de Janeiro, bluntly stated, "Guanabara Bay does not offer the boating safety conditions, nor water quality to [host] the events of the Olympics." He added that local officials "never had any real interest to do anything to please the Bay's environment." Moscatelli advised Olympic athletes to receive vaccinations for Hepatitis A before Olympic competition.[73] In early 2016, the United States Olympic Committee advised that athletes participating in outdoor water sports do just that.[74] In contrast, IOC officials joked about the situation. When asked whether she'd be willing to swim in the polluted waters to prove they were safe, Nawal El Moutawakel, head of the IOC's Coordination Commission in Rio, shrugged off the suggestion with a chuckle, commenting, "We will dive together" as she gestured toward other Olympic luminaries. IOC Executive Director Christophe Dubi went further, taking partial credit for the impact of AP's water-quality investigation: "Thanks to the games, the level of awareness regarding the bay has been raised to unprecedented levels, which is a good thing."[75]

Other dangers lurked in Rio's waterways. One competitive Brazilian sailor reportedly chanced upon human corpses on four separate occasions in Guanabara Bay. Another told the *New York Times*, "It can get really disgusting, with dog carcasses in some places and the water turning brown from sewage contamination."[76] Human corpses bobbing in the water is not uncommon; one was photographed near the Olympic sailing venue in late February 2016.[77] Rio 2016's Olympic motto, "Green Games for a Blue Planet," was shaping up to be a cruel farce, especially for cariocas who believed the Olympics would finally help remediate their iconic waterways. Even Rio

Mayor Eduardo Paes publicly stated that Rio's sewage-infested waters were "a missed opportunity," though he also claimed it was "not an Olympic issue," despite the fact that cleaning the waters was an Olympic promise.[78] Mario Andrada, spokesperson for the Rio 2016 Organizing Committee, echoed IOC Executive Director Dubi when he said in February 2016 that even though the water cleanup goals for Guanabara Bay would not be met, "we finally got something that the bay has been missing for generations, which is public will for the cleaning."[79] Dubi went further, asserting that Brazil's sharp economic downturn undercut the Rio Organizing Committee's ability to achieve its stated water cleanup goals. "It's not 80 percent," he said, "but it has improved since 2009. I say it's already a super-achievement."[80]

The Olympic golf course, which was built specifically for the Rio 2016 Olympics, also gained attention from environmentalists. Golf courses have long raised questions about water consumption, water quality, and pesticide use.[81] Rio de Janeiro already featured two elite golf courses—Gávea Golf Club and Itanhangá Golf Club—that have staged major tournaments, a fact included in Rio's Olympic bid.[82] But instead of renovating an existing course to meet Olympic standards, Rio's Olympic Delivery Authority decided that Gávea Golf Club didn't have enough space to expand and Itanhangá Golf Club did not have the requisite drainage and irrigation systems. Olympic officials argued that retrofitting these courses would cost as much as building a brand new course.[83]

Mayor Paes led the charge to build the new golf course in Barra da Tijuca along coastal marshland adjacent to the Marapendi Lagoon. In fact, the course boundary encroached on the Marapendi Nature Reserve, home to numerous threatened species like a rare tree iguana and the Fluminense swallowtail butterfly.[84] Vegetation and natural habitat were compromised during the construction of the golf course. This sparked activism from groups like *Ocupa Golfe* (Occupy Golf) and *Golfe Para Quem?* (Golf For Whom?), which united scientists, lawyers, and grassroots environmentalists to challenge the construction and press Rio 2016 organizers to sync up their actions with their publicly touted environmental ethos. Activists experienced significant repression and the golf course was built.[85]

Most of these environmental issues were bumped, if temporarily, from the top of the mass-media docket in early 2016 when the Zika virus became omnipresent on the North American mediascape. The mosquitos that transmitted the virus—the Aedes aegypti, which also transmitted dengue—could breed in bottle caps, thereby making the stagnant water that accumulated in Rio after intense rains due to the lack of proper sewage systems potential breeding grounds for the virus. Concerns about the virus led some athletes to consider skipping the Games. In February 2016, U.S. soccer goalkeeper Hope Solo told *Sports Illustrated*, "If I had to make the choice today, I wouldn't go" to the Rio Olympics.[86] Meanwhile, Rio Mayor Eduardo Paes deflected the Zika issue, stating that while he did not want to minimize the seriousness of the virus, it was "a Brazil problem, not an Olympic problem."[87]

CONCLUSION

In September 2015 IOC President Thomas Bach spoke at the UN Sustainable Development Summit in New York, where in addition to his standard rhetoric about the IOC's goal "to make the world a better place through sport," he offered full-throated support for the UN's 2030 Agenda for Sustainable Development. He stated, "Olympic Agenda 2020 addresses progress with regards to sustainability, credibility, and youth in the context of the Olympic Movement. Therefore, with this Olympic Agenda 2020 the IOC is absolutely in line with the objectives of the 2030 Agenda for Sustainable Development."[88] In part due to such broad-sweeping statements, critics have argued that the UN and IOC have created a symbiotic echo chamber. Byron Peacock wrote:

> the relationship between the IOC and IGOs [intergovernmental organizations] has, in some cases, become so intimate that, when the latter have awarded the former with honours for 'doing good', suspicion must be aroused as to the objectivity of a selection process that may amount to little more than the nonprofit equivalent of insider trading (with legitimacy gains replacing the conventional monetary ones).[89]

Beyond mutually beneficial backslappery, the problem also emerges from the verbal arms race to offer the grandest, most robust environmental promises during the bid phase in order to both impress IOC members and to attract support from the local population that is keen to see the megaevent jumpstart ecological improvements. Caitlin Pentifallo and Rob VanWynsberghe have argued convincingly that the "coercive, mimetic and normative pressures operating in the organizational field of the Olympic Movement have created an environment in which BOCs [Bid Organizing Committees] are motivated to not only take up similar environmental programmes of previously successful Olympic bids but also surpass sustainability and environmental considerations."[90] This dialectic of escalation can lead to overhyped environmental pledges that are difficult, if not impossible, to meet. Rio 2016 places this dialectic in high relief; in March 2015 the Brazilian press was reporting that *none* of the major environmental projects related to the Olympics would be completed before the Games commenced.[91]

The Olympic movement sets itself up for charges of greenwashing by failing to institute oversight mechanisms and concrete standards that would enhance accountability. In fact, Olympic luminaries obfuscate matters by conflating internal sustainability measures with bigger-picture environmental legacy. The IOC and local organizers have made advances in instituting environmental standards for the internal running of Olympic events and preparations through recycling, building with green materials, and lowering waste. As early as 1993, IOC member Richard Pound suggested that the group reduce paper consumption and "encourage environmentally-responsible behaviour and actions around the world," which he viewed as "a responsibility as well as an opportunity."[92] Since then, the IOC has bolstered its commitment to international reporting standards such as the Sustainable Development Index and the United Nations Human Development Index.[93] However, relying on international standards is sometimes not enough, as when Rio organizers stuck to WHO standards on bacterial testing of water rather than adopting virus tests, which the WHO does not require. More broadly, the IOC has allowed local organizers to make big promises about social and environmental legacy and has not enforced accountability to follow through on these pledges.

When in late January 2016 the Rio Organizing Committee was bestowed with the honor of a sustainability award, these dynamics were thrown under the spotlight. To great fanfare, Rio organizers were awarded recognition and a certificate for meeting the ISO 20121 international standard, which was created in 2012 for the London Olympics in order to institute sustainability criteria for event organization and to offer advice on best green practices. This acknowledgment allowed Tania Braga, the head of Rio 2016 sustainability initiatives, to state, "The certification it's an international standard that ensures we have a good management in place to integrate sustainability in everything we do." Rio organizers tacked a commemorative plaque to their office wall and claimed total success. Braga even said, "I think the main legacy is to prove to people that it is possible to organize such a huge event according to international recognized standards."[94] To be sure, Games organizers instituted sustainable sourcing for materials used to make the decorative cushions for the Olympic village and media facilities. The Olympics medals came from more than 30 percent recycled materials. Dining halls served sustainably harvested fish and zero-deforestation beef.[95] But these sustainability practices hardly affected everyday people in the Olympic city. The brand of environmental legacy that is limited to the internal workings of Olympic organizing is markedly weaker than the type of ecological legacy that was widely touted in Rio 2016 bidding materials. The awarding of the sustainability certificate to Rio 2016 symbolizes the disjointed relationship that can develop between internal environmental practices and wider sustainability goals.

Creating international standards, and then ostensibly meeting them, is clearly not enough. As Pentifallo and VanWynsberghe put it, "Although the IOC has taken steps to institutionalize environmentally friendly practices and promote more sustainable methods of Games procurement from its position of authority, these measures fail to operate beyond the level of rhetoric and rule making, providing guidance, yet lacking enforcement." Independent monitoring of the IOC is key. "Without mechanisms for oversight and methods for recourse in the event of unfulfilled bid pledges," they write, "Candidature Files will fail to be anything more than promises tactfully deployed as a way of attracting IOC votes." Olympics bids and their bold promises may make splashy headlines, but, they argue, the "follow-up into the post-Games period has been historically neglected, with neither the IOC nor the OCOGs volunteering to report on long-term outcomes once the Olympic flame has moved on to the next host."[96] In short, the IOC not only needs to ramp up accountability expectations but stringent enforcement as well. The IOC needs to obtain independent monitors to keep local organizing committees in check so they follow through on big environmental promises they float during the bid stage. This watchdog must have the power to ensure that proper budgeting has been planned, to enforce sustainability promises, and to impose penalties if need be. Rio 2016 highlights the fact that it has become far too easy to make big green promises only to ignore them when the Games finally roll around, let alone when IOC powerbrokers jet off to the next venue. The IOC has wedged open this door in its Olympic Agenda 2020 recommendations by suggesting that it might be acceptable to organize "preliminary competitions outside the host city, or in exceptional cases, outside the host country." Multicity and even multicountry Games bids should become standard practice. Environmental legacies could be a valuable element for communities that offer great outlays to host the Olympic Games. Unfortunately, host cities have not benefited as much as they could or should. For too long, the Olympic movement has squandered the chance to create lasting sustainability legacies. For the good of the Olympics—not to mention the planet—this needs to change.

NOTES

1. Rio 2016 Organizing Committee, "Dilma Rousseff Presents the '10 Commandments' of the Rio 2016 Olympic and Paralympic Games," *Rio 2016*, November 10, 2015 (www.rio2016.com/en/news/dilma-rousseff -presents-the-10-commandments-of-the-rio-2016-olympic-and-paralympic -games).

2. "Candidature File for Rio de Janeiro to Host the 2016 Olympic and Paralympic Games, Volume 1–3," *Rio 2016*, 2009.

3. *The XI Olympic Winter Games: Sapporo 1972*, official report, parts 1 and 2 (The Organizing Committee for the XIth Olympic Winter Games,

1972) (http://library.la84.org/6oic/OfficialReports/1972/orw1972pt1.pdf); ibid., (http://library.la84.org/6oic/OfficialReports/1972/orw1972pt2.pdf), p. 116.

4. Ibid., p. 268.

5. Ibid., p. 246.

6. Jules Boykoff, *Activism and the Olympics: Dissent at the Games in Vancouver and London* (New Brunswick, NJ: Rutgers University Press, 2014), pp. 22–24.

7. World Commission on Environment and Development, *Our Common Future* (Oxford University Press, 1987), p. 43.

8. United Nations General Assembly, "Report of the United Nations Conference on Environment and Development," August 12, 1992 (www.un .org/documents/ga/conf151/aconf15126-1annex1.htm).

9. *Sustainability Through Sport: Implementing the Olympic Movement's Agenda 21—2012* (Lausanne, Switz: International Olympic Committee, Commission for Sport and Environment, 2012), p. 9 (www.olympic.org /Documents/Commissions_PDFfiles/SportAndEnvironment/Sustainability _Through_Sport.pdf).

10. Hart Cantelon and Michael Letters, "The Making of the IOC Environmental Policy as the Third Dimension of the Olympic Movement," *International Review for the Sociology of Sport* 35, no. 3 (2000), pp. 294–308.

11. Jon Helge Lesjø, "Lillehammer 1994: Planning, Figurations and the 'Green' Winter Games," *International Review for the Sociology of Sport* 35, no. 3 (2000), pp. 290–91.

12. Ibid., p. 292.

13. Ibid.

14. Juan Antonio Samaranch, "Sport and Environment," *Olympic Review* 25, no. 4 (1995), p. 3.

15. International Olympic Committee, "XII Olympic Congress— Paris, 1994," *Olympic.org*, n.d. (www.olympic.org/paris-1994-olympic -congress).

16. *Olympic Charter* (International Olympic Committee, June 15, 1995), p. 13 (www.olympic.org/Documents/Olympic%20Charter/Olympic_Charter _through_time/1995-Olympic_Charter.pdf).

17. Graeme Hayes and John Karamichas, "Introduction: Sports Mega-Events, Sustainable Development and Civil Societies," in *Olympic Games, Mega-Events and Civil Societies: Globalization, Environment, Resistance,* edited by Graeme Hayes and John Karamichas (New York: Palgrave Macmillan, 2012), p. 9.

18. International Olympic Committee, "Cooperation with the UN," *Olympic.org*, n.d. (www.olympic.org/cooperation-with-the-un).

19. "Agenda 21 of the Olympic Movement," *Olympic Review* 26, no. 30 (1999), pp. 42–43 (http://library.la84.org/OlympicInformationCenter/Olympic Review/1999/OREXXVI30/OREXXVI30ze.pdf).

20. *Manual on Sport and the Environment* (Lausanne, Switz.: International Olympic Committee, 2005), p. 43 (http://www.olympic.org/Documents /Reports/EN/en_report_963.pdf).

21. Hayes and Karamichas, "Introduction," p. 9.

22. Graeme Hayes and John Karamichas, "Conclusion: Sports Mega-Events: Disputed Places, Systemic Contradictions and Critical Moments," in *Olympic Games, Mega-Events and Civil Societies: Globalization, Environment, Resistance*, edited by Graeme Hayes and John Karamichas (New York: Palgrave Macmillan, 2012), p. 257.

23. Helen Jefferson Lenskyj, *The Best Olympics Ever?: Social Impacts of Sydney 2000* (Albany, NY: State University of New York Press, 2002), p. 156.

24. *Official Report of the XXVII Olympiad*, vol. 1, *Preparing for the Games* (Sydney Organising Committee for the Olympic Games, 2001), p. 353 (http://library.la84.org/6oic/OfficialReports/2000/2000v1p3.pdf).

25. Adrian Bradley, "Three Mascoteers an Olympic Hit, Naturally," *The Weekend Australian*, January 25, 1997, p. 3.

26. Lenskyj, *The Best Olympics Ever?*

27. Marc Zemel, "How Powerful Is the IOC?—Let's Talk about the Environment," *Chicago-Kent Journal of Environmental and Energy Law* 1, no. 2 (2011), pp. 182, 220.

28. Egidio Dansero, Barbara Del Corpo, Alfredo Mela, and Irene Ropolo, "Olympic Games, Conflicts, and Social Movements: The Case of Torino 2006," in *Olympic Games, Mega-Events and Civil Societies: Globalization, Environment, Resistance*, edited by Graeme Hayes and John Karamichas (New York: Palgrave Macmillan, 2012), p. 216.

29. Arthur P. J. Mol and Lei Zhang, "Sustainability as Global Norm: The Greening of Meg-Events in China," in *Olympic Games, Mega-Events and Civil Societies: Globalization, Environment, Resistance*, edited by Graeme Hayes and John Karamichas (New York: Palgrave Macmillan, 2012), pp. 134–36.

30. T. Wang et al., "Air Quality During the 2008 Beijing Olympics: Secondary Pollutants and Regional Impact," *Atmospheric Chemistry and Physics Discussions* 10 (2010), pp. 12433–63.

31. D. Q. Rich et al., "Differences in Birth Weight Associated with the 2008 Beijing Olympic Air Pollution Reduction: Results from a Natural Experiment," *Environmental Health Perspectives* 123, no. 9 (2015), pp. 880–87.

32. J. C. Witte et al., "Satellite Observations of Changes in Air Quality During the 2008 Beijing Olympics and Paralympics," *Geophysical Research Letters* 36, no. 17 (2009), pp. 1–6.

33. Rob VanWynsberghe, Inge Derom, and Elizabeth Maurer, "Social Leveraging of the 2010 Olympic Games: 'Sustainability' in a City of Vancouver Initiative," *Journal of Policy Research in Tourism, Leisure and Events* 4, no. 2 (2012), p. 198.

34. David Whitson, "Vancouver 2010: The Saga of Eagleridge Bluffs," in *Olympic Games, Mega-Events and Civil Societies: Globalization, Environment, Resistance*, edited by Graeme Hayes and John Karamichas (New York: Palgrave Macmillan, 2012), p. 220.

35. London 2012 organizers named BP a "sustainability partner" prior to the Gulf Coast environmental disaster.

36. "Breaking the Tape: Commission for a Sustainable London 2012 Pre-Games Review (Annual Review 2011)" (London: Commission for a Sustainable London 2012, 2011).

37. Boykoff, *Activism and the Olympics.*

38. Ban Ki-moon, "Secretary-General's Remarks at the 126th Session of the International Olympic Committee Session," Sochi, Russia, February 6, 2014, *United Nations Secretary-General* (www.un.org/sg/statements/index.asp?nid =7446).

39. Jules Boykoff, "Celebration Capitalism and the Sochi 2014 Winter Olympics," *Olympika: The International Journal of Olympic Studies* 22 (2013), p. 56.

40. Ibid.

41. International Olympic Committee, "Olympic Agenda 2020: 20+20 Recommendations," *Olympic.org*, December 2014, p. 7 (www.olympic.org /documents/olympic_agenda_2020/olympic_agenda_2020-20-20 _recommendations-eng.pdf).

42. Bruce Stokes, Richard Wike, and Jill Carle, "Concern about Climate Change and Its Consequences," *Pew Research Center*, November 5, 2015 (www.pewglobal.org/2015/11/05/1-concern-about-climate-change-and-its -consequences/).

43. *2016 Candidature Procedure and Questionnaire* (Lausanne, Switz.: International Olympic Committee, 2008), p. 10 (www.olympic.org/Documents /Reports/EN/en_report_1318.pdf).

44. Demian Garcia Castro, Christopher Gaffney, Patrícia Ramos Novaes, Juciano Martins Rodrigues, Carolina Pereira dos Santos, and Orlando Alves dos Santos Junior, *Rio de Janeiro: Os Impactos da Copa do Mundo 2014 e das Olimpíadas 2016* (Rio de Janeiro: Observatório das Metrópoles— IPPUR/UFRJ, 2015), pp. 16–17.

45. *Candidature File for Rio de Janeiro to Host the 2016 Olympic and Paralympic Games*, vol. 1, Rio 2016, 2009, p. 21.

46. Christopher Gaffney, "Between Discourse and Reality: The Un-Sustainability of Mega-Event Planning," *Sustainability* 5 (2013), p. 3932.

47. *Candidature File*, vol. 1, p. 37.

48. Ibid., p. 93.

49. Ibid., p. 95.

50. *Report of the 2016 IOC Evaluation Commission* (Lausanne, Switz.: International Olympic Committee, 2009), p. 49 (www.olympic.org/Documents /Reports/EN/en_report_1469.pdf).

51. Ibid., pp. 84, 85.

52. Martin Curi, Jorge Knijnik, and Gilmar Mascarenhas, "The Pan American Games in Rio de Janeiro 2007: Consequences of a Sport Mega-Event in a BRIC Country," *International Review for the Sociology of Sport* 46, no. 2 (2011), pp. 140–56.

53. *Candidature File*, vol. 1, pp. 33, 35.

54. See, for example, Michael Joseph Gross, "Jumping Through Hoops," *Vanity Fair*, June 2012 (www.vanityfair.com/culture/2012/06/international -olympic-committee-london-summer-olympics).

55. *Candidature File*, vol. 3, p. 97.

56. Ibid., p. 109.

57. Ibid., p. 97.

58. Juan Pablo Spinetto and Tariq Panja, "2016 Rio Olympic Games Hinge on Down-to-Wire Subway Construction," *Reuters*, October 7, 2015.

59. Roberto Maltchik and Luiz Ernesto Magalhães, "Prefeito Alerta Para Risco de Atraso na Linha 4 e Propõe Corredor de Ônibus," *O Globo*, February 20, 2016.

60. *Megaeventos e Violações dos Direitos Humanos no Rio de Janeiro: Olimpíada Rio 2016, Os Jogos da Exclusão*, (Rio de Janeiro: Comitê Popular da Copa do Mundo e das Olimpíadas, November 2015), pp. 43–53.

61. *Candidature File*, vol. 3, p. 97.

62. Nick Butler, "Public Access Threatened During Rio 2016 After Plans to Limit Peak Travel to Those with Olympic Transport Card," *Inside the Games*, January 22, 2016.

63. Gabriel Barreira, "Tarifa Sobe de R$3,70 para R$4,10 no Metrô do Rio em Abril," *O Globo*, February 29, 2016.

64. *Candidature File*, vol. 1, p. 33.

65. "Rio 2016 and Dow to Implement Most Comprehensive Carbon Programme in Olympic Games History," *Rio 2016*, September 23, 2014 (www .rio2016.com/en/news/rio-2016-and-dow-to-implement-most -comprehensive-carbon-programme-in-olympic-games-history).

66. See the Rio 2016 Sustainability website (www.rio2016.com/sustenta bilidade/en/partners/).

67. Vinicius Konchinski, "RJ Prometeu 34 Milhões de Árvores para Rio-2016: Deve Plantar 8 Milhões," *UOL*, May 22, 2015 (https://olimpiadas

.uol.com.br/noticias/2015/05/22/rj-prometeu-plantar-34-mi-de-arvores
-para-rio-2016-deve-plantar-8-mi.htm).

68. *Candidature File*, vol. 1, p. 97.

69. Jenny Barchfield, "Away from Olympics, Sewage Blights Vast Swaths
of Rio," Associated Press, September 10, 2015 (http://summergames.ap.org
/article/away-olympics-sewage-blights-vast-swaths-rio).

70. Vinicius Konchinski, "Rio Rescinde Contrato e Abandona Último
Legado Ambiental da Olimpíada," *UOL*, March 17, 2016 (https://olimpiadas
.uol.com.br/noticias/2016/03/17/rio-rescinde-contrato-e-abandona-ultimo
-legado-ambiental-da-olimpiada.htm).

71. Brad Brooks and Jenny Barchfield, "Olympic Teams to Swim,
Boat in Rio's Filth," Associated Press, July 30, 2015 (http://www.summer
games.ap.org/article/ap-investigation-filthy-rio-water-threat-2016
-olympics).

72. Brad Brooks, "AP Test: Rio Olympic Water Badly Polluted, Even Far
Offshore," Associated Press, December 2, 2015 (https://www.usnews.com
/news/world/articles/2015/12/02/ap-test-rio-olympic-water-badly-polluted
-even-far-offshore).

73. Aaron Bauer, "Conditions 'Not Safe' for Rio 2016 Regatta," *Around
the Rings*, April 28, 2015 (http://aroundtherings.com/site/A__51111/title__
Conditions-Not-Safe-for-Rio-2016-Regatta/292/Articles).

74. Bonnie D. Ford, "The Promise Rio Couldn't Keep," *ESPN Outside
the Lines*, February 18, 2016 (http://www.espn.com/espn/feature/story/_/id
/14791849/trash-contamination-continue-pollute-olympic-training
-competition-sites-rio-de-janeiro).

75. Jenny Barchfield, "IOC Rules Out Viral Testing of Rio's Olympic
Waters," Associated Press, August 12, 2015 (https://www.usnews.com/news
/sports/articles/2015/08/12/ioc-rules-out-viral-testing-of-rios-olympic
-waters); Rob Harris, "Rio Head Vows to Introduce Viral Testing in Olympic Waters," Associated Press, September 1, 2015 (https://www.usatoday
.com/story/sports/olympics/2015/09/01/rio-head-vows-to-introduce-viral
-testing-in-olympic-waters/71516146/).

76. Simon Romero and Christopher Clarey, "Note to Olympic Sailors:
Don't Fall in Rio's Water," *New York Times*, May 19, 2014, p. A1.

77. Cristina Boeckel, "Braço É Fotografado Boiando na Baía de Guanabara, no Rio," *O Globo*, February 25, 2016.

78. "Rio Mayor: Great Change Happening Because of Olympics," video,
ESPN, February 18, 2016 (www.espn.go.com/video/clip?id=14794223).

79. Ford, "The Promise Rio Couldn't Keep."

80. Tom Farrey, "Q&A: IOC Executive Director Christophe Dubi on
Rio Water Issues, Zika Virus," *ESPN*, February 18, 2016 (http://www.espn

.com/olympics/story/_/id/14801125/2016-rio-olympics-ioc-executive
-director-christophe-dubi-rio-water-issues-zika-virus).

81. Brad Millington and Brian Wilson, *The Greening of Golf: Sport,
Globalization, and the Environment* (Manchester University Press, 2016);
Stuart Cohen, Amelia Svrjcek, Tom Durborow, and N. LaJan Barnes, "Ground
Water Quality: Water Quality Impacts By Golf Courses," *Journal of Envi-
ronmental Quality* 28 (1999), pp. 798–809.

82. *Candidature File*, vol. 2, p. 165.

83. "Prefeitura Esclarece Dúvidas Sobre Campo de Golfe," *Autoridade
Pública Olímpica*, March 26, 2015 (www.apo.gov.br/index.php/prefeitura
-do-rio-esclarece-duvidas-sobre-campo-de-golfe/).

84. Juliana Barbassa, *Dancing with the Devil in the City of God: Rio
de Janeiro on the Brink* (New York: Touchstone, 2015), pp. 154–55.

85. Gaffney, "Between Discourse and Reality."

86. Grant Wahl, "Solo: As of Now, I Wouldn't Go to Olympics Over
Zika," *Sports Illustrated*, February 9, 2016.

87. Leonardo Filipo, "Paes Vê Exagero em Zika e Diz Que Doença Não
É Problema Olímpico," *O Globo*, February 12, 2016.

88. Thomas Bach, "Remarks on the Occasion of the Adoption of the
UN Sustainable Development Goals UN Sustainable Development Sum-
mit," New York, September 26, 2015 (www.olympic.org/Documents/IOC
_President/UN-SDG-speech-2015.pdf).

89. Byron Peacock, " 'A Secret Instinct of Social Preservation': Legitimacy
and the Dynamic (Re)constitution of Olympic Conceptions of the 'Good,' "
Third World Quarterly 32, no. 3 (2011), p. 490.

90. Caitlin Pentifallo and Rob VanWynsberghe, "Blame It on Rio: Iso-
morphism, Environmental Protection and Sustainability in the Olympic
Movement," *International Journal of Sport Policy and Politics* 4, no. 3
(2012), p. 428.

91. Konchinski, "Rio Rescinde Contrato."

92. Richard W. Pound, "The IOC and the Environment," *Olympic
Message* 35 (1993), pp. 14, 18.

93. *Candidature File*, vol. 1, p. 105.

94. Aaron Bauer, "Sustainability Award Highlights Rio 2016 Progress,
Legacy," *Around the Rings*, January 28, 2016 (http://aroundtherings.com
/site/A__54571/Title__Sustainability-Award-Highlights-Rio-2016-Progress
-Legacy/292/Articles). Also see "Rio 2016 Receives Top Global Sustainability
Certificate for Organisation of Major Events," *Rio 2016*, January 27, 2016
(www.rio2016.com/en/news/rio-2016-receives-top-global-sustainability
-certificate-for-organisation-of-major-events); and "SGS Awarded Rio 2016
Olympics with ISO 20121 Certification," *SGS*, August, 24, 2016 (www.sgs

.com/en/news/2016/08/sgs-awarded-rio-2016-olympics-with-iso-20121 -certification). For more details on the ISO 20121 standard, see www.iso.org /iso/iso20121.

95. Ann Duffy, "Rio2016 Olympics: A Sustainability Summary," *To- ronto Sustainability Speaker Series*, August 25, 2016 (http://tsss.ca/2016 /08/rio2016-olympics-a-sustainability-summary/).

96. Pentifallo and VanWynsberghe, "Blame It on Rio," p. 443.

NINE

The Economic Legacy of Rio 2016

ANDREW ZIMBALIST

It should surprise no one that those responsible for inflicting the 2016 Olympics on Rio de Janeiro have declared the Games a resounding economic success. Indeed, IOC President Thomas Bach said history will record the Games as a turning point in Rio's development and that the Games were "iconic" and a "miracle." He added paternalistically, and some would say condescendingly, that the residents of Rio, *cariocas*, should be happy and proud.[1]

To be sure, some IOC executives gloated that the Rio Games have proven that even developing countries are capable of hosting the Olympics. As I will show in this chapter, such a conclusion is unwarranted. The reality is that the less developed a country, the more it has to invest in transportation, telecommunications, hospitality, security, and sports infrastructure. Building tens of billions of dollars of infrastructure to meet the demands of the IOC and the international sports federations (IFs) does not typically correspond with the development needs of a city. The ensuing waste of scarce resources is massive.

When Bach ended his speech at the closing ceremony of the Rio Games, he thanked Rio and said goodbye. He did not speak about the coming Paralympic Games, which he did not attend. He did not speak about the next phase of the Games: the implementation of the heralded "legacy." No, he just said goodbye. What would happen in Rio after Bach flew back to Europe was not the IOC's concern.

SHORT-RUN COSTS

The first step in assessing the impact of hosting is to consider the costs incurred and the revenues received during the period leading up to and going through the Games. This step is not as straightforward as one might imagine. There are different budgets: operations (managed by the local organizing committee, or ROCOG), security, sport facilities, nonsport facilities, and infrastructure. And the money to pay for all this comes from different sources: the city, the state, and the federal governments and the private sector. Moreover, often the "money" is opaque because it comes in the form of public land grants, tax benefits, or low-interest loans. Further, there is always what economists call opportunity costs, which means that each of the resources used may have had a better or more productive use that imposes an unforeseen cost on the host city. Lastly, there are social and environmental costs, which are also often hidden, at least in the short run. Counting revenues poses another set of conundrums.

But before entering into the calculus of costs and benefits, it is necessary to consider the genesis of the Rio Games and the accompanying historical expenses that were incurred. Rio's first foray into the Olympic-hosting competition was back in the early 1930s when it bid against twelve other cities worldwide to host the 1936 Games. The winner was Berlin, with forty-three votes; Barcelona received sixteen; the other eleven cities got no votes. Then a long dry period ensued, which included a rude dismissal of the Olympics by Brazil's last military president, João Baptista de Oliveira Figueiredo (1979–85), who exclaimed that the Olympics are "political propaganda for nations who needed that sort of thing."[2] Brazil's next bid came for the 2004 Games, but the germ for this bid dates back to 1993. Rio's mayor, César Maia, was intrigued by Barcelona's apparent success in hosting the 1992 Olympics. Maia called in consultants from Barcelona to help him formulate a plan to present to the IOC. Rio's bid did not make it to the final round. The president of Brazil's National

Olympic Committee, Carlos Nuzman, became a member of the IOC and got the message that Rio first had to prove itself as a host of a lesser sports megaevent. Thus was born Rio's successful bid to host the Pan American Games in 2007. The Pan Am Games is a regional mini-Olympics over seven days involving almost 6,000 athletes. Unlike the failed master plan for the 2004 Olympics, which focused development in the downtown area of Rio, the Pan Am focused construction in the western suburb of Barra da Tijuca.

The original budget for the Pan Am Games was R$390 million. The final cost was almost ten times greater, R$3.58 billion. (In July 2007, when the Pan Am competition was held, the Brazilian currency, the real (R$, or plural reais) was worth approximately $0.53 in U.S. dollars.) Much of the construction was rushed and of low quality.[3] Today, as a result of poor foundation work, what was the athletes' village is sinking. Nonetheless, the Games were pulled off successfully from the perspective of the athletic competition and seemed to signal to the IOC that Rio had proven its mettle as a megaevent host. While some of the facilities renovated or built for the Pan Am Games were deemed inadequate for Olympics competition (the R$60 million velodrome had a seating capacity of 1,500, whereas the IOC required 5,000, and the R$85 million Maria Lenk Aquatics pool was undersized for swimming), some of the facilities were found suitable for Rio 2016. These included: the Maria Lenk pool for water polo, the Olympic Stadium (also called the Engenhão) for track and field, and the Maracanã Stadium for the opening and closing ceremonies and for soccer. Thus, when discussing the cost of hosting the 2016 Olympics, it is important to keep in mind that it would have been considerably higher had Rio not hosted the Pan Am Games nine years earlier. Indeed, since the Pan Am Games were held as a stepping-stone to hosting the Olympics, it might be argued that the cost of these Games should be added to the cost of hosting the Olympics.

Maintenance on facilities and infrastructure also went to support Rio's and Brazil's hosting of the World Military Games with its 5,650 athletes during August 12–19, 2011, FIFA's Confederations Cup during June 15–30, 2013, and FIFA's World Cup during June 12–July 13, 2014.

Cost-Counting Conundrums

Depending on the article one reads and the day it is read, one might come away with the impression that the Rio Olympics cost $2 billion, $7 billion, $12 billion, $20 billion, or more. The real number, in my view, is above $20 billion (and rising). A good place to start unpacking the bundle of contradictory data is the bid budget that the Rio organizing committee submitted to the IOC in 2009.

In table 9-1, the costs refer to the expenses of the Rio Organizing Committee for the Olympic Games (ROCOG). The non-ROCOG costs attributed to the Games refer to everything else. Note that the non-ROCOG costs explicitly specify that only costs directly attributable to the staging of the games are included. That is, the construction costs for work at the downtown port, the international airport, the highways and Bus Rapid Transits (BRTs), and the metro, inter alia, are not included in this budget, even though they were planned for and timed for the Games. The argument for excluding these items is that they contribute to the long-run development of the city and were needed whether or not Rio hosted. If that were true, then it would possibly be understandable to exclude these costs.

Media stories about the cost of the Games sometimes refer only to the ROCOG costs and sometimes to the ROCOG costs plus non-ROCOG costs (directly attributed to the Games). The former were estimated in 2008 prices to equal R$5.63 billion or $2.815 billion (with reais converted to dollars at 50 cents). The latter were estimated in 2008 prices to equal R$13.01 billion or $6.505 billion. In estimated 2016 prices (that is, with inflation added in), the estimates for "grand total costs" were R$17,465 billion or $7.545 billion (reais are now converted into dollars at 43.2 cents, indicating that more inflation is expected in Brazil than in the United States between 2008 and 2016).

Rio's 2009 bid, however, also included estimates of the infrastructural costs that were not directly attributable to the Games. These estimates are included under non-ROCOG costs in table 9-2.

In U.S. dollars of 2016, the Rio bid anticipated expenses of $1.16 billion in modernizing the international airport and the downtown port, $5.16 billion in building roads and railways, $495 million in constructing the Olympic village, $942 million for the media village,

TABLE 9-1. Rio 2016 Cost Matrix

ROCOG Costs	Millions (R$=reais)			
	R$ 2008	US$ 2008	R$ 2016	US$ 2016
Sports venues	635.0	317.5	852.5	368.3
Olympic village and other villages	565.0	282.5	758.4	327.6
MPC	42.5	21.3	57.1	24.7
IBC	45.1	22.6	60.6	26.2
Other non-competition venues	82.3	41.2	110.5	47.7
Workforce	683.9	342.0	918.1	396.6
Information systems	569.8	284.9	764.8	330.4
Telecommunications	356.0	178.0	477.9	206.5
Internet	50.8	25.4	68.2	29.5
Ceremonies and culture	250.0	125.0	335.6	145.0
Medical services	40.2	20.1	53.9	23.3
Catering	152.2	76.1	204.3	88.2
Transport	329.6	164.8	442.5	191.1
Security	46.7	23.3	62.7	27.1
Paralympic Games	340.1	170.1	456.6	197.2
Advertising and promotion	283.0	141.5	379.9	164.1
Administration	338.9	169.4	454.9	196.5
Pre-Olympic events and coordination	89.1	44.6	119.6	51.7
Other	730.1	365.0	980.1	423.4
TOTAL ROCOG COSTS	5,630.3	2,815.2	7,558.0	3,265.0

Note: The value of the real has varied greatly over time. The following gives the value of the real in dollars on August 1 from 2009 to 2016:

YEAR	VALUE	YEAR	VALUE
2009	$0.533	2013	$0.435
2010	$0.570	2014	$0.442
2011	$0.646	2015	$0.306
2012	$0.490	2016	$0.309

avg. 2009–16	$0.466
avg. 2011–16	$0.438
2008 avg.	$0.555

Non-ROCOG Costs (directly attributed to Games)	Millions (R$=reais)			
	R$ 2008	US$ 2008	R$ 2016	US$ 2016
Capital costs				
Airport and ports	0.0	0.0	0.0	0.0
Roads and railways	2,141.3	1,070.6	2,874.4	1,241.7
Accommodation	111.6	55.8	149.8	64.7
Sports Venues				
— Competition venues	485.9	243.0	652.3	281.8
— Training venues	21.9	11.0	29.4	12.7
Olympic village	0.0	0.0	0.0	0.0
Barra media village	0.0	0.0	0.0	0.0
Power/electricity infrastructure	0.0	0.0	0.0	0.0
Environmental management	890.0	445.0	1,194.8	516.1
Medical	20.0	10.0	26.9	11.6
Security	731.7	365.8	982.2	424.3
Telecommunications	0.0	0.0	0.0	0.0
IBC/MPC	405.9	202.9	544.8	235.4
Urban legacy	1,454.7	727.4	1,952.8	843.6
Subtotal Capital Costs	6,263.0	3,131.5	8,407.3	3,631.9
Operating costs				
Security	874.7	437.4	1,174.2	507.2
Transport	0.0	0.0	0.0	0.0
Medical	0.0	0.0	0.0	0.0
Environmental management	0.0	0.0	0.0	0.0
Cultural programming	45.2	22.6	60.7	26.2
Decoration of the city	24.0	12.0	32.2	13.9
Special projects	173.2	86.6	232.5	100.4
Subtotal Operating Costs	1,117.1	558.6	1,499.6	647.8
TOTAL NON-ROCOG COSTS	7,380.1	3,690.0	9,906.9	4,279.7
GRAND TOTAL COSTS	13,010.4	6,505.2	17,464.9	7,544.7

TABLE 9-2. Non-ROCOG Costs, Total Reported

	Millions			
	R$ 2008	US$ 2008	R$ 2016	US$ 2016
Capital costs				
Airport and ports	2,002.5	1,001.3	2,688.1	1,161.2
Roads and railways	8,903.0	4,451.5	11,951.2	5,162.8
Accommodation	111.6	55.8	149.8	64.7
Sports venues				
—Competition venues	958.6	479.3	1,286.8	555.9
—Training venues	21.9	11.0	29.4	12.7
Olympic village	854.1	427.1	1,146.5	495.3
Barra media village	1,624.8	812.4	2,181.0	942.2
Power/electricity infrastructure	1,540.0	770.0	2,067.3	893.0
Environmental management	2,409.6	1,204.8	3,234.6	1,397.3
Medical	20.0	10.0	26.9	11.6
Security	1,625.9	813.0	2,182.6	942.9
Telecommunications				
IBC/MPC	405.9	202.9	544.8	235.4
Urban legacy	1,640.4	820.2	2,202.1	951.3
Subtotal capital costs	22,118.2	11,059.1	29,691.0	12,826.3
Operating costs				
Security	874.7	437.3	1,174.2	507.2
Transport				
Medical				
Environmental management				
Cultural programming	45.2	22.6	60.7	26.2
Decoration of the city	24.0	12.0	32.2	13.9
Special projects	173.2	86.6	232.5	100.4
Subtotal operating costs	1,117.1	558.6	1,499.6	647.8
TOTAL NON-ROCOG COSTS	23,235.4	11,617.7	31,190.6	13,474.1
GRAND TOTAL COSTS	28,865.7	14,432.8	38,748.6	16,739.1

$235 million for the international broadcasting and media center, and so on. Now, including the indirect infrastructure, the total costs rise to $14.43 billion, measured in 2008 prices, or $16.74 billion, measured in estimated 2016 prices.

Note that if we take the 2016 estimate in reais of R$38.75 billion and convert it into U.S. dollars at the actual exchange rate in 2016 of approximately R$1=$0.30, then the dollar cost becomes $11.63 billion, or around the $12 billion figure often cited in the press. The problem, however, with using the 2016 exchange rate is that much of the construction was performed between 2009 and 2015 (and some of it was contracted in dollars, not reais). It makes economic sense to use the conversion rate at the time the expenditures were made. As an approximation, the average exchange rate during 2009–16 of R$1=$0.466 can be used, yielding a dollar estimate of grand total costs of $18.1 billion. One problem with such an estimate is that it is based on initial cost estimates (plus inflation) and, hence, excludes any real cost overruns.

One study out of England's University of Oxford estimated the cost overrun for the Rio Olympics (not counting infrastructure) at 51 percent in real terms.[4] If we apply this estimate to the grand total in dollars, it comes to $21.8 billion (in 2008 dollars). Yet, based on recent data, it appears that the Oxford study may have been too conservative in its estimate of overruns. Consider what is shown in table 9-3.

Detailed data for all the venues is not publicly available. Table 9-3 includes the original dollar value (in 2016 prices) of five construction projects connected to the Olympics, which showed an average cost overrun of 101.6 percent (more than doubling of costs). This is based on cost estimates from early 2016, so, if anything, the final cost would be still higher as kinks were worked out, finishing touches added, and unforeseen problems arose. It is notable that at a press conference at the unveiling of the Olympic village in late June, Mario Andrada, Rio 2016 communications director, declined to answer a question about the construction cost of the village.[5] A sixth construction project, the media center (or MPC), shows a mammoth overrun of over twenty-eight times the initial projected cost. I did not include that in the average because it is unclear in the source whether the

TABLE 9-3. Cost Overruns at Rio 2016 in Millions

Venue costs	US$ 2008 bid (2008 prices)	US$ 2016 bid (2016 prices)	US$ 2016 projected in Jan 2016* (2016 prices)	Percent cost overrun
Olympic tennis center	46.1	51.7	83.7	62.0%
Olympic aquatics Stadium	37.9	42.5	98.7	132.4%
Olympic velodrome	35.1	39.3	62.9	60.0%
Olympic village	427.1	478.7	1,274.4	166.2%
Metro to Barra		1,600.0	3,000.0	87.5%
AVERAGE				101.6%
MPC		25.0	738.0	2,852.0%

*Converted from reais at the average exchange rate for 2011–16, R$1= $0.438.

Sources:

1. *Candidature File for Rio de Janeiro to Host the 2016 Olympic and Paralympic Games,* vol. 1, January 2009, pp. 125–31.

2. www.rio2016.com/transparencia/en/budget.

3. "Jogos Olímpicos e Paraolímpicos Rio 2016: Governo Municipal," *Plano de Políticas Públicas,* April 24, 2015 (www.apo.gov.br/wp-content/uploads /2015/05/Plano_Politicas_Publicas_Municipio.pdf).

4. "Jogos Olímpicos e Paraolímpicos Rio 2016: Governo Estado," *Plano de Políticas Públicas,* April 24, 2015 (www.apo.gov.br/wp-content/uploads /2015/05/Plano_Politicas_Publicas_Estado.pdf).

5. "Jogos Olímpicos e Paraolímpicos Rio 2016: Governo Federal," *Plano de Políticas Públicas,* April 24, 2015 (www.apo.gov.br/wp-content/uploads /2015/05/Plano_Politicas_Publicas_GovFederal.pdf).

6. "Responsibility Matrix," *Brasil 2016,* n.d. (www.brasil2016.gov.br/en/ legacy/responsibility-matrix).

final reported cost also includes the international broadcast center. Also not included is security, the total dollar value for security costs estimated in the bid in 2016 prices was $1.48 billion. However, numerous press reports appeared during 2016 that state Rio 2016 had cut its security budget by $550 million and characterized this as 20 percent of the overall budget. This implies that the security budget had risen to $2.75 billion but was now, in the wake of financially dictated budget cuts, reduced to $2.2 billion, or $720 million higher than in the 2009 bid budget.[6] The $2.2 billion figure appears to make sense given that there were at least 85,000 security personnel working the Rio Games (more than double the number in London in 2008), extensive use of international security consulting firms (such as Giuliani Security and Safety), and large volumes of military-grade hardware that were purchased by Rio (including Black Hawk and Sabre helicopters as well as A-29 Super Tucano aircraft outfitted for aerial surveillance and counterinsurgency). In any event, the University of Oxford estimate of an average real overrun of 51 percent seems rather conservative in light of this data.

Further, non-cash expenditures or government subsidies for Olympics construction via public-private partnerships (PPPs) amount to an additional billions of dollars of value. For instance, "In the case of Porto Maravilha, the [PPP] contract expects a public monthly counterpart of R$10 million, over fifteen years, paid in cash or [development rights]. In the case of the Olympic park, the PPP contract expects public compensation of R$528 million, paid in instalments over fifteen years, plus a plot of land measuring 800,000 square meters, located where the park is being constructed."[7] The estimated value of the land for the Olympic park was R$2.7 billion and that of the private consortium's tax exemption was R$3.0 billion.[8] The land was turned over in 2010, when one real was worth 57 cents, so the land's dollar value was $1.5 billion and that of the tax benefits was $1.7 billion. In addition to land grants and tax privileges, PPPs also include heavily subsidized interest rates from the state development bank, BNDES. These billions of dollars appear nowhere in the Olympics budgets.

Next, it appears that the extended budget including infrastructure has not counted all Olympics-related costs: for instance, the wall that was erected to block the view of the Maré favela complex on the road from the airport; the furniture for the Olympic village; the payments to, the land purchases for, and building for the resettlement of *favelados*; the stadia that were built for the Pan Am Games; the costs of the Units of Pacifying Police (UPP) program after 2009; the costs of dismantling temporary facilities and maintaining others, among other expenditures. These costs do not appear anywhere in the Olympics budget.

It should also be considered that after the $14.4 billion bid budget was accepted, the IOC added two sports to the Olympics competition: golf and rugby sevens. Each of these added facilities and personnel costs to the original budget. Although cariocas have shown little interest in golf and Rio already had two private golf courses,[9] according to mayor Paes the IOC and the international golf federation required ROCOG to build a new course on protected wetlands in Barra da Tijuca.[10] Other than the environmental degradation that this entailed, the course cost some $20 million to construct (not counting the land value) and continues to add expenses because of the required watering and upkeep, as will be discussed below.

Finally, there were also indirect costs caused by horrific traffic and additional work vacation days. Regarding the traffic problems, the *Wall Street Journal* reported that commuters around the city complained of routine journeys "taking double or triple their usual time."[11] The informal sector of tens of thousands of street vendors, food kiosk owners, and others was decimated as highways tore through their stations, formerly public land was turned over to private management, and officials pushed them away from Olympics venues.[12]

Public versus Private Costs

From early on Rio's politicians pledged that there would be no public funds encumbered to defray the hosting costs. Even after the event Thomas Bach maintained: "There is no public money in the organization of this Olympic Games."[13] Bach is guilty on a daily basis of spinning the news; in this case he is guilty of intentional, outright distortion. As already indicated, there are several distinct budgets for the Games. The smallest of these budgets is the operating budget of the local organizing committee, ROCOG in the case of the Rio Games. The operating budget essentially refers to the cost of operating the games for the seventeen days of competition; that is, it includes items such as transporting the athletes, trainers, coaches, and judges from their home countries and around Rio, lodging and feeding the athletes and others, maintaining health and other services, wining and dining members of the IOC and Olympics sponsors, providing power to the Olympics venues, erecting and running temporary facilities, preparing

opening and closing ceremonies and other cultural events, part of security, information systems, catering, advertising, administration,
and the Paralympic Games, inter alia. These operating costs for Rio
were approximately $3 billion—less than 15 percent of the total
costs. The operating costs are usually covered by the combination of
Olympics-generated revenue from ticket sales, local sponsorships,
and the TV money and international sponsorships shared by the IOC
with the host city. In the case of Rio, however, both the ROCOG and
the state government ran out of money, requiring a last-minute financial transfer of nearly a billion dollars from the federal government
(in part for security and in part to finish the Line 4 metro) and then
another from the city government of $61 million (for the Paralym-
pics).[14] Beyond this emergency public money, usually reserved for
natural disaster relief or other states of crisis, there were also the much
larger public expenditures for infrastructure, permanent venues, and
the PPP contracts.

Because of all the public subsidies, many of them hidden, and in-
complete reporting, it is difficult to measure the net contribution of
the private sector to the overall financing burden of hosting the
Games. There is, however, a study by the Olympic Public Authority
(Autoridade Pública Olímpica or APO) of Rio 2016 that finds the private sector's contribution to the construction of Olympics venues was
a mere 9.2 percent of the total cost.[15]

SHORT-RUN REVENUES

Rio 2016's budget included the following revenue items:

International television (share from IOC)	$758 million
International sponsorships (share from IOC)	$361 million
Local sponsorships	$1.21 billion
Ticket sales	$484 million
Licensing and other	$209 million
TOTAL REVENUE	$3.02 billion

Although at this writing final figures have not been published, it is
known that ticket sales and local sponsorships did not meet their bud-

getary targets. This was in significant measure due to the serious economic recession in Rio and Brazil during 2015–16. In all likelihood, total Games-related revenue was below $3 billion.

In addition to revenues that flowed directly to ROCOG, the Rio and the Brazilian economy might also have benefitted from net increments to tourism. That is, if more people from outside Rio or Brazil traveled to Rio and Brazil during August 2016 than people who avoided Rio and Brazil because of fears of congestion, Zika, higher prices, or security incidents, there would be a net gain to the Rio or Brazilian economies. Such a gain should also be part of the calculation of the economic return or loss from hosting.

There is available data on arrivals at Rio's international airport (Galeão) that allows us to estimate the possible impact of the Games on tourism. The evidence is mixed but, in the end, does not suggest a boost from the Olympics. The average number of passengers at Rio's Galeão airport during the month of August for the 2012–15 period was 1,411,706. During August of 2016, the number of passengers was 1,577,879, or an increase of 166,173 above the average over the previous four years. This increase at first pass indicates a positive impact of the Games on tourism. However, if we consider the average monthly number of passengers between January and August in 2015 and 2016, we find that the average is 1,405,178 in 2015 and 1,338,994 in 2016. That is, the total number of passengers at Galeão airport was lower for the first eight months of 2016 than for 2015. This statistic suggests that there was time switching in 2016—people who were planning to visit Rio in 2016 made their visit in August instead of visiting in earlier months. Such a pattern is not indicative of an overall boost in Rio tourism from the Olympics.

One other fact stands out. Considering Brazil's nine international airports together, the total number of airline passengers was 11,481,759 in August 2015 and 11,009,131 in August 2016. That is, total airline travel in Brazil was 472,628 lower in August 2016 than in the previous year, suggesting that travelers to Brazil in 2016 substituted visiting Rio for other Brazilian cities. Hence, it is hard to conclude that there was a net increase in spending occasioned by Olympics-related tourism either in Rio or in Brazil overall.[16]

In January 2017, the National Tourism Office of Brazil released data indicating that the number of foreign tourism visitors in 2016 in

Brazil increased by 4.8 percent above that in 2015. This figure does not seem compatible with the airport arrival numbers, unless many of the foreign tourists came from neighboring countries via bus or car. The official statistics on bus travel into Rio in August 2016, however, do not support the idea of increased tourism via buses: the total number of bus seats occupied in trips to Rio was 249,842 in August 2015 and 231,963 in August 2016; that is, the number of bus travelers to Rio fell by 7.2 percent during the month of the Olympic Games.[17] However, even if we were to accept the official claim from the Brazilian National Tourism Office, the total increase in foreign tourism spending in Brazil in 2016 was only $360 million for the entire year, hardly sufficient to make up for the deficit of over $10 billion.[18]

It is important to keep in mind that approximately 80,000 of the visitors to Rio were part of the extended Olympics family, that is, the athletes, trainers, coaches, judges, executives, and families of participants. Of these, ROCOG was responsible for paying for the transportation to and within Rio, lodging, and meals for the athletes. The athletes, then, did not bring in new spending for the most part. On the contrary, the spending that did occur on the construction of facilities, on imported inputs and goods for the Games, and on income to the participants was not subject to local or national taxation. This tax exemption is part of the package that the IOC requires of the host city.[19] Thus, tax revenues that would normally accrue to the city, the state, and the federal government did not materialize—an important factor contributing to the bankruptcy of the Rio state government.[20]

Economic impact studies of sports stadiums and megaevents are notorious for the use of multipliers. The multiplier is a concept in macroeconomics that measures the total impact from a net increase in (exogenous) spending (to an economy in equilibrium). The idea is that if new spending occurs, it generates new income to those who produced the products that were sold, and the recipients of this income then spend a portion of this income on other products, which generates new income, and the virtuous cycle continues. The total impact of all this activity compared to the initial increase in spending is the multiplier.

Economic impact studies are usually performed by consulting firms hired by the promoters of the new stadium or the event. Not surprisingly, such a study was performed for Rio 2016, commissioned by Brazil's Ministry of Sport. The study took the estimated gross increase in spending and then multiplied this inflated number by a multiplier of 4.26. This procedure is puzzling in the extreme. First, even economic impact studies, performed under hire, typically use a multiplier around 2 or 2.5, but never above 3. Second, macroeconomic models of the large U.S. economy find multipliers closer to 1.2, and cities have lower multipliers than whole countries. Third, because of larger leakages, sports' facilities multipliers are still smaller than city multipliers and are often estimated to be close to 1 or lower. We can only conclude that the multiplier for new spending from the Olympics would be close to 1.

We now have the elements to estimate the financial balance for Rio from hosting the Games. The total cost, on a conservative basis, was $20 billion or above, and the total revenue was on the order of $3 billion. Thus, the short-run negative financial balance was at least $15 billion and probably a good deal more. If hosting the Games, then, is to find an economic justification, there must be a very appreciable long-term economic gain to offset this acute short-term loss.

LONG-TERM IMPACT

The claim of a long-term positive impact from hosting the Olympics usually runs along the following lines. First, the Games burnish the image of the host city, thereby promoting tourism, foreign investment, and trade over time. Second, the Games leave behind an improved transportation, telecommunications, hospitality, sports, and security infrastructure. Third, the Games yield intangible benefits, improving or modernizing cultural traits, the feel-good factor, management abilities and administrative efficiency. Fourth, for the Rio Games, the city, the state, and ROCOG claimed that the Olympics would enable the successful implementation of the favela pacification (UPP) and modernization (Morar Carioca) programs.

There is a sad irony in contemplating these arguments in the case of Rio. Let us consider them one by one. First, prior to hosting the World Cup and the Olympics, Rio de Janeiro was known worldwide as the *cidade maravilhosa* (marvelous city) because of its extraordinary physical beauty and perpetual Carnivalesque atmosphere. The 2014 and 2016 megaevents in Brazil, however, brought the world news of a different Rio: a city wracked by violence, inequality, disease and pollution, extensive corruption, political instability, recession, and inefficiency. Any reasonable observer had to conclude that the city's image was tarnished, not burnished.

Moreover, the city, state, and federal government were overwhelmed with debt and would not be able to offer the tax incentives to which developers and investors had grown accustomed; rather, the budget deficits were so severe that sharp cuts in pensions, wages, and employment became the fiscal medicine. Violence increased: the murder rate in Rio from January through October of 2016 was up 18 percent above 2015 and the robbery rate was up 48 percent.[21] Militant political protests became commonplace. These conditions are not auspicious for promoting tourism, trade, or investment. To be sure, as has been true of many past Olympics host cities, Rio overinvested in hotel rooms in order to accommodate the anticipated increase in tourism. The result has been reductions in hotel capacity utilization, falling room rates, and likely hotel bankruptcies—since hotel construction was underwritten by loans from BNDES, the state may not recoup its investments. Rio's stock of hotel rooms grew by almost 30,000, or by 40 percent, between 2012 and 2016. By the time of the Paralympics in September 2016, hotel occupancy rates in Rio stood at 49 percent, compared to the September average in recent years of 65 percent.[22]

Second, what about the additions to Rio's infrastructure? New transportation infrastructure and the renovated port top the lists of boasts by officials about the Olympics legacy. Rio added several BRT (bus rapid transit) routes. These routes connect the international airport to the main Olympics cluster (Olympic park) in Barra da Tijuca, the Olympics cluster in Barra to that in Deodoro (a military base converted into several Olympics venues), the new metro stop in Barra to the Olympic park, and the Olympic park to its west. These routes all serviced the Olympics project and respond only in a minimal way to the daily, severe transportation bottlenecks that confront the local population. In fact, in many respects these BRT routes exacerbate the problem by reducing the number of lanes for normal car traffic, impeding pedestrian crossings, reemphasizing dependence on car (rather than metro) transportation, and restructuring existing bus routes inconveniently. The restructuring of traditional bus routes catered to the wealthier neighborhoods that did not want the noise and pollution from buses passing on their streets and forced many workers to take two buses to work when they used to take one.[23] While some commuters will benefit from shortened travel time, all commuters will face substantially higher fares, doubling in many cases due to the BRT's lack of integration with the metro system.[24]

But, most significantly, these BRT routes cut through dense, low-income residential zones, forcing the evictions of thousands of families and either eliminating or reducing the favelas. The emblematic cases were the favelas Recreio II and Camorim, both removed for the Transoeste BRT but then used as a deposit for machinery or left empty. The evicted families were often obligated to relocate up to thirty-five miles to the west, making it nearly impossible for the man or woman of the household to retain his or her job or for the children to stay in their schools. Of course, their neighborhood life was upended. All told, over 77,000 *favelados* were evicted from their homes between 2009 and 2015.[25]

The international human rights group Terre des Hommes published a report on the impact of these evictions on children and family life, which concluded the following:

> Children that faced forced evictions have missed out on school places, moved to dangerous areas, and lost contact with friends and the social fabric of their previous communities. *Terre des Hommes'* interviews reveal strong evidence that indicates increase of police violence against adolescents in street situations and the intention of "cleaning up" the streets as the games approached. Rio saw a devastating increase in number of overcrowded juvenile detention centers when compared to last year and a deterioration of the condition of the units.[26]

Another transportation project was the Line 4 metro, roughly a ten-mile transit that linked the Olympics cluster around Copacabana and Ipanema beaches (*Zona Sul*) with Barra da Tijuca. Barra da Tijuca is a tony Rio area. It is the Rio district with the highest per capita income and the lowest level of employment. Spending $3 billion plus on a metro to link Barra to the beaches,[27] while raising property values in Barra, does little to alleviate Rio's transportation problems. The main point, however, with both the BRTs and the Line 4 metro is that any rational planner would have had them at the bottom of a long list of transportation investment projects for Rio. The Line 4 metro itself does not aggravate Rio's transportation problems, but for a city and a state strapped for resources and with dire transportation needs, it represented a gross misallocation of public funds and quixotic inversion of priorities.[28]

The Line 4 metro typifies another problem that afflicted all Olympics-related construction, as well as most government contracts in this century: the construction-government complex. The principal contractor of the metro was Odebrecht. Brazilian expert and geographer Christopher Gaffney writes about Odebrecht: "The company at the center of the Lava Jato corruption scandal, Odebrecht, was found to have paid at least R$500,000 in bribes to secure their participation in the metro project. The same company was or is involved in at least seven other Olympic-related projects."[29] As noted in chapter 3, "Brazil's Olympic Rollercoaster" by Juliana Barbassa, the CEO of Odebrecht was found guilty of bribery and kickbacks and is serving a nineteen-year jail sentence. While Odebrecht was involved in at least eight Olympics construction contracts, several of Brazil's other giant construction companies partnered with Odebrecht and with each other for multiple contracts, and many of their CEO's are also in prison.[30] These companies colluded to avoid bidding competition with each other, charged higher prices for their work, and benefitted from land grants, major tax exemptions (contributing to the parlous fiscal condition of Rio's city and state governments), and low interest loans. The loans generally permitted the construction companies to avoid advancing their own capital for the projects. The construction consortia also gained by being granted or offered long-term management rights and control over BRTs, metros, rail lines, and entire development projects. Such was the case with the redevelopment of Rio's downtown port.

Thomas Bach singled out Rio's renovated port as evidence that the city benefitted from hosting the Games. It is peculiar that Bach takes credit for the development of the "Porto Maravilhosa" because none of the construction in the fifteen-year port project had any relationship to the Games. Further, when the IOC or ROCOG publicly presented the budget for Rio 2016, they invariably separate out expenditures that were not directly related to the Games and, hence, do not include the R$5 billion that had been spent on the port development as of the end of 2015.[31]

One of the more controversial elements in the port renovation was the building of a cable car up to and across the Morro da Providência favela, Rio's oldest favela. Despite promises that favela residents would be consulted about any such construction and its location, they were not. Through political organizing and protests the residents were able to alter the original plan for the R$75 million gondola, which would have dislocated 5,000 *favelados*. The final plan resulted in the destruction of approximately 200 homes. The cable car permitted tourist visits to the quaint favela. Meanwhile, Cosme Felippsen, a Providência resident and tour guide, lamented: "Basic sanitation would have been more useful. But there was no dialogue and the government just did what it pleased."[32] The Providência cable car stopped operating the first week of December 2016 and there is no timetable for its return. At least it was functioning for the seventeen days of the Olympics.[33]

Another element of the port project is the development of a light rail network (veículo leve sobre trilhos or VLT). The port area, however, is one of the only parts of Rio that has been well served by metro and bus lines. Only a small part of the VLT design had been implemented by August 2016. The balance is being undertaken at a snail's pace, disrupting life in the neighborhood.[34]

The central core of the port region has been modernized with two new museums and a highway overpass that was replaced by tunnels and commercial buildings. Still to come are condos and more commercial buildings. The Trump Organization had advanced plans to build a Trump Towers Rio and a Trump Hotel Rio de Janeiro but abandoned those projects in December 2016. The development is managed by an Odebrecht-led consortium. Its success depends on being able to attract some 70,000 wealthy Brazilians to relocate to the area over the next ten years, as well as dozens of businesses.[35]

There has also been the claim that there will be a legacy of new sports facilities from the Olympics. While there are scheduled to be a few new training facilities at the Olympic park, they will only become functional if a private operator is found to redesign, prepare, and manage the park's facilities. The Maracanã Stadium has existed since 1950, though it has undergone several expensive remodelings and does not constitute a new facility. Until May 2013 the Maracanã was always under public management. As of that date, the management of the stadium was turned over to the private sector, the Maracanã Consortium, via a thirty-five-year lease. This consortium is 90 percent owned and controlled by Odebrecht. The average ticket prices for soccer matches at the Maracanã went from R$14 in 2012 to R$45 after the consortium took over; that is, they more than tripled.[36] The Maracanã had to undergo another facelift for the 2016 Games and, hence, was closed to the public. During the Maracanã's renovation, the nearby track and field stadium Célio de Barros, used by schools for competitions and professional athletes for training, was shut down during 2013–15. The Célio de Barros Stadium was used as a staging ground for the work on the Maracanã. The Olympic Stadium (commonly called the Engenhão) was also closed to the public during 2013–15 for renovations.

The third putative positive legacy is the improvement in managerial and administrative efficiency. Any impact in this area defies quantification, but it seems reasonable to argue that the opposite occurred in Rio. Namely, the organization and administration of the Olympic Games placed such a burden upon the governmental capacities of the Rio city and state that the system fell into deeper patterns of corruption and dysfunction.

The promised legacy of better security, safer streets, modern sewerage and electricity for the favelas, and cleaner waterways did not come to pass. On the contrary, violence has increased in Rio in 2016 and the Guanabara Bay remains heavily and dangerously polluted. The Guanabara Bay continues to receive 169 million gallons of untreated human waste daily and only 49 percent of the sewage that flows into the Bay is treated. The promise by the organizers was that the treatment level would reach 80 percent by 2016. The failure of the police pacification units (UPP) and the Morar Carioca to reduce violence and modernize services for the favelas is primarily due to the fact that the city and state ran out of resources to effectively implement these programs. The scarce public resources were being squandered on Olympics constructions and operations, as well as being wasted on bribes and kickbacks to Brazilian politicians.

Thus, the four anticipated positive legacies had little to show for themselves in Rio at the end of 2016. There are, however, many not-so positive legacies that Rio now has to confront. One of these is environmental degradation, which is discussed at some length in chapter 8 by Jules Boykoff, "Green Games: The Olympics, Sustainability, and Rio 2016."

The new golf course in Barra is emblematic of the disdain for sound environmental practices of Rio 2016. The decision to build a new golf course for the Olympics was taken after the president of Rio's Itanhangá Golf Club offered to allow his course to be used for the Games. The new course was built on wetlands in a wildlife conservation zone within an environmental protection area. The affected acreage is composed of mangrove-associated ecosystems, beaches, sandbanks, dunes, and a lagoon, which shelter rare or endemic species of fauna and flora, some in danger of extinction. After the Olympics competition, the plan was to build a luxury condo community at the course's edge, with individual units running from two to thirty million dollars. In order to build the condos, it required another easing of environmental protection legislation and the implementation of this process was full of irregularities. One glaring omission was the absence of an environmental impact study either for the course or for the condos.[37]

Now that the Games are over, the predictable is happening. The greens fees at the course are sky high, at $74–$82 per person for residents and $192 for foreign visitors, and the course is getting little play.[38] Meanwhile, the maintenance of the course requires vast amounts of water as well as chemicals, and the course is running monthly operating deficits over $80,000.[39] The course's condition has been reported to be sharply deteriorated. Rumors abound that the course will close. It has all the markings of a white elephant—expensive to build, costly to maintain, with little use. Its despoliation of the environment was underscored by a state court's decision in early December 2016, when it froze the assets of Rio mayor Eduardo Paes. Rio's state court opened an inquiry in March 2016 into whether the mayor had granted "excessive" and "unjustified" benefits to the course's builder, Fiori Empreendimentos, which never paid the required environmental impact fee of R$1.8 million.[40] (The following day, as part of a plea bargain, a former top executive of Odebrecht stated that Odebrecht contributed $8.95 million to Paes's reelection campaign in 2012, explaining: "The purpose of the payments made, as detailed in the initial topic of this report, was to keep the company's privileged access to Paes' agenda, allowing us to deal directly with him, without any red tape or any difficulty, on payment delays or any problem in the execution of our contracts."[41])

The wider environmental degradation caused by the Olympics was recognized in ROCOG's plans, which included the intention to plant thirty-four million tree seedlings to offset the Games' carbon footprint. As of the end of September 2016, only a reported 5.5 million seedlings had been planted.[42]

Beyond the golf course, Rio has to contend with other white elephants. The Maracanã Stadium, renovated for the World Cup and the Olympics at a cost of $600 million, was described as having fallen into "a state of abandonment" by the Brazilian newspaper O Globo. The newspaper wrote that the "smell of mold is noticeable," numerous cats roam the stadium's grounds, and holes in walls and exposed wires are widely visible, along with destroyed furniture.[43] The $65 million cable car in Complexo do Alemão, a purported legacy project for the poor in Rio's north zone, was shut down indefinitely in October, two months after the Games.[44] The future of the half-disassembled International Broadcasting Center (IBC), a massive structure with a footprint of roughly four city blocks and costing close to a half billion dollars, is up in the air as of this writing in February 2017.[45] The IBC, of course, is part of the Olympic park, where other facilities are boarded up.

Of the projected 3,604 condos that are planned out of the Olympic village (with an average price of approximately $450,000), as of mid-February 2017 only 260 have been sold.[46] The management of the entire 300-acre-plus main Olympic park in Barra da Tijuca, including its nine venues, was put out to private bidding. The manager would be responsible for not only leasing and selling properties within the park but also for operating it and carrying out the conversion of some facilities from Olympics venues into a public use. One such conversion plan that was widely publicized was the conversion of the Olympics handball venue at the Future Arena into municipal schools. Others included the Carioca arenas, where Olympics basketball, judo, and wrestling events were held, which are supposed to be converted into sports training facilities and a concert hall. Other facilities are to be dismantled by the management company.

Despite the fact that the municipality offered to subsidize the prospective management company to the tune of R$30 million per year, grant a full tax exemption, and provide public investment on the park's conversion of nearly R$1 billion, no bona fide companies were ready to take on the project.[47] Press reports in early December 2016 indicated that there was only one bidder to manage the Olympic park. The bidding company was Sanerio Construction, and it was in bankruptcy proceedings. Moreover, Sanerio had had several run-ins with the city in the past. Sanerio's bid was deficient because it had not submitted the requisite R$3.8 million security deposit. It was not regarded as a legitimate bid. The Brazilian government was forced to announce on December 23, 2016, that it would take over management of the park for the time being. On January 11, 2017, the government announced that the secondary Olympic park at the Deodoro cluster, including its legacy public swimming pool (in the heat of Rio's summer), was being closed indefinitely.

A related problem is that the Olympics venues and infrastructure were mostly built in a hurry. From the collapsing bicycle path to the apartments' plumbing and electricity in the Olympic village, problems with shoddy construction abounded. Such quality issues are not uncommon for Olympics hosts.

Perhaps the most prominent and troubling Olympics legacy is the horrific state of Rio's economy. While the Brazilian recession of 2014–17 has its roots in the plummeting price of crude oil (Brazil's main export) and reduced demand from China, the economy continued to go downhill even as the oil market partially recovered in 2016. The financial and employment conditions in Rio were not brought on by the burden of hosting, but they were certainly exacerbated by it.

The December 2, 2016, issue of *USA Today* ran an article on Rio after the Olympics that began as follows:

> From the front steps of Rio de Janeiro's Municipal Theater, the ballet company danced, and opera singers belted out the strident "Carmina Burana."
>
> It was last month, and the show was an artistic public protest. The performers, all state employees, haven't been paid for weeks and won't be getting paychecks until Dec. 5.
>
> The same day, outside a state-run hospital in Rio's Tijuca neighborhood, a doctor shrugged when asked about the long lines of people waiting to be treated. "It's total chaos in there," he says.
>
> And in Rocinha, Brazil's largest favela, or marginalized neighborhood, 10-year-old Railene de los Santos frowns and gives a faraway look when asked about the threat of her local library closing, to save money.
>
> "If anyone closes my library I'll kill them," she says. "I love my library."
>
> Three months since the Rio de Janeiro Summer Olympics, the "marvelous city," as it's known, is unraveling.
>
> The state of Rio is broke. It hasn't been able to pay its bills since long before the games. A federal bailout kept police on the streets and hospitals open while Olympics tourists were in town. But now the money has dried up, and public employees aren't being paid.
>
> The state government is voting on an austerity package that could slash state workers' wages and pensions by 30%. That's triggered violent protests and led demonstrators to briefly storm the state Legislature last month. Meanwhile, crime is surging across the state. From January to October, murders increased by 18%, and street robberies jumped by 48% compared to the same time last year, according to the state's security institute.[48]

The state of Rio owes the federal government over \$30 billion. The federal government, in turn, is running an annual budget deficit of 10 percent of GDP—the equivalent in the United States to a $1.9 trillion budget deficit![49] In September, Fitch downgraded Rio's debt to "C" status, which is solidly in the junk bond category. S&P downgraded Rio's debt from B- to CCC-. The federal government has frozen Rio state's bank accounts.

Ignacio Cano, a professor of sociology at the State University of Rio de Janeiro, told the *Washington Post* in December 2016, "You have an economic crisis, a political crisis, a moral crisis. There is a general perception of a very dark time."[50]

And opera singer Ciro d'Araujo, who was protesting at the Municipal Theater, told *USA Today*: "I think the Olympics were like the last ball of the empire. We threw a party but we knew that this was going to happen afterwards."[51]

With few exceptions, hosting the Olympics has not turned out well economically for the chosen cities. The international bidding among cities to convince the IOC monopoly that a particular city is most worthy of the hosting "honor" sets the chosen city up for a winner's curse. The immense volume of venue and infrastructure construction spending easily surpasses ten billion dollars, while the comparatively meager generation of revenues falls considerably short of that. Unless there is a preexisting, rational plan for developing a city that is fully congruent with the investment needed to host the Games, the finances of hosting are not auspicious.

When this dynamic is foisted upon an emerging economy, the amount of infrastructural and venue preparation spending magnifies, and the political and administrative means to implement the Olympics plan are deficient. The IOC and Rio boasted that the 2016 Summer Olympics would be the first Games hosted in South America. The continent should hope it won't happen again for a long time; it has more urgent matters to which to attend.

NOTES

1. See, for one, Nick Butler, "Bach Claims No Public Funding Used for Rio 2016," *Inside the Games*, August 20, 2016.

2. R. M. Levine, "Sport and Society: The Case of Brazilian Futebol," *Luso-Brazilian Review* 17, no. 2 (1980), p. 250.

3. See Jamile Chequer, "Especial PAN 2007," *Democracia Viva*, no. 35 (June 2007), pp. 32–41; and, Tribunal de Contas da União, "Relatório de acompanhamento das ações e obras relacionadas aos jogos pan e parapan-americanos de 2007," Acompanhamento TC-014.800/2007-3 (Brasília: Tribunal de Contas da União, 2008).

4. Bent Flyvbjerg, Allison Stewart, and Alexander Budzier, *The Oxford Olympics Study 2016: Cost and Cost Overrun at the Games* (Oxford, UK: Saïd Business School, University of Oxford, July 2016), p. 1.

5. "Rio Olympic Organizers Unveil Village Where Athletes to Stay," Associated Press, June 23, 2016.

6. See, for instance, "Major Cuts to Security Budget Put Olympics at Risk, Official Says," Associated Press, May 6, 2016.

7. Andre Mantelli and others, *Rio 2016 Olympics: The Exclusion Games* (Rio de Janeiro: World Cup and Olympics Popular Committee of Rio de Janeiro, November 2015), p. 141.

8. Ibid, p. 145.

9. To be sure, a major reason why cariocas do not play golf is its expense. The new Olympics course does not remedy this problem.

10. Reality might be a bit more complicated. The approval for the new golf course came in an extraordinary session of the city council on December 20, 2012. Bach has claimed that he was surprised that mayor Paes said the IOC required the new course be built, asserting instead that it was Paes who wanted the new course. So, choose your poison: believe Paes or believe Bach. AFP, "IOC 'Surprise' at Rio Mayor Golf Course Criticism," *Yahoo! Sports*, February 25, 2015 (http://sports.yahoo.com/news/ioc-surprise-rio-mayor-golf-course-criticism-214600338—oly.html).

11. Paul Kiernan and Will Connors, "Rio's Traffic Jams Force Last Minute Holiday for Olympics," *Wall Street Journal*, August 2, 2016.

12. Rio city government approved a law in 2009 that forbids vendors from working within a two-kilometer radius of Olympics venues. Such treatment of informal workers has been found at many sports megaevents in cities around the world. See Mantelli and others, *Rio 2016 Olympics*, pp. 56–60.

13. Nick Butler, "Bach Claims No Public Funding Used for Rio 2016 despite Bailout as Pays Tribute to 'Iconic Games," *Inside the Games*, August 20, 2016.

14. To be sure, this $61 million was pledged, but it appears that the city was not able to contribute this sum, at least by the end of November 2016. As a result, Rio 2016 was $3.7 million in arrears in making payments to national paralympic teams for travel to and from Brazil for their athletes. Rio 2016 blamed the late payments on the failure of the city government to transfer the promised funds. The national paralympic teams, in turn, have

had to borrow the money from the International Paralympic Committee or from local financing sources. See, for instance, Nick Butler, "IPC Forced to Bailout Five National Paralympic Committees after Rio 2016: Miss Latest Deadline for Travel Payments," *Inside the Games*, December 13, 2016.

15. APO, *Matriz de Responsabilidades Rio 2016* (http://www.apo.gov .br/index.php/matriz/). Also see Marcelo Weishaupt Proni and Raphael Brito Faustino, "Economic and Sorting Legacy of Olympics 2016," *ICSSPE Bulletin*, no. 70 (May 2016), p. 27.

16. Further, to keep the potential impact of additional tourists in realistic proportions, it is interesting to note that the first Olympic Games impact report that was required by the IOC in January 2014 estimated that the average spending per day of tourists in Rio was $66.27. So, if the average Olympics tourist spent five days in Rio, she would spend $331.35. If the Olympics brought 100,000 net new tourists to Rio, the total value of their spending would be $33.135 million. To be sure, some of this spending would have been on items that were imported into Rio, so the net new activity in Rio would have been below $33 million. Impacts of this magnitude are rounding errors when the investment is on the order of $20 billion. For context, Rio's annual Carnival draws an estimated six million visitors (900,000 from other countries) into the city. The costs of Carnival are *de minimus* in relation to the Olympics.

17. It is interesting to note that Brazil's bus companies expanded the number of bus trips by 17.2 percent in August 2016, anticipating stronger travel demand for the Olympics.

18. "Olympic Games Push Tourism to Record," *Wall Street Journal*, January 5, 2017. There is ample room for statistical legerdemain in counting foreign tourism spending. For instance, ROCOG was responsible to cover the lodging, transport, and room and board expenses of the Olympics athletes. This spending could be counted as foreign tourism spending even though it was paid for locally. The potential rationale for this treatment could be that even though the money was local, it was received as part of the sharing television and sponsorship revenue from the IOC.

19. IOC, "Host City Contract: Games of the XXXI Olympiad in 2016," 2009.

20. Of course, the reduction of tax revenues was further exacerbated by the endemic tax exemptions, kickbacks, and theft in Rio's political culture. For instance, an auditor found that Rio missed out on R$138 billion (about $42 billion) in corporate taxes between 2008 and 2013 from this special treatment. That's almost twice the state's annual budget of about R$80 billion. See, for one, Will Carless, "Three Months After the Olympics, Rio de Janeiro is Broke," *USA Today*, December 2, 2016.

21. Ibid.

22. Nelson Belen, "Rio Hotel Occupancy for Paralympics Less Than 50 Percent," *The Rio Times*, August 30, 2016. Leslie Josephs, "Rio Built Too Many Hotel Rooms (Again)," *Quartz*, August 3, 2016 (http://qz.com /748669/brazil-built-too-many-hotel-rooms-again/).

23. See, for one, Mantelli and others, *Rio 2016 Olympics*, pp. 52–53.

24. See, for instance, Luiza Franco and Lucas Vettorazo, "Após Jogos, linha do Metrô do Rio abre sem integração de tarifas com BRT," *Folha de S. Paulo*, September 19, 2016 (www1.folha.uol.com.br/cotidiano/2016/09 /1814738-carioca-reclama-de-falta-de-integracao-de-tarifas-em-linha-4-do -metro-do-rio.shtml). The commuter who takes the BRT and metro will spend $316 per month, or about 36 percent of the minimum wage.

25. In an op-ed in the *New York Times*, Brazilian columnist Vanessa Barbara wrote: "Homeless people in Rio told me that police officers are forcing them off sidewalks and dragging them to filthy shelters to start 'cleaning up' the streets before the influx of visitors. The evictions often take place at 3 a.m. with the help of police dogs and pepper spray, and sometimes horses. There are also reports that street children have been arbitrarily placed in juvenile detention centers." "Brazil's Olympic Catastrophe," *New York Times*, July 1, 2016.

26. Terres des Hommes, *Breaking Records: Child Rights Violations during the 2016 Rio Olympics* (Geneva: Terres des Hommes International Federation, September 2016), p. 3.

27. At least one Brazilian source found the Line 4 metro construction costs to be in excess of $3 billion. See "Emprestimos para obras da Linha 4 do metro custarao R$12 bilhoes," *Extra Globo: Noticias Economicas*, April 4, 2016 (http://extra.globo.com/noticias/economia/emprestimos-para -obras-da-linha-4-do-metro-custarao-12-bilhoes-19009461.html).

28. One study found that the number of journeys made by BRT did not equal 10 percent of those by regular bus services. See Mantelli and others, *Rio 2016 Olympics*, p. 50. Also see Christopher Gaffney and Erick Silva, "Mega Eventos Esportivos: Resstruturacao Para Quem?" *Proposta* 121, no. 1 (2010), pp. 49–93. Also see the blog posts of Christopher Gaffney, *Hunting White Elephants/caçando elephantes brancos: Critical Reflections on Brazil 2014 and Rio 2016* (http://geostadia.blogspot.com/).

29. Christopher Gaffney, "Transforming Rio—For the Benefit of Whom?" *ICSSPE Bulletin*, no. 70 (May 2016), p. 40.

30. After Odebrecht, no other company has more than two Olympics projects. The companies tied in second place with two contracts are: Andrade Gutierrez, Carioca Engenharia, Carvalho Hosken, Queiroz Galvão, Invepar, and OAS. The investigation into the depths of the construction company

scandal and its impact on the Olympics is ongoing. In early December 2016, Marcelo Odebrecht signed a plea bargain with the government, agreeing to provide information in exchange for allowing Odebrecht to once again bid for government contracts (it had been prohibited from bidding for new contracts since 2014 but allowed to continue in its preexisting ones). Marcelo Odebrecht is one of seventy-seven former and current executives of the company who have signed plea bargains. Marcelo Odebrecht, who is forty-eight years old, is also hoping that his nineteen-year prison sentence will be reduced. See, for one, Luciana Magalhaes and Reed Johnson, "Magnate's Plea Deal Spurs Brazil Graft Probe," *Wall Street Journal*, December 2, 2016.

31. "Special Report: Rio 2016," *The Guardian*, July 19, 2016.

32. Ibid.

33. Karine Ferreira, "E o Teleférico da Providência?" *ANF*, January 10, 2017 (www.anf.org.br/e-o-teleferico-da-providencia/).

34. "Port Region Suffers with Ceaseless Light Rail Construction," *RioOnWatch*, n.d. (www.rioonwatch.org/?p=33799).

35. Land transfers are key here as new forms of governance of public space. See Fernanda Sánchez and Anne-Marie Broudehoux, "Mega-Events and Urban Regeneration in Rio de Janeiro: Planning in a State of Emergency," *International Journal of Urban Sustainable Development* 5, no. 2 (2013), pp. 132–53.

36. Mantelli and others, *Rio 2016 Olympics*, p. 69.

37. Ibid., p. 89. If there were such a study, it was never made public. See also Christopher Gaffney, "Between Discourse and Reality: The Un-Sustainability of Mega-Event Planning," *Sustainability* 5, no. 9 (2013), pp. 3926–40.

38. Sebastian Smith, "Rio Olympic Golf Course Eerily Empty Three Months On," *Agence France Presse*, November 25, 2016.

39. Associated Press, "Rio's Olympic Golf Course: Who Plays It? Who Pays for It?" *Boston Herald*, December 16, 2016 (www.bostonherald.com /sports/other/olympics/2016/12/rios_olympic_golf_course_who_plays_it _who_pays_for_it). This article also describes the course's dismal environment: "Once through the rutted parking lot and inside the clubhouse, there's no pro shop, few furnishings, no local club professional and no restaurant. And few players. Only four middle-age men were on the course one morning this week."

40. Sebastian Smith, "Court Freezes Rio Mayor's Assets Over Olympic Golf Course," *Agence France Presse*, December 9, 2016.

41. Aaron Bauer, "Rio Mayor Named in Connection to Ongoing Corruption Case," *Around the Rings*, December 12, 2016 (http://aroundtherings

.com/site/A__58393/Title__Rio-Mayor-Named-in-Connection-to-Ongoing
-Corruption-Case/292/Articles).

42. "Reforestation Is Below the Target Provided as a Legacy of the 2016
Games," *Jornal do Brazil*, September 28, 2016. Also see "Olimpíadas 2016:
Legado do plantio de 24 milhões de árvores em atraso," *ProMudasRio*, n.d.
(http://promudasrio.com.br/olimpiadas-2016-legado-do-plantio-de-24
-milhoes-de-arvores-em-atraso/); Alana Gandra, "Reflorestamento fica
abaixo da meta prevista como legado dos Jogos 2016," *EBC Agência Brasil*,
September 24, 2016 (http://agenciabrasil.ebc.com.br/rio-2016/noticia/2016
-09/reflorestamento-fica-aquem-da-meta-prevista-como-legado-dos-jogos
-2016); and Vinicius Konchinski, "RJ prometeu 34 milhões de árvores para
Rio-2016. Deve plantar 8 milhões," *UOL 20 Anos*, May 22, 2015 (http://
olimpiadas.uol.com.br/noticias/2015/05/22/rj-prometeu-plantar-34-mi-de
-arvores-para-rio-2016-deve-plantar-8-mi.htm).

43. "Iconic Rio Stadium Has Fallen Into 'A State of Abandonment' After
Olympics," *Huffington Post*, January 5, 2017.

44. "Cable Car Suspension and Violent Police Operations Leave Residents Stranded—and Threatened—in Complexo do Alemão," *RioOnWatch*,
n.d. (www.rioonwatch.org/?p=33224).

45. One excellent discussion of the utter state of disrepair of multiple Rio
Olympic venues is Anna Jean Kaiser, "Legacy of Rio So Far Is Series of Unkept Promises," *New York Times*, February 16, 2017. Also see Renata Latuf
de Oliveira Sanchez, "Olympic Games in Rio 2016: A Discussion about Its
Legacy," *ICSSPE Bulletin*, no. 70 (May 2016), p. 46.

46. The billionaire developer of this village is Carlos Carvalho. He has
infuriated many because he has said his condos are for refined Brazilians
only and has called his village "Ilha Pura" or Pure Island. See "Bad Economy May Spoil Future Plans for Rio's Olympic Park," Associated Press,
August 22, 2016; and Stephen Eisenhammer, "Rio Risks Empty Olympic Legacy as Real Estate Market Stalls," *Reuters*, July 19, 2016 (www.reuters.com
/article/us-olympics-rio-realestate-insight-idUSKCN0ZZ179). Even though
the plan is for several thousand families to reside at Ilha Pura, the project has
no space allocated for schools, day care centers, or clinics. Also see Kaiser, "Legacy of Rio."

47. See Marcelo Moreira e Monica Teixeira, "Rio 2016: comitê deve R$100
milhoes a fornecedores e instalações tem abandono," *Globo*, March 25,
2017 (http://g1.globo.com/rio-de-janeiro/noticia/rio-2016-comite-deve-r-100
-milhoes-a-fornecedores-e-instalacoes-tem-abandono.ghtml; http://olimpiadas
.uol.com.br/noticias/redacao/2016/07/08/rio-vai-gastar-ate-r-11-bilhao-em
-parque-olimpico-apos-olimpiada.html.

48. http://us.lalalay.com/news/world/-8837-three-months-after-the
-olympics-rio-de-janeiro-is-broke/.

49. In December the Brazilian senate passed an austerity program that mandated no real spending increases for government social spending over the next twenty years. A UN official called this the most socially regressive austerity package in the world. Dom Phillips, "Brazil Senate Approves Austerity Package to Freeze Social Spending for 20 Years," *The Guardian*, December 13, 2016.

50. Dom Phillips, "After Olympics, Rio Mired in Crisis," *Washington Post*, December 9, 2016.

51. Will Carless, "Three Months After the Olympics."

Contributors

Juliana Barbassa is an award-winning journalist and the managing editor of *Americas Quarterly*, a publication about politics and business in Latin America. She is also the author of *Dancing with the Devil in the City of God: Rio de Janeiro on the Brink*, based on her years as the Associated Press's Rio correspondent.

Jules Boykoff has written three books on the Olympic Games, most recently *Power Games: A Political History of the Olympics*. In fall 2015 he was a Fulbright research fellow in Rio de Janeiro. In the 1990s he represented the U.S. Olympic Soccer Team in international competition.

Jamil Chade is the European correspondent for the newspaper *O Estado de S. Paulo*. Honored as the best Brazilian foreign correspondent, he was chosen as one of the forty most influential journalists in Brazil. A member of the network Anti-Corruption Solutions and Knowledge (ASK), led by Transparency International, Chade has written four books and visited more than sixty countries.

Stephen Essex is associate professor in human geography at the School of Geography, Earth, and Environmental Science, Plymouth University (UK). His teaching and research focus on urban and rural planning, especially the infrastructure implications of the Olympic Games. He has coauthored a number of journal articles and book chapters on the urban impacts and planning of both the Summer and Winter Olympic Games with Brian Chalkley (also at Plymouth University).

Renata Latuf de Oliveira Sanchez is a Brazilian architect and urbanist based in São Paulo currently working on the urban design legacy of Rio Olympics. Supported by the São Paulo Research Foundation, she was a guest researcher in Copenhagen and England in 2016.

Theresa Williamson, a city planner, is the executive director of Catalytic Communities, a Rio de Janeiro–based organization that provides media and networking support to favela communities. An advocate on behalf of Rio de Janeiro's favelas, she helps to ensure they are recognized for their heritage status and their residents fully served as equal citizens.

Andrew Zimbalist is the Robert A. Woods Professor of Economics at Smith College and a noted sports economist and sports industry consultant. He has published twenty-six books, most recently *Circus Maximus: The Economic Gamble Behind Hosting the Olympics and the World Cup* and *Unwinding Madness: What Went Wrong with College Sports and How to Fix It* (with Gerald Gurney and Donna Lopiano.)

Index